# STEEL
# VICTORY

# STEEL VICTORY

## The Heroic Story of America's Independent Tank Battalions at War in Europe

## HARRY YEIDE

PRESIDIO
PRESS

BALLANTINE BOOKS • NEW YORK

# TO THOSE WHO FOUGHT

A Presidio Press Book
Published by The Random House Publishing Group
Copyright © 2003 by Harry Yeide

All rights reserved under International and Pan-American Copyright
Conventions. Published in the United States by The Random House
Publishing Group, a division of Random House, Inc., New York, and
simultaneously in Canada by Random House of Canada Limited, Toronto.

Presidio Press and colophon are trademarks of Random House, Inc.

ISBN 0-89141-782-6

*Book design by Joseph Rutt*

Manufactured in the United States of America

# CONTENTS

*Preface*                                                                    vii

*Acknowledgments*                                                             xi

*Maps*                                                                      xiii

1  General McNair's Children                                                   1

2  DDs at D Day                                                               37

3  The Bocage:
   A School of Very Hard Knocks                                              57

4  Open-Field Running                                                        93

5  Hitting the West Hall                                                    127

6  Two Grim Months                                                         145

7  Hitler's Last Gamble                                                     191

8  The Reich Overrun                                                       229

Appendix A  Battalion Profiles                                             255

Appendix B  Independent Tank Battalion/
            Armored Group Attachments to
            Infantry and Airborne Divisions, ETO                           271

Appendix C  Independent Tank Battalions
            by Campaign                                                     283

*Glossary*                                                                  285

*Bibliography*                                                              287

*Notes*                                                                     291

*Index*                                                                     309

# PREFACE

I was inspired to take up this task by *Combat Mission: Beyond Overlord* (Big Time Software at Battlefront.com), which, as of this writing, is the best computer war game ever written— period. The player experiences in near real time many of the challenges faced by the American tank-infantry team of World War II. Most of the time, such teams consisted of elements of an infantry division and an attached separate tank battalion. I began going through the records of those tank battalions in search of historically accurate information to serve as the basis for scenarios for *Combat Mission*. I quickly realized that those files contained an incredible story. So far as I can determine, no one has ever told this story in its entirety.

This work provides a portrait of those tank battalions as much as it does a history. It explores how they fought the war, as often as possible in the tankers' own words recorded at the time. I do not want those words to remain locked in dusty archives forever. Moreover, it is impossible to provide a running account of each and every tank battalion in the European Theater; it was a big war! The reader will find some such accounts, but to the extent possible, I have selected material that either illustrates experiences common to many battalions or highlights the more singular experience of an individual unit or sector of the front.

That said, I recognize that even the original accounts are not always entirely accurate. As the police know, eyewitnesses are notoriously unreliable. Particularly in cases where something went wrong, such as a breakdown in tank-infantry cooperation, the various parties to the events are likely to have come away with—and recorded—different views of reality. My tale is told from the tankers' perspectives, and I have not attempted the daunting task of cross-checking tank battalion after-action reports (AARs) with those of other units involved in each action. I leave that to those who, interested in a particular event, are welcome to sort out any differences in accounts, if that is even possible after a half century.

The quality of the surviving records varies tremendously from battalion to battalion. Some, such as the 743d, left exhaustive records. Others left skimpy and uninformative files. The disparity largely accounts for the relative frequency of citations drawn from the experiences of the various units.

I offer one suggestion to the reader. Keep in mind that the success or loss of any given tank was a drama for the five men inside. Newly arriving battalions generally kept close track of individuals. After all, these were men that the recording officers knew and had trained with for months. As the war dragged on and casualties became routine, battalion records tended to give less attention to individuals and more to the status of the fighting force as measured in tanks available and aggregate casualty figures. I suppose that this is natural. Faceless replacements would appear and maybe disappear quickly. The infantry commander was most interested in how many vehicles would show up to support his men. Who might be inside was not his concern. Thus, the tank to some extent became the collective surrogate for the crew in the historical record.

For those seeking a deeper look at an independent tank battalion, I offer several suggestions. The best place to get a feel for the life of the tankers is a work of fiction by Wayne Robinson—who served in the 743d Tank Battalion—published under the titles *Barbara* (Doubleday, 1962) and *Hell Has No Heroes* (Warner Paperback Library, 1964). Unfortunately, the work is long out of print under both titles. Tankers penned a spate of unit histories shortly after the war, such as *Move Out, Verify* (743d), *Daredevil Tankers* (740th), and *Up From Marseille* (781st), but these are difficult to obtain at any price, let alone a reasonable one. As of this writing, the 741st Tank Battalion veterans association was still selling copies of that outfit's informal history, *We'll Never Go Over-Seas*. Several recent works are available following a long drought: *The 761st "Black Panther" Tank Battalion in World War II* by Joe Wilson, *The View From the Turret* (743d) by William Folkestad, *Strike Swiftly!* (70th) by Marvin Jensen, and *Tanks for the Memories* (712th) by Aaron Elson.

This work is not a history of American military operations in the European Theater, although those operations are obviously the framework in which the story of the independent tank battalions unfolds. I have relied heavily on the excellent works of the U.S. Army Center of Military History to relate the big picture. I have also leaned on the work of the West Point Department of History (Thomas E. Griess, ed.), *The Second World War: Europe and the Mediterranean*. Reliance on U.S. Army perspectives doubtless introduces certain biases, but that is a risk I willingly accept. Moreover, I note cases in which the tank battalion records conflict with the official histories.

Harry Yeide
January 2002

# ACKNOWLEDGMENTS

I would like to thank my wife, Nancy, who is first in my book and makes me better in every endeavor, including this one. Michael Ard, friend and colleague, who after hearing me rant on about how fascinating this all is, said, "Well, write a book." "Wild Bill" Wilder opened a door at the right time. John Walker, a platoon commander with the 750th Tank Battalion during the war, not only offered many interesting observations based on his experiences but kindly reviewed the entire draft manuscript. Lieutenant Colonel Mark Reardon, U.S. Army, also reviewed the draft and offered the valuable insights of a man combining historical scholarship and service in today's armored force. This work would not be as good if it were not for their contributions. All remaining errors are mine.

Many thanks to Mrs. Betty Wilkes and Mrs. Hilda Rubel, who graciously granted permission to use excerpts from their late husbands' histories of the 747th and 740th Tank Battalions, respectively. I tip my hat to Al Heintzleman, too, who gave permission to use excerpts from his informal history of the 741st Tank Battalion. Thanks also to the tank battalion veterans who shared their experiences and insights and in some cases reviewed parts of the manuscript, including Whit

Blanchard, Harold Bradley, Phil Fitts, Henry Peters, and Paul Ragan.

I would also like to acknowledge the cheerful and efficient public servants at the National Archives and Records Administration's document and still-photo reading rooms in College Park, Maryland. The taxpayer is getting a good deal.

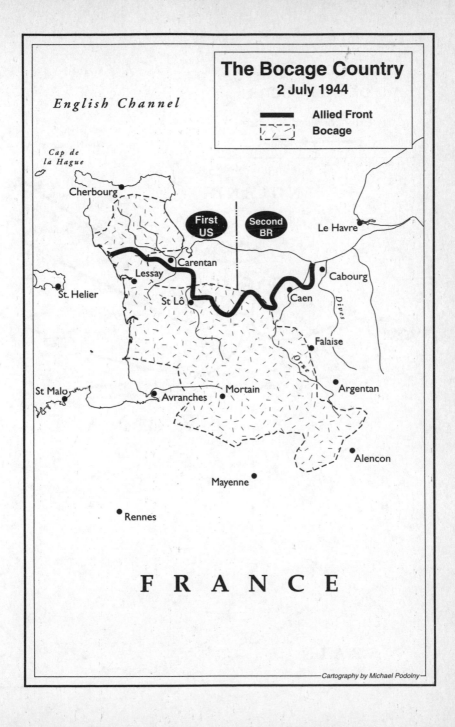

The Bocage Country
2 July 1944

Allied Front
Bocage

English Channel

Cap de
la Hague

Cherbourg

First US

Second BR

Le Havre

Carentan

Lessay

Cabourg

St. Helier

St Lô

Caen

Dives

Falaise

Dive

St Malo

Mortain

Argentan

Avranches

Alencon

Mayenne

Rennes

F R A N C E

Cartography by Michael Podolny

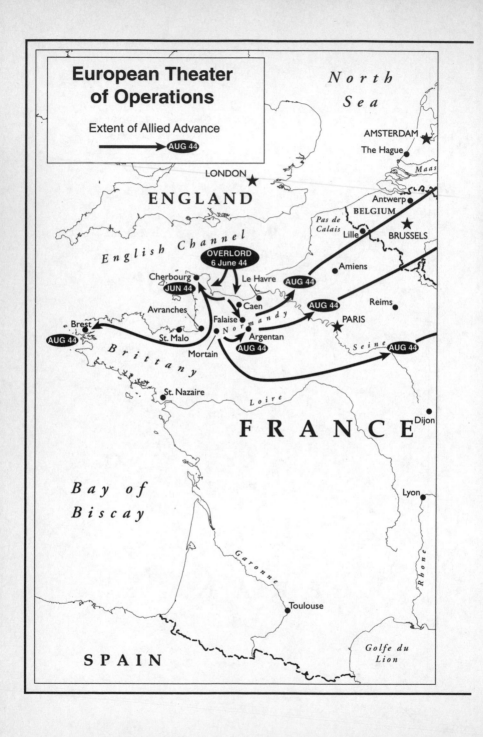

**European Theater of Operations**

Extent of Allied Advance
→ AUG 44

*North Sea*

AMSTERDAM ★
The Hague

*Maas*

LONDON ★

**ENGLAND**

Antwerp

**BELGIUM**

*Pas de Calais*

Lille

**BRUSSELS** ★

*English Channel*

OVERLORD
6 June 44

AUG 44

Amiens

Cherbourg
JUN 44

Le Havre

Reims

Avranches

Caen

AUG 44

PARIS ★

Brest

Falaise

*Normandy*

St. Malo

Argentan

AUG 44

*Seine*

AUG 44

Mortain

AUG 44

*Brittany*

St. Nazaire

*Loire*

**FRANCE** Dijon

*Bay of
Biscay*

Lyon

*Garonne*

*Rhone*

Toulouse

**SPAIN**

*Golfe du
Lion*

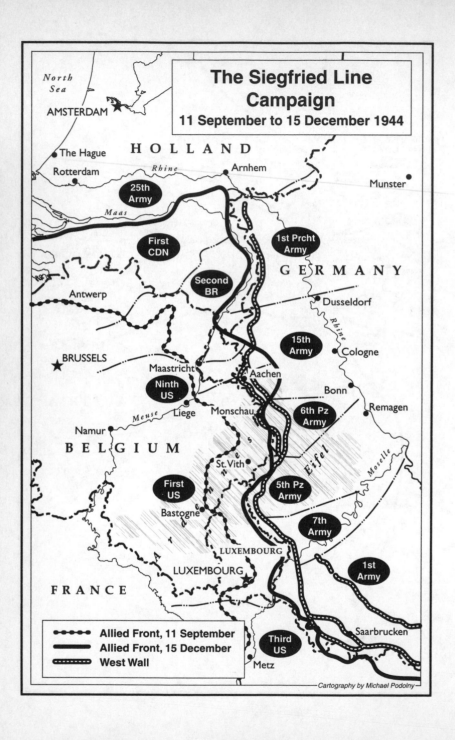

The Siegfried Line Campaign
11 September to 15 December 1944

North Sea

AMSTERDAM

The Hague

Rotterdam

HOLLAND

Rhine

Arnhem

Munster

Maas

25th Army

First CDN

1st Prcht Army

GERMANY

Second BR

Antwerp

Dusseldorf

Rhine

15th Army

Cologne

BRUSSELS

Maastricht

Aachen

Ninth US

Bonn

Meuse

Liege

Monschau

6th Pz Army

Remagen

Namur

BELGIUM

St.Vith

Eifel

Moselle

First US

5th Pz Army

Bastogne

7th Army

LUXEMBOURG

LUXEMBOURG

1st Army

FRANCE

Saarbrucken

Third US

Metz

•••• Allied Front, 11 September
▬▬▬ Allied Front, 15 December
□□□□ West Wall

Cartography by Michael Podolny

**Beating the Bulge**
December 1944 to January 1945

Aachen

GERMANY

Liege

BELGIUM

*Meuse*

Stoumont

Malmedy   Rocherath

First
US

St Vith

Second
BR

German
Penetration

Houffalize

Bastogne

Wiltz

Echternach

LUXEMBOURG

Arlon

Third
US

*Meuse*

★

LUXEMBOURG

*Moselle*

FRANCE

Metz

Cartography by Michael Podolny

## Mobilization: The Big Picture

General [George C.] Marshall and Secretary of War Henry L. Stimson made plans to expand the [U.S.] Army to 1.5 million men. On 27 August 1940, Congress approved inducting the National Guard into federal service and calling up the reserves. A few weeks later the lawmakers passed the Selective Service and Training Act, the first peacetime draft in American history. By mid-1941 the Army had achieved its planned strength, with twenty-seven infantry, five armored, and two cavalry divisions; thirty-five air groups; and a host of support units. But it remained far from ready to deploy overseas against well-equipped, experienced, and determined foes.

On 7 December 1941, while German armies were freezing before Moscow, Japan suddenly pushed the United States into the struggle by attacking the American naval base at Pearl Harbor, Hawaii. Four days later Hitler declared war on the United States. President Roosevelt called on Congress for immediate and massive expansion of the armed forces. Twenty years of neglect and indifference, however, could not be overcome in a few days. . . .

In early 1942 the Joint Chiefs of Staff emerged as a committee of the nation's military leaders to advise the President and to coordinate strategy with the British. In March the War Department General Staff was reorganized and the Army divided into three major commands: the Air Forces, Ground Forces, and Service Forces. Thirty-seven Army divisions were in some state of training, but only one was fully trained, equipped, and deployable by January 1942. Army planners of the time estimated that victory would require an Army of nearly 9 million men organized into 215 combat divisions—estimates that proved accurate regarding overall manpower but too ambitious for the ninety divisions that eventually were established and supported on far-flung battlefields.

Lieutenant General Lesley J. McNair, head of Army Ground Forces and an ardent advocate of mobile war, oversaw the development of armored and airborne divisions. . . . A serious and continuing shortage of Allied shipping space placed absolute limits on the size and capabilities of Army units. New tables of organization stressed leanness and mobility, sometimes at the expense of fighting power and endurance.

*A Brief History of the U.S. Army in World War II,* Center of Military History, United States Army, Washington, D.C., 1992

# GENERAL McNAIR'S CHILDREN

> By the time dirt-grimed tankers rolled up to the assembly
> area south of Isigny and staff officers had gone out to report
> that the 743d had arrived as ordered, the XIX Corps had al-
> ready planned an attack for the 30th [Infantry] Division. . . .
> *Move Out, Verify:*
> *The Combat History of*
> *the 743d Tank Battalion*

Fifty-four medium tanks, model M4 Sherman; 6 assault guns,
model M4 mounting 105mm howitzers; 17 light tanks, usually
model M5 Stuart; 750 officers and men. Mere "attachments"
to the infantry divisions and unglamorous step-sisters to the
storied armored divisions, the U.S. Army's separate tank battalions carried a heavy load in the European Theater of Operations (ETO) in World War II, but tend to get little attention.
Their tanks fought beside—and often in front of—the "doughs"
of the Big Red One, the Old Hickory Division, and other outfits
whose well-earned reputations would not have been as grand
were it not for the contributions made by the tank crews and
their supporting troops. Soldiering in tanks that many considered outmoded death traps, they gave as good as they got (and
often more) against a battle-honed foe who could deploy Panthers, Tigers, and other menacing war machines that excelled
at killing from a distance and shrugging off American armor-
piercing shells.

Wayne Robinson, who served with and wrote the informal
history of the 743d Tank Battalion, described a battalion's role
in these terms:

A separate tank battalion assigned to work with an infantry division fought at the foot soldier's pace. Its job was to give the doughboy's attack the added punch that tanks have, to bull ahead when the going got rough, to knock down houses Jerry tried to use as forts, to stop enemy tanks in the counterattacks, to spearhead a way for the doughboy and his rifle, his machine gun, and his mortar. . . . Often the doughboy regiment and its attached tank battalion slugged it out with the Jerry on the line for days, inching painfully ahead to engineer an opening in the enemy defenses through which the star ball carriers, the armored divisions, could do their free and fancy open-field running. When this happened, it became the job of the doughboy and his supporting tanks to follow up as fast as they could, moving behind the swift, surging, twenty-mile-a-day drives. The infantry moved and fought, mopping up the pockets of resistance always left in the wake of such drives. But mostly, while the big armor waited in reserve for the quarterback to call their number and set them going through the line, the infantry and the separate tank battalion were in the thick of the line play, fighting and getting hurt, always under fire, within enemy artillery range, doing their work ever at the front of the division's sector.[1]

The mission of the separate tank battalion as outlined in FM 17-33, 19 December 1944, was as follows:

- To lead the attack.

- To support by direct fire the advance of light tanks, other medium tanks, and ground troops.

- To feel out the enemy and develop weak spots.

- To serve as a reserve for exploiting a success or breaking up a counterattack against the supported unit.

- To accompany the infantry and assist the advance by destroying or neutralizing automatic weapons and pillboxes holding up the advance.

- To fight enemy tanks when necessary.

- To destroy dug-in pillboxes as necessary.

- To reinforce artillery fires.

- To assist the infantry in mop-up.

By the end of the war, infantry and tank commanders appended an additional role on the basis of combat experience: transporting infantry on tanks in fast-moving operations.[2]

A mere four years separated the creation of the first tank battalions from the grueling combat of Normandy, France. Starved of resources, the U.S. Army had allowed its tank force to fade into irrelevance after World War I. Stunned by the German Wehrmacht's Blitzkrieg through Poland and France, Congress found the money, and the Army re-created an Armored Force on 10 July 1940.[3] The independent tank battalions were part of the scheme from the start, albeit initially as a side show. That they existed at all was the result of a doctrinal dispute between a group consisting mostly of cavalry officers who thought in terms of armored divisions and German-style Blitzkrieg, and a group who viewed tanks as an important infantry-support weapon.

The armored divisions look back on cavalry officers such as George Patton, Adna Chaffee, and Daniel Van Voorhis as their forebears; all were men who realized the tank's potential in warfare and argued their cause. Chaffee became the first

commander of the Armored Force, and the swashbuckling
Patton became the U.S. Army's most effective practitioner of
mechanized warfare in the ETO. Despite the establishment of
a separate Armored Force (in part to end the wrangling between the cavalry and infantry over the control and use of
tanks), cavalry officers largely determined the organization,
doctrine, and mission of the armored divisions.[4]

Fittingly for the independent tank battalions, their most
important patron during the early evolution of the Armored
Force was the decidedly unglamorous, hard-of-hearing Lt.
Gen. Lesley J. McNair, who, as commander of the General
Headquarters (GHQ), lacked any clear authority over the
newly created organization. His views on the subject nevertheless carried great weight at the War Department. Along
with other senior infantry officers, McNair continued to cham-
pion the traditional infantry-support role of armor, which had
a pedigree dating back to World War I. Whether or not this
was wise lies in the eye of the beholder and admits to no au-
thoritative answer. Military historian David Johnson, in an
innovation-themed study of the Army during this period, concluded, "The GHQ [i.e., separate] tank units were memorials
to the War Department's reluctance to completely discard its
conventional tank wisdom for a new concept." Johnson himself concedes, however, that the cavalry officers in the Armored
Force were perfectly comfortable with an infantry-support role
for some of the tank battalions.[5] And infantry commanders
throughout the war expressed strong support for the concept.
As a pragmatic answer, the arrangement worked in the ETO.

As of 1940, the War Department contemplated the activation of only fifteen GHQ tank battalions organized under three
Reserve (later Tank and then Armored) Group headquarters.
McNair was convinced from the start that the Armored Force
was the most wasteful of the ground arms in its use of men
and equipment, and he argued in 1942 and 1943 that the ar-

mored divisions were bloated and unwieldy. Combat experience helped McNair make his case by showing that tanks frequently needed escort by foot troops to locate and destroy antitank defenses. In 1943, McNair wrote in a memorandum: "It is believed that our 1943 troop basis has entirely too many armored divisions, considering their proper tactical employment, and too few GHQ tank battalions. It is particularly important that the latter be available in quantities to permit all infantry divisions to work with them freely and frequently."[6]

In part due to McNair's influence, the armored divisions were reorganized twice, first in March 1942 and again in September 1943. The latter affected all but the 2d and 3d Armored divisions and released two battalions per division into the GHQ pool. Standard separate battalions were made identical to the divisional battalions and hence could theoretically be attached to armored divisions—although that did not occur directly in even a single case in the European campaign. Prior to the reshuffle, a sharp distinction existed between medium and light tank battalions. Afterward, although a few light tank battalions continued to exist, the vast majority were mixed. Each had three medium tank companies (seventeen tanks each), one light tank company (seventeen tanks), and six assault guns (Shermans mounting a 105mm howitzer in place of the normal 75mm cannon). The battalions also became administratively self-contained, each receiving a service company and a headquarters company.[7]

Several tank battalions (701st, 736th, 738th, 739th, 740th, and 748th) were organized as special battalions under T/O & E (Table of Organization and Equipment) 17-45S and equipped largely with M3 Grants mounting special searchlights and code-named Canal Defense Lights (CDLs). Each CDL battalion had a headquarters company, a service company, and three medium-tank companies, each with three platoons consisting of six CDL tanks and one standard fighting tank. Each company also had two standard tanks as command tanks, and battalion headquarters had three more.

Developed by the British in 1939, the CDL project was shared with the United States in 1942 with the proviso that American forces would not use the equipment without checking with London first. Moreover, the components would be manufactured by different firms and assembled under military supervision in order to maintain secrecy. The primary mission of CDL tanks was to provide illumination for aimed fire at night. Secondary missions included dazzling enemy soldiers with a flicker effect and protecting friendly foot troops in triangles of darkness formed between adjacent lights. Training, conducted in strictest secrecy at Fort Knox, Kentucky, and the Desert Training Center at Indio, California, was completed between December 1943 (736th and 748th) and April 1944 (739th). No CDL battalion was used in combat as such. In light of the need for more standard battalions to support infantry divisions, the U.S. European command on 23 October 1944 requested permission to convert four special battalions to standard battalions. The War Department agreed, and the 701st, 736th, 740th, and 748th were so converted; the 738th and 739th were converted to mine exploder battalions.[8]

The separate battalions, then, came from three sources. The first independent tank battalion, the 70th, was created alongside the 1st and 2d Armored divisions on 15 July 1940, originally as a light tank battalion. From the start, it was to support infantry divisions and operate under their command.[9]

A second wave of independent battalions was activated in 1941–43 to fill out the pool of units that McNair envisioned as a flexible force to strengthen infantry or armored divisions as needed. Indeed, the Armored Force initially referred to these units as *reserve* tank battalions. These included the 191st–194th (pulled together from National Guard tank companies), 701st–702d, 735th–764th, 766th–767th, and 781st–785th battalions.[10]

The third group of independent battalions resulted from the reorganization of the armored divisions in late 1943. These included the 706th–718th, 771st–780th, and 786th–788th.[11] The 712th and 777th Tank battalions, for example, were separated from the 10th Armored Division on 20 September 1943.[12]

From the initially planned fifteen separate battalions, the number of such units rose to twenty-six by late 1942, forty-one by mid-1943, and sixty-five by late 1944. The separate battalions by that time outnumbered the fifty-four battalions incorporated into armored divisions.[13] As of 1 January 1945, thirty-one separate battalions were in the ETO: the 70th, 191st, 701st, 702d, 707th, 709th, 712th, 735th, 736th, 737th, 738th MX (mine exploder), 739th MX, 740th, 741st, 743d, 744th Light, 745th, 746th, 747th, 748th, 749th, 750th, 753d, 756th, 759th Light, 761st, 771st, 774th, 778th, 781st, and 784th.[14] (Rich Anderson's list— corrected here—mistakenly includes the 40th, which was actually part of the 7th Armored Division, and omits the 784th, which is reported attached to the 104th Infantry Division beginning 31 December 1944.)

## THE ARMORED GROUP

Independent tank battalions initially were subordinated to an armored group headquarters. McNair envisioned armored groups as performing the role of armored divisions. He thought that battalions of tanks, armored infantry, and armored artillery from nondivisional pools could be flexibly attached to the headquarters, but this did not work out in practice.[15]

Armored groups wound up playing a rather peculiar role, generally as the coordinator of armor-related issues within a corps. The after-action reports (AARs) of the tank battalions indicate that the armored group headquarters now and again exercised tactical control over tanks in combat. More generally, however, they provided services such as coordinating equipment upgrades; scheduling chaplain services, Red Cross Clubmobile visits, stage shows, and movies; obtaining replacement tanks and ammo; and arranging for special equipment such as mine-clearing tanks. They collected information on and inspected their battalions, exercised command authority when those battalions were between attachments to infantry divisions, and sometimes passed orders from the corps or division to the battalions.

Some armored groups played different roles. The 4th Armored Group, for example, specialized in preparing tank and amphibious units for operations in the Pacific.[16] The 5th Armored Group was organized solely to oversee the activation of several battalions manned by black enlisted men and largely white officers, including the 758th Light, 761st, and 784th Tank battalions; it was deactivated in December 1944.[17]

Beginning October 1944, armored groups in the ETO were judged redundant and were gradually attached to armored divisions to provide a more robust headquarters capability for their combat command reserve (CCR) elements. A small detachment was carved off each group to remain as the corps armored section. The first so treated was the 3d Armored Group, which was attached to the 5th Armored Division. By the end of the war, this practice had become general.[18]

## FROM ACTIVATION TO INVASION

As the independent tank battalions stood up, they often obtained cadre troops—those needed to form the organizational skeleton of a unit—from another battalion. An order from Headquarters, Armored Force on 16 March 1942 indicated that ten of the twelve then existing independent tank battalions were to be manned at their T/O & E strength "plus a cadre equivalent over strength" in order to provide trained troops later to newly activated battalions.[19] The 746th Tank

Battalion, for example, drew its activating officers from the 760th Tank Battalion and its initial cadre of enlisted men from the 70th Tank Battalion.[20]

Newly formed battalions typically went through a basic-training regimen of about thirteen weeks and qualification on tank weapons, but the details varied from battalion to battalion. Most courses were at the unit's home base, but some officers and men attended the Armored Training Center at Fort Knox, Kentucky. Some battalions had to conduct their own basic training for raw recruits received directly from replacement centers. The Army's assumption was that six months was the time required to train a unit for combat.[21] First furloughs followed the completion of basic training. For most men, this was the first opportunity to visit their homes as soldiers.[22] Maneuvers followed, normally in combination with a permanent change of station for the battalion. Major maneuver areas included Camp Polk, Louisiana; and the Desert Training Center, including Camp Young in Indio, California, and Camp Laguna, thirty miles north of Yuma, Arizona.

The country was at war, but despite their warlike preparations, the men were an ocean away—psychologically and physically—from what was to come. The history of the 741st Tank Battalion for 6 April 1942 records: "A demonstration of a company of tanks in attack was given at 1:00 P.M. that day. This demonstration was witnessed by a number of civilians and the remainder of the battalion. Immediately following this, tanks were available for members of this battalion to give tank rides to members of their families." On 10 November 1942, notes the 743d Tank Battalion diary, one tank and two halftracks took part in a scrap drive in Centralia, Washington, and on 14 November Lieutenant Linsroth took one tank and a halftrack to Seattle to participate in the half-time show of a

University of Washington football game. In April 1943, the 747th
Tank Battalion hosted a dance for a newly arrived WAAC (Wom-
en's Army Auxiliary Corps) detachment, which the unit diary
brags was a "big success."

The training that the independent tank battalions underwent was to some extent appropriate for what would come.
Brand-new outfits were able to learn the basics of fire-and-
maneuver as coherent units. The records of the 741st Tank
Battalion, which would land in Normandy on D day, indicate
that this unit conducted maneuvers with the infantry-heavy
7th Mechanized Division in October 1942 and underwent amphibious training in July 1943. The 70th, another D day assault
battalion, underwent amphibious training in June 1941 and
practiced tank-infantry cooperation with the 1st Infantry Division in a series of maneuvers later that year.

The tankers in some cases were already learning critical
lessons such as the need to establish direct liaison contact
with the infantry. There is no indication in the records, however, that such lessons were pulled together and shared among
the tank battalions.

In other aspects, the training did not give the soldiers in
most outfits a realistic appreciation for, and preparation to
handle, the realities they would face in France. In the worst
cases, the training appears to have been simply inadequate or
to have created unrealistic notions about the likely course of
battle.

Homer Wilkes, a lieutenant in the 747th, recalls that for
his outfit, "there was no training with the infantry, no training
with artillery, no training with air support, and no amphibious
training. (However, the men were taught indirect fire with
tank cannons by their own officers.) In that condition, the
command sailed for England in February 1944."[23]

The diary of the 743d offers the following account of exercises that probably encouraged the tankers to view them-

selves as invulnerable less than one year before the battalion would be taking heavy losses in Normandy: "Battalion participated in a maneuver from 27 June 1943 to 14 July 1943. . . . When the enemy armored division attacked just after daybreak, they were stopped with loss of thirty-six tanks, five halftracks, and six wheeled vehicles. The battalion lost one tank and one halftrack. During the remainder of the day, the enemy continued its attacks, hitting at the flanks, but it encountered stubborn resistance each time and sustained losses at the ratio of 20 to 1."

Training did not include the use of tanks in towns, which was common in European combat.[24]

Battalion records provide no evidence that units were given any practice dealing with known German capabilities (beyond basic enemy vehicle identification training) in the tactical or technical sense. This was true despite contact with the enemy, which for the independent tank battalions occurred as early as 29 December 1942, when the Afrika Korps mauled a platoon of Company A, 70th Tank Battalion, northeast of Pichon, Tunisia.[25]

## CHARIOTS OF IRON

The Sherman M4 tank—the nickname adopted from the British, who named American armored equipment after famous Civil War generals—is probably the most simultaneously praised and criticized armored vehicle in history. The M4 in its many variants was the only medium tank used by the independent tank battalions in the ETO. (A few of the M26 Pershing tanks—a medium tank dubbed "heavy" to improve troop morale—saw service with the armored divisions shortly before the end of the war.) Standardized in 1941, the Sherman represented the cutting edge of tank technology. Critics argue, however, that by 1944 the Sherman was effectively obsolete

when compared to tanks fielded in western Europe by the
Germans. Others argue that the M4 was a remarkably versa-
tile and reliable tank well suited to the American combined-
arms approach to war.

The tank battalions landing in Normandy initially were
equipped mostly with M4 or M4A1 Shermans (the former had
a welded hull, and the latter a cast hull with rounded con-
tours). The thirty-four-ton vehicle had a crew of five (commander, gunner, cannoneer/loader, driver, and assistant driver/
bow gunner or "bog"). Its main armament consisted of a 75mm
gun in a fully traversing turret supplemented by a coaxial
.30-caliber machine gun, a second .30-caliber mounted in the
hull at the assistant driver's position, and a .50-caliber machine gun mounted outside the commander's hatch on the
turret. The front plate (glacis) of the Sherman had two inches
of armor (later increased to two and a half inches), the sides
and rear were one and a half inches thick; and the front of the
turret was three and a half inches at its thickest. The power
plant was a Wright Whirlwind aircraft engine that could push
the vehicle close to thirty miles per hour under optimal conditions; M4A3s using Ford engines entered the battalions, too,
and the records of some units indicate that these became the
preferred variant.

The Sherman was undeniably a compromise to the realities
of American production capabilities and shipping capacity—a
compromise that arguably lasted longer than necessary. The
Sherman, for example, inherited the chassis and engine of its
predecessor, the M3 (referred to as the General Lee in American service and the General Grant in British service). The M3
itself had been a massive compromise with the mounting of its
main gun in a side sponson that provided only limited traverse. Moreover, Army regulations prohibited vehicles wider
than 124 inches because of shipping constraints.[26] These re-
strictions affected how wide the turret could be, which in turn

limited the size of the main gun, and how wide the tracks could be, which in turn helped determine the vehicle's "flotation," or ability to distribute its weight for maximum maneuverability on soft surfaces such as mud. The need to mount the Wright Whirlwind engine forced a relatively tall design in relationship to the vehicle's other dimensions.

The Sherman also initially fell victim to official U.S. Army doctrine, formulated by McNair, which saw the role of the tank as infantry support and for fast, deep penetrations of the enemy's rear once infantry had cracked the main line of resistance. Tank destroyers—not tanks—were supposed to deal with enemy tanks. The close-support role led directly to the selection of a low-velocity 75mm gun for both the M3 and M4.[27] The Army gave little emphasis to providing the Sherman with the kind of armament it needed to kill the latest generation of German tanks until it became clear that, in the real world, American tanks were running into German tanks with some regularity— and often with unhappy results.

## The Sherman as Impotent Deathtrap

American tankers had been assured by the Army that they had the finest tank in the world, but it took only a few encounters— particularly with German Panther tanks—for them to realize they had problems. The Sherman's 75mm gun could deal effectively with the still widely used Panzerkampfwagen IV (always referred to by tankers as the "Mark IV"), but it could not penetrate the glacis of the Panther (Mark V) or Tiger (Mark VI) from *any* range. All tanks common in German service, meanwhile, could penetrate the thickest armor of the Sherman at all ordinary combat ranges and had superior optics that allowed accurate gunnery at longer distances.[28] Indeed, the literature is rife with tales of rounds from the Panther's long-barreled, high-velocity 75mm cannon and the Tiger's powerful 88mm gun penetrating Shermans and exiting the other side of the tank. Major Welborn G. Dolvin, commanding officer of the 191st Tank Battalion, summarized the situation from the tanker's point of view in August 1944 after his outfit had been in action for only two weeks: "The Sherman tank, equipped with the 75mm gun, is no match for . . . the German Mark IV, V, or VI. On numerous occasions, hits were obtained on German tanks with no noticeable results. On the other hand, German high-velocity tank guns never failed to penetrate the Sherman tank. This situation has a tremendous effect on the morale of the tank crews. This was evidenced by reluctance of crews to fire on German tanks, feeling that it would do no good and would result in their being promptly knocked out. Crews soon became ultracautious where German tanks were in the vicinity."[29]

Shermans also had a nasty tendency to catch fire and burn out completely when hit, which conditioned crews to abandon them at the first sign of trouble. The 743d Tank Battalion, for example, lost ninety-six medium tanks from 6 June 1944 to 8 May 1945, sixty-five of which burned.[30] Crews believed that the use of a gasoline-powered engine, rather than diesel, was the reason for this, but investigation by the Army concluded that burning ammunition propellant from rounds in the Sherman itself was the main cause.[31] Whatever the cause, the following account from the history of the 737th Tank Battalion could describe the experience of any other battalion at one time or another: "[On 3 March] 2d Platoon of Company B working with the 3d Battalion of the 10th Infantry [Regiment of the 5th Infantry Division] advanced toward Ordorf. Suddenly the tanks were subjected to a terrific barrage from five well-camouflaged 88mm AT [antitank] guns [and all] five tanks were set aflame."

American tankers generally thought that German tanks, with their wide tracks on models subsequent to the Mark IV, had better mobility in mud or snow than theirs did. Tests showed that the Panther was capable of speeds similar to the Sherman's on surfaced roads.

The Sherman had some irritating mechanical peculiarities, too. In order to prevent hydrostatic lock in tanks with the Whirlwind power plant, for example, a crewman had to hand-crank the engine about fifty turns (which actually turned the engine over five times) before starting. The engine also needed to be operated at above 1,200 rpm to avoid fouling its 18 spark plugs; during periods when advances were measured in yards, there was much engine idling and many fouled plugs.[32] Nonetheless, particularly as compared with German tank engines, the Sherman's engine variants were all reliable workhorses.

Sherman crews complained of one more characteristic: the Sherman's high silhouette, which they said was inferior to that of the German tanks. But this gripe, at least, stands up poorly to examination. The Sherman was tall relative to its other dimensions, but not as compared with German tanks. The Sherman equipped with the 75mm gun was nine feet tall (76mm-equipped Shermans were slightly taller), while the Panther was nine feet eight inches high and the Tiger was nine feet five inches. Perhaps tankers should have been grateful that the Sherman presented relatively less target area in the other two dimensions than did their foes.

## The Sherman as Effective War Machine

The Army was more than a little defensive about the fighting qualities of the Sherman. Let us stipulate: The Sherman was not capable of going toe-to-toe with Panthers or Tigers on equal terms, particularly at long ranges. Although this problem loomed large in the minds of tankers, such encounters were not the typical daily activity of the infantry-support tank crew, and the Sherman would arguably have been no better at its other missions had it been a Panther. Moreover, the historical record shows that the Sherman was hardly helpless against German armor.

The Army offered a strategic-level defense of the Sherman that probably struck many tankers as a massive rationalization. Nonetheless, wars are won or lost in the big picture. General Patton offered the following observations in a 19 March 1945 letter to *The Army and Navy Journal*, published on 31 March:[33]

Since 1 August 1944, when the Third Army became operational, our total tank casualties have amounted to 1,136 tanks. During the same period we have accounted for 2,287 German tanks, of which 808 were the Tiger or Panther variety, and 851 on our side were the M4. These figures of themselves refute any inferiority of our tanks, but let me add that the Third Army has always attacked, and therefore better than 70 percent of our tank casualties have occurred from dug-in antitank guns and not enemy tanks, whereas a majority of the enemy tanks have been put out by our tanks.

In the current operation, had the 4th Armored Division been equipped with Tiger and Panther tanks and been required to make the move from Sarreguemines to Arlon, then through to Bastogne, from Bastogne to the Rhine, and now to Mainz, it would have been necessary to re-armor it twice; and furthermore, it would have had serious if not insurmountable difficulty in crossing rivers.

Finally, we must remember that all our tanks have to be transported on steamers, and the difference between forty tons and seventy tons is very marked. The seventy-ton tank could never have been brought ashore in landing boats as many of our medium tanks were. Nor could they have marched from the Cotentin Peninsula to the Rhine as practically all of our tanks have been required to do.

The experiences of at least one independent tank battalion, which kept unusually good aggregate records, seem to support aspects of Patton's case. The 743d, while losing ninety-six medium tanks during the European campaign (many to antitank guns or bazookas) reported forty-one Mark IV, twenty-six Mark V, four Mark VI, and ten self-propelled guns (eighty-one total) positively destroyed. The battalion also destroyed approximately one hundred pillboxes and machine-gun nests, thirty-six antitank guns, nine field pieces, four armored cars, and approximately one hundred twenty-five miscellaneous wheeled vehicles— the targets expected of the infantry-support tank. On the other hand, the 3d Armored Division reported dramatically higher loss rates in proportional terms. The 3d, one of two "heavy" armored divisions with more tanks than the standard reorganized armored division, entered combat in Normandy with 232 Shermans. The division during the European campaign lost 648 completely destroyed and another 700 knocked out, repaired, and put back into service.[34]

Long-range mobility was, as Patton suggested, a real strength of the Sherman. The M4 used half as much gasoline as did the heavier German tanks, and the Sherman's track was good for about 2,500 miles, as compared with about 500 miles for the Panther and Tiger.[35]

Moreover, separate tank battalion loss rates suggest that one of the Sherman's main weaknesses was inexperienced crews. Units tended to suffer a substantial portion of their total losses for the war in their first few weeks of combat, after which the tankers who survived evidently learned how to fight more effectively. Consider the following examples. The sixteen tanks lost by the 743d on D day alone accounted for

17 percent of its total Sherman losses for the war; the 737th, attached to the 35th Infantry Division, entered combat on 14 July. It lost twenty-three Shermans in its first three days of fighting, 35 percent of its total losses for the war.[36] The 750th, attached to 104th "Timberwolf" Infantry Division, endured its first real combat on 16 November 1944 near Aachen and lost thirty-five tanks in the first seven days of fighting, an astonishing 61 percent of the battalion's total medium tank losses; the battalion's AAR specifically draws attention to inexperience as a contributing factor in the losses.[37]

Tankers nonetheless made it clear that they wanted more armor, better maneuverability, and a more lethal main gun. The Army was working on it, which makes it difficult to compare the Sherman, in its many guises and various modifications, to a Tiger or Panther. The M4 of D day was far outclassed in tank-versus-tank terms, but late production Shermans offer a more ambiguous comparison. Moreover, the production of the improved models began before or slightly after D day. It was to a large extent a problem of deploying equipment in the pipeline, rather than a failure to respond to the challenges posed by German tanks, that accounts for the seemingly outmoded Shermans being left to duke it out with Panthers, Tigers, King Tigers, and other deadly foes until the war's end.

## Protection

Where the Sherman initially offered two inches of steel up front, the Panther sported 80mm (a bit more than three inches) of better-sloped armor, and the Tiger offered 100mm, or about four inches. Matching German armor would not have been a cure-all solution, however. Although tank crews would have preferred to be invulnerable, even some tankers acknowledged that this would have been impossible against superb German weaponry.[38] Tankers knew that German antitank rounds could punch through even ten inches of armor in the corner where the Sherman's turret was thickest.[39] Moreover, American tankers faced two major armor-piercing threats.

The 88mm main gun used in the Tiger and several other tanks and self-propelled guns could penetrate the thick frontal armor of the Tiger—which weighed fifty-five tons—out to about two thousand yards.

German light antitank weapons were also highly effective. The crew-served 88mm Panzerschreck bazooka, in tests performed by the 17th Armored Engineer Battalion, reliably penetrated the frontal armor of the Panther—which weighed nearly forty-six tons—at ranges up to two hundred yards.[40] Lieutenant Belton Cooper, an ordnance officer with the 3d Armored Division, demonstrated that an ordinary Panzerfaust—a one-man antitank weapon—could penetrate the turret front of a Royal Tiger.[41]

Tankers and the Army nevertheless had every incentive to take measures to reduce the danger of penetration. Even before the invasion of France, the Army welded on one-inch thick steel plates to add protection to vulnerable ammunition storage bins and shot traps (armor angled in such a way as to maximize the penetrating power of an incoming round) in front of the driver's and bow gunner's hatches on early model Shermans.

The crews turned to field solutions in hope of adding protection, at least against Panzerfausts and other light antitank weapons. The first expedient was sandbagging. The bags were initially held on with chicken wire or some other quick fix, but service companies later welded brackets intended for the purpose onto many tanks. The 743d Tank Battalion, for example, sandbagged all of its tanks between 18 and 22 July 1944, and its records show that the unit re-sandbagged old tanks and outfitted newly received tanks during down times for much of the rest of the war.[42] There is considerable debate as to whether sandbagging was all that effective. Some field tests suggested not.[43] But some showed promising results: A day after test-firing a German bazooka and antitank grenade against a sandbagged Sherman on 28 July in the 3d Armored Group, trucks headed back to the beach to collect sand for bags for the tanks.[44] If nothing else, as the commanding officer of the 756th Tank Battalion noted, "Sandbagging the front of the tank greatly improves the morale of the crew."[45]

Later in the war, some units actually tried pouring concrete on the front plates of their Shermans. The 750th Tank Battalion, for example, had to use jackhammers at the end of hostilities to remove six inches of reinforced concrete it had added during combat.[46] Experiments conducted by the 709th in February 1945 indicated that poured concrete did not stop bazookas from penetrating the armor plate, but that it did reduce the splash of molten steel inside the tank caused by the warhead to "negligible" proportions.[47] Based on combat experience, tankers in the 753d concluded that antitank rounds that hit concrete-reinforced armor had a reduced chance of killing the crew, even if they knocked the tank out of action.[48]

The Army, meanwhile, produced one-inch armor kits to be welded onto the front of midproduction Shermans with a 47-degree glacis, which had been introduced in 1943 to correct the shot trap caused by protruding hatches. That new glacis design had reduced the slope from 56 degrees, and in order to compensate for the lost ballistic protection, the front armor was increased to two and a half inches.[49] In March 1944— even before the hard lessons of Normandy—Army Ordnance also ordered a limited production run of M4A3E2 assault tanks, nicknamed Jumbos. These tanks began reaching independent tank battalions in October 1944. The Jumbo carried about six inches of armor up front (the lower hull was somewhat thicker than the upper hull) and, combining armor and the gun mantlet, thirteen inches of protection on the turret front.[50] The extra armor reduced the top speed slightly to twenty-two miles per hour. The records of the independent tank battalions demonstrate a certain futility in this armor race; although the Jumbos clearly took more punishment than stock Shermans, they nevertheless regularly fell prey to guns of 75mm and higher, bazookas, and mines.

The Army also introduced "wet" storage for ammunition (racks surrounded by water) into newer models of the Sherman to reduce the probability of burning. A study conducted in 1945 showed that only 10 to 15 percent of Shermans so equipped burned when penetrated, as compared with 60 to 80 percent of those with the original stowage system.[51] Wet storage was not a cure-all, in part because of the tankers' practice of carrying more ammunition than the official combat load (ninety-seven rounds for a 75mm Sherman with a welded hull), with the excess often stacked on the floor.

## Maneuverability

The tank battalions saw the first Army effort to improve mobility during the winter of 1944, when grouser kits, also known as "duck bills," became available. The duck bills were attached to the edge of the tracks, making them wider and thus better distributing the tank's weight. This expedient proved only somewhat successful, however, because the grousers were prone to snap off or bend.

The main step forward was the production of the M4A3E8, which began in August 1944.[52] The final production model of the Sherman, the "Easy 8" had an improved horizontal volute suspension and wider tracks. Major General Isaac D. White, commanding general of the 2d Armored Division, said of this vehicle, "The M4A3E8 has comparable speed and maneuverability to any German tank."[53] (This was not strictly true because German tanks could pivot in place, while U.S. tanks had to turn like a car.) Unfortunately, the Easy 8 did not begin to reach the independent tank battalions until early 1945—and then only in very small numbers.

## Lethality

For the infantry support tank, machine guns were usually the most important weapon in the vehicle (indeed, the very first Shermans had two additional forward-pointing fixed .30-caliber machine guns in the hull). Tankers were happy enough with their .30-calibers, which fired more slowly than the German counterpart but were more accurate.[54] Most units carried 50 percent more .30-caliber ammo than could be contained in organized stowage. The 740th Tank Battalion went into combat with fifty thousand rounds of .30-caliber ammunition per day—and spent them. The tanks had stowage space for only fifteen thousand rounds, so the tankers carried the rest in boxes fastened to the bustle and stacked on the floor.[55] In one day's engagement near Etouvy, France, during the breakout from Normandy, tanks of the 741st expended one hundred thousand rounds of .30-caliber ammo.[56] Tankers had mixed feelings regarding the .50-caliber mounted on the turret top; German soldiers were afraid of it, but a tank could carry only five or six hundred rounds of .50-caliber ammunition.[57]

The main point of contention was the cannon. The Army began testing a 76mm tank gun with a much higher muzzle velocity than the 75mm in August 1942, and the results were so good that the weapon was standardized and accepted into inventory as the 76mm gun M1 in September 1942. Although the project languished until a new turret was developed in

1943, the Army Ground Forces ordered production of one thousand Shermans with the new weapon. Serial production began in January 1944 and expanded that May.[58] A few 76mm Shermans made it to England in time for D day, but commanders were not enthused until stung by the bad experiences of tankers in France.

Like many equipment upgrades, the appearance of 76mm Shermans in the independent tank battalions varied tremendously. At one extreme, the 774th Tank Battalion entered combat in August fully equipped with 76mm-equipped Shermans, and the 70th drew 76mm Shermans on 10 August (all of which went to Company A).[59] On 19 October 1944, the 737th received a single tank with a 76mm gun, which it decided to use as an assault gun attached to Headquarters Company and shuttle among the line units as needed.[60] The 741st drew its first 76mm Shermans on 1 January 1945,[61] and the 743d received its first five M4s with 76mm guns on 2 January.[62] The 3d Armored Group noted on 7 January 1945, "The issue of M4 medium tanks mounting 76mm cannon . . . was noteworthy only in the sense of promise, for separate tank battalions [have been] issued only a few of them."[63] It was not until February 1945 that the independent tank battalions moved to the top of the list, ahead of armored divisions, for allocation of 76mm tanks arriving in theater.[64]

Although better against armor than the 75mm, the 76mm gun was not the solution for which tankers had hoped. It, too, proved to be generally ineffective against the frontal armor of the Panther and Tiger, except at close ranges, thanks to a botched assessment of the gun's penetration ability by the Ordnance Department during development.[65] The gun's effectiveness improved significantly with the introduction of tungsten-core high-velocity armor-piercing (HVAP) rounds, with which the Sherman finally gained the ability to kill Panthers and Tigers from the front at typical combat distances.

Once again, deployment of equipment in the pipeline caused the Sherman to remain weaker than it had to be. HVAP rounds began to reach independent tank battalions by September 1944 at the latest,[66] but the new ammunition remained extremely scarce for the entire war. In late March 1945, when the U.S. Ninth Army notified the 3d Armored Group that HVAP would henceforth be available as a standard issue, it indicated that one-half round per tube per month could be drawn.[67] Nevertheless, as Lt. Col. Stuart Fries of the 747th Tank Battalion observed in a "Battle Lessons" report on 1 January 1945, "The 76mm gun firing HVAP ammunition is a good step forward toward battlefield parity with the heaviest German armor."

A drawback to the 76mm gun was that it fired a far less effective high-explosive (HE) round than did the 75mm. For infantry support tanks, this was a major sticking point. At least some infantry commanders seemed to want to keep a preponderance of 75mm guns around. Indeed, Maj. Gen. Alvan C. Gillem, who became commander of the Armored Force in May 1943, was an infantry officer and believed that no more than one-third of Shermans should have the 76mm gun because of its less-effective HE round.[68]

The 76mm gun also produced a muzzle blast so large that crews had trouble tracking the rounds in order to correct their aim. It was not until the Easy 8 was delivered that a muzzle brake (a pineapple-shaped device on the end of the gun tube with vents that diverted blast force to the sides) corrected the problem. In February 1945, the 709th Tank Battalion experimented with the field expedient of cutting muzzle brakes off German 88mm guns and welding them on to Sherman 76mm cannons—with good effect.[69]

Tankers also complained that the 76mm gun turret had a semicircular floor with a flat edge that, in combat, could jam against spent shell casings or trap the loader's foot.[70]

The Sherman had one key advantage over German tanks

when mounting either the 75mm or 76mm cannon: a faster turret rotation speed. The Sherman had power traverse, while German tanks had a manual system and heavier turrets. This factor could determine who got off the first shot, and American tankers valued their advantage in this area.[71] The Sherman also had a longer gun-tube life than the high-velocity German tank guns, but as the Army admitted, "Due to the short battle life of [our] tanks, the present accuracy life of gun tubes greatly exceeds that of the tanks in which they are mounted."[72]

Some observers have lamented that the Sherman was not provided with a 90mm gun. Lieutenant Colonel George Rubel of the 740th Tank Battalion, however, described his view on the subject, which he shared with the War Department in March 1945:

> My personal opinion is that tanks must fight tanks, and must be able to knock them out with their firepower. Our 90mm gun could not do this for the reason that it lacked sufficient velocity. I would much rather have a 75mm tank gun with an extremely high-velocity projectile than a 90mm or larger gun for several reasons: First, very few rounds of 90mm ammo can be carried in a tank; second, it lacked penetrating power; third, that the great weight of the gun prevented fast traverse; and fourth, that the extreme length of the barrel made it impossible to traverse to the side in narrow streets or on roads lined with trees or telephone poles. The present M26 tank has accumulated all of these disadvantages and is worthless in street fighting, fighting in woods, or in fact anywhere except wide-open spaces.[73]

Actually, HVAP ammunition was available in very small quantities for the 90mm gun, too. Nevertheless, postwar Army surveys of tankers indicated that, in most cases, they believed 90mm ammunition was too large for easy handling in battle. They appeared to want something equivalent to the Panther's high-velocity 75mm gun. A survey of tank battalion commanders conducted about the same time indicated a decided lack of enthusiasm for the M26 heavy tank introduced just before the end of the war, with most expressing a preference for the Easy 8—perhaps with add-on armor like that of the Jumbo— or for a new tank entirely.[74]

## Other Armored Members of the Team

Six Shermans in every battalion, usually grouped in a platoon attached to the battalion headquarters, carried 105mm howitzers. (Battalions landing on D day for some reason equipped their assault gun platoons with 75mm Shermans until established ashore.) These assault guns at times played the role of an artillery battery, but they could generally only do so when the infantry division to which the battalion was attached integrated the pieces into its fire-direction system. The assault guns also often provided direct-fire support to infantry. They proved effective as antitank weapons when called upon, although they were somewhat hampered by the absence of power traverse. During the Battle of the Bulge, 3d Armored Group informed its battalions that 105mm high-explosive antitank (HEAT) ammo was "very effective" against Tiger tanks.[75] Tests carried out by the 736th Tank Battalion against a captured Panther showed that assault guns firing HEAT ammo reliably penetrated the front hull at 350 yards, but the flight path of the round was erratic, precluding great accuracy.[76]

Company D in each standard battalion was equipped with M5 light tanks, although by the end of the war some had been equipped with Shermans. As of 9 February 1945, for example, the 701st had seventy M4 tanks, instead of the usual fifty-four.

The thinly armored M5 had a crew of four and carried a small 37mm cannon and two .30-caliber machine guns. The M5 showed itself to be of some value in Normandy thanks to the canister round for the main gun, which was quite effective against machine-gun nests and snipers. M5s in the 735th Tank Battalion, for example, carried 70 percent of their ammo load in the form of canister during the hedgerow fighting. The M5's superior speed and mobility (compared with the Sherman) made it a competent spearhead for tank-infantry task forces during the race across France.[77] But the degree of its vulnerability and limited all-around usefulness was reflected in the fact that many battalions pulled crewman from Company D to man Shermans in the other companies after suffering heavy losses. After the 746th suffered heavy casualties battling the 17th SS Panzergrenadier Division and the veteran 6th Fallschirmjäger Regiment near Carentan in early July 1944, the battalion went so far as to stand down Company D completely and transfer its crews into medium tanks.[78] (The 70th, in contrast, incorporated Company D tanks directly into the battered medium tank companies about the same time.) At the end of the war, according to an Army survey, infantry division commanders recommended that light tank companies either be replaced by medium tanks or eliminated; tank battalion commanders, on the other hand, favored deployment of the M24 light tanks.[79]

The M24, featuring an improved suspension and a low-velocity 75mm main gun, began arriving in the ETO in late 1944 as a replacement for the M5, but only a minority of the separate battalions received any. Tankers referred to the M24 as the "Panther Pup" because its suspension system and sloped front armor somewhat resembled that of the much larger Panther.

Where the M5 could not stand up to any German tank, the M24 could. According to the records of the 3d Armored Group, on 20 April 1945 the 5th Armored Division reported that an M24 had knocked out a Tiger tank from close range with two rounds.

Records of the 3d Armored Group indicate that M24s were flagged for armored cavalry units, with the exception of the 736th Tank Battalion, which was to receive a company's worth. Several other battalions also received M24s by May 1945, and the 740th Tank Battalion obtained two M24s by accident in mid-December 1944. As a footnote, the 745th reported on 13 April 1945 that while conducting operations in the Harz Mountains, its tanks destroyed one Mark IV and one enemy-driven M24. If this is true, it indicates that German forces fielded more M24s than did most American separate tank battalions.

Headquarters company had a small M4 tank section used as a pool of replacement tanks for the line companies, for training replacements, and for combat operations on bad days. A mortar platoon, equipped with three 81mm mortars, was mounted in M3 halftracks. Opinion varied with regard to how much use these few tubes were in combat. A survey conducted at the end of the war indicated that infantry division and tank battalion commanders viewed the platoon as superfluous.[80]

Service company ran T2 (later replaced by the M32) recovery vehicles, which were converted M3 tanks lacking main armament. They were a huge force multiplier by playing a key role in the American system of recovering, repairing, and reusing damaged tanks. The service company men who drove unarmored trucks full of gas and ammo—often to the front lines under fire—performed an incredibly demanding duty without which armor could not have fought at all.

## INTO THE UNKNOWN

Once trained, independent tank battalions usually moved to holding bases in the northeastern United States, such as Camp Shanks, New York, and Fort Dix, New Jersey, before shipping out for the United Kingdom and more training or, after the invasion of France, directly for the Continent. The first independent tank battalions—including the 70th, 743d, and 745th—arrived in the United Kingdom between August and November 1943. Describing a typical deployment, the diary of the 747th Tank Battalion recalls that the unit on 10 February 1944 moved to Staten Island, where it boarded the USS *Charles Carrol.* A convoy departed the next day and combined with ships out of Boston. There were twenty-eight transports, the battleship *Nevada,* two escort carriers, and twelve destroyer escorts. The *Charles Carrol* had a displacement of 13,500 tons and carried approximately 1,600 men. On 22 February, after a smooth voyage, the convoy dropped anchor off Scotland, and the *Charles Carrol* docked at Glasgow on 23 February. On 26 February, the battalion moved by train to Fairford, England, although companies B and D would go separately to Stow on the Wold. The battalion was quartered at Palmer Estate in hutments. The headquarters of the 6th Tank Group, the 746th (which had shipped to the United Kingdom in January), and 747th were jointly quartered in the estate mansion. On 6 March, the battalion drew its allotment of medium tanks from Ordnance.

Preparation in the United Kingdom before D day included refresher training, exercises with partner infantry divisions, familiarization with landing craft, waterproofing of equipment for any unit that would go ashore across the beach, and orientation with special equipment built for the invasion. Three battalions selected to go ashore with the first invasion wave in Operation Overlord received special and secret training for a

scheme that embodied the purpose of the independent battalions: giving the infantry close-in gun support throughout combat operations. Two companies each of the 70th (Utah Beach),
741st (Omaha Beach), and 743d (Omaha Beach) Tank battalions were to land minutes before the first infantry, riding special amphibious duplex drive (DD, also known as "Donald
Duck") Sherman tanks to shore. The third medium tank company and battalion tank dozers (Sherman tanks with bulldozer
blades attached) would follow in landing craft.

Developed by the British, the DD conversion to the M4
Sherman added a collapsible screen and thirty-six inflatable
rubber tubes or pillars attached to a boat-shaped platform
welded to the hull of the waterproofed tank. When inflated,
the tubes raised the screen, which was locked into position by
struts. The assembly acted as a flotation device, allowing the
tank to displace its own weight in water and giving the vehicle
about three feet of freeboard. The tank was driven through
the water at seven to eight miles per hour by two eighteen-
inch movable screw propellers, which also acted as rudders,
attached to the back of the hull and powered through a bevel
box off the track idler wheel. Between 15 March and 30 April
1944, the 743d Tank Battalion conducted 1,200 test launches
from landing craft at Slapton Sands, losing only three tanks
and three lives.[81]

Training focused on getting ashore in France rather than
what to do afterward. For example, even though the 70th Tank
Battalion exercised in an inland area that somewhat resembled the hedgerow country of Normandy, all training was invasion related; infantry and tanks had no opportunity to work
on coordination or tactics in hedgerow country, or anywhere
else.[82] The unit history of the 746th Tank Battalion suggests that
maneuvers with the partner 4th Infantry Division routinely
ended on the same day or the day after landing exercises.

The diary of the 747th Tank Battalion indicates that the

unit conducted tactical problems with the 29th Infantry Division, but Homer Wilkes judged this preparation to be inadequate. Wilkes had been a cowboy before joining the Army, where he had risen through the ranks to become platoon sergeant before going to Officer Candidate School in 1942. Always ready to apply the jaundiced eye of practicality and common sense, Wilkes later recalled, "The next training, other than road marches, was taking infantry for tank rides on the Devon moors. I objected vociferously to the battalion commander, then Stuart G. Fries. I practically demanded tactical training, because we had been told they were the infantry we would hit the beaches with. The battalion commander became extremely angry with me, stating there was not a thing I could do about it, for the 29th Infantry Division operations officer said this would be done."[83] Pre-invasion maneuvers gave the Army forewarning that the tank-infantry team was going to have trouble once ashore in France, but commanders took no steps to remedy the situation. American forces conducted a series of landing exercises on the beaches of Slapton Sands. One of these, Beaver, took place on 28 March 1944. Following preparatory fire from all classes of ships of the Royal Navy, companies B and C of the 746th hit the beach in the leading wave. The assault troops moved toward objectives several miles inland, and the unit history reported that "The attack was resumed on the second day ashore and terminated in the afternoon. During this phase of the exercise a new difficulty arose: that of infantry-tank communication. Up to this point the infantry-tank teams had worked with close coordination, due to a prearranged system of smoke signals, but the unexpected situations arising after the successful assault landing created some disruption in contact between infantry and tanks. This was temporarily solved by the use of radio."[84]

The infantry and tanks, however, did not use interoperable

radio equipment; in the above case, one partner physically loaned a radio to the other.

In one respect, the time in the United Kingdom prepared the men in some units for the war ahead; for several battalions, the companies were seldom all in one place at one time, being separated for special training. In the 743d, after several months of this the officers and men of some of the companies were almost strangers to the others.[85] The war of the independent tank battalions was to be one of companies, platoons, or sections. The battalions almost never maneuvered in combat as a unit. Indeed, with his companies and platoons parceled out to support infantry elements, the battalion commander often had little idea what his troops were doing. The 745th, which landed on D day, reassembled all of its elements in one place for the first time on 15 July.[86] The 753d Tank Battalion commander controlled all of his units for only one three-day span between 15 August 1944 and 10 May 1945.[87] A postwar study conducted in the ETO concluded that by the end of the war, the separate tank battalion headquarters had tended to become an administrative unit and advisory staff section only.[88]

Invasion briefings began for battalion officers in early May 1944. In the 747th Tank Battalion, Lt. Col. Stuart Fries and selected officers down to the rank of first lieutenant were cleared for Top Secret bigot (meaning on the access list for) Neptune on 11 May and allowed to read the invasion field order of the 29th Infantry Division, issued on 21 April. On 23 May, all officers were briefed on the invasion orders, and the 29th Infantry Division commanding general spoke to the battalion. On 26 May, the men were briefed and confined to "the park" for security reasons.[89] Homer Wilkes describes the scene:

Toward the end of May [the battalion] was sealed in camp. This consisted of having its English friends string concertina wire around the park. Outside this, British Army guards were posted. . . . A briefing tent was erected. It too was surrounded by barbed wire and guarded by the English. Admission was by positive identification only.

Within this tabernacle, a terrain table depicted the Norman coast from Vierville to Gaborg. This area's code name was Omaha.[90]

The briefing for the 746th officers and men took place on 25 May. The battalion history records: "As the magnitude of the undertaking unfolded before us we felt that we were virtually standing at the entrance of a new era in the annals of mankind." For the 746th, the destination would be a beach code-named Utah.

## D Day: The Big Picture

By early 1944 an Allied strategic bombing campaign so reduced German strength in fighters and trained pilots that the Allies effectively established complete air superiority over western Europe. Allied bombers now turned to systematic disruption of the transportation system in France in order to impede the enemy's ability to respond to the invasion. At the same time, American and British leaders orchestrated a tremendous buildup in the British Isles, transporting 1.6 million men and their equipment to England and providing them with shelter and training facilities. . . .

The Allies would land in Normandy and seize the port of Cherbourg. They would establish an expanded lodgement area extending as far east as the Seine River. Having built up reserves there, they would then advance into Germany on a broad front. Ground commander for the invasion would be General Montgomery. The British Second Army would land on the left, while the American First Army, under Lt. Gen. Omar N. Bradley, landed on the right. Intensive exercises and rehearsals occupied the last months before the invasion. An elaborate deception plan convinced the Germans that the Normandy landings were a feint, and that larger, more important landings would take place farther east, around the Pas de Calais. Here the Germans held most of their reserves, keeping their armored formations near Paris.

Developments on the eastern front also aided the success of the invasion. . . . By March 1944 Soviet forces had reentered Polish territory, and a Soviet summer offensive had prevented the Germans from transferring troops to France.

On 5 June 1944, General Eisenhower took advantage of a break in stormy weather to order the invasion of "fortress Europe." In the hours before dawn, 6 June 1944, one British and two U.S. airborne divisions dropped behind the beaches. After sunrise, British, Canadian, and U.S. troops began to move ashore. The British and Canadians met modest opposition. Units of the U.S. VII Corps quickly broke through defenses at a beach code-named Utah and began moving inland, making contact with the airborne troops within twenty-four hours. But heavy German fire swept Omaha, the other American landing area.

*A Brief History of the U.S. Army in World War II,* Center of Military History, United States Army, Washington, D.C., 1992

# DDs AT D DAY

TOP SECRET
"Neptune"

Hq. 741st Tank Battalion      BIGOT
APO #230, U.S. Army      TOP SECRET
21 May 1944      -Authority: CG
     -1st US Inf. Div.
     -21 May 1944
F.O. #1

    1.      a. See annex #2 to F.O. #1, Hq 741st Tank Battalion.
     b. The British Second Army on the left, the American V Corps in the center, and American VII Corps on the right, together with combined Allied Naval and Air Forces, land simultaneously on the coast of FRANCE with the mission of establishing a beachhead on the continent from which further offensive operations can be developed. . . .
     2. This Bn, less Companies D and Hq. and Ser[vice]. (incl. Med[ical] Det[achment]) will land on Beach OMAHA— Easy Red and Fox Green in direct support of the 2d and 3d BLTs [Battalion Landing Teams], CT [Combat Team] 16,

Companies B and C (DD) landing at H-5, D-day, and Company A landing at H-hour, D-day. Companies abreast with
Companies B and C on the right and left flanks, respectively,
Company A in the center. All companies not participating
in the assault will land on order of the div. commander. . . .

3.       a. Company A will land on Beach OMAHA—
astride the boundary between Beaches Easy Red and Fox
Green at H-hour, D-day, with the mission of directly supporting the attack of the 3d BLT. Prior to landing, Company A will provide fire from landing craft afloat on
orders from Naval authority. When beach defenses are reduced and the beach is cleared, Company A will leave the
beach head by exit E-3 and proceed to assembly area, reorganize and service and prepare to support the 3d BLT
in its attack on objectives to the east. Company commander, Co A, will call upon the company commanders of
Companies B and C for replacement tanks, if necessary, to
insure that Co A is at full strength for further opns. Exit
from the beach and preparation of route to assembly area
will be accomplished by Co A, 37th Engr [Battalion].

            b. Co B, attached to the 2d BLT, CT 16, will land
on Beach OMAHA—Easy Red at H-5, D-day, and support
by fire the landing of the 2d BLT 16th CT. When the beach
defenses are reduced and beach is cleared, attachment to
2d BLT ceases and Co B reverts to bn. control. Leave the
beach by exit E-3 and proceed to assembly area, reorganize, service, and prepare to move to 2d BLT objectives to
reinforce defensive sectors.

            c. Co C, attached to the 3d BLT, CT 16, will land
on Beach OMAHA—Fox Green at H-5, D-day, and support
by fire the landing of the 3d BLT, 16th CT. When the beach
defenses are reduced and beach is cleared, Co C will exit
from the beach by E-3 and follow Co B to assembly area.

After reorganizing and servicing, Co C will proceed with Co B to 2d BLT objectives and be prepared to reinforce defensive sectors. Attachment to 3d BLT ceases upon departure from the beach.

      *d.* (1) All assault units of the bn will land on beaches with intervals of sixty yards between vehicles.

      (2) The traffic circulation plan will be strictly adhered to. Continental traffic moves on the *RIGHT* side of the road. All vehicles will keep to the right.

      (3) DD equipment on tanks of Companies B & C will not be removed or damaged.

      (4) Conservation of gasoline and ammunition will be practiced by all individuals. Engines will not be idled without necessity. Ammunition will not be needlessly wasted.

      (5) All tanks will take every precaution so as not to damage roads or cause them to become un-servicable for use by wheeled vehicles.

      (6) All tanks will avoid damaging telephone field wire, causing the breakdown of important channels of communication.

      (7) Machine gun fire will be concentrated on enemy strong points and pillboxes in addition to cannon fire.

      (8) Efforts will be made to explode antipersonnel mines attached to element C barricades, if they are present, by machine gun fire.

      (9) Extreme caution must be used by all commanders in firing at enemy positions after friendly assault infantry has passed through the tanks. Fire should not be placed, under any consideration, where friendly troops will be endangered.

      (10) Crossfire on the beach will be avoided after passage of the inf.

(11) American fighter support will consist of the P-38 plane only. . . .

OFFICIAL:                SKAGGS
       KING                     Cmdg
       S-3

The 743d, also landing at Omaha Beach, and the 70th Tank Battalion, off Utah Beach, held similar orders. After delays caused by awful weather, the date was set: D day was to be 6 June 1944, and H hour was 0630. A massive flotilla off the coast of Normandy readied itself to launch the largest amphibious operation in history. At 0400 hours, soldiers of the assault wave in the 743d awoke and prepared equipment and vehicles for landing. At 0430, hot coffee and K rations were issued to all men.[1] Tankers in the 741st were getting ready, too, and at 0445 turned over their engines.[2] In the 70th, men downed their last cup of hot java in the galley at 0530.[3]

The invasion plan called for elements of one corps to land at each of the two American beaches: V Corps at Omaha and VII Corps at Utah. Later, XIX Corps would become active in the area between the two lead corps, and an element of XIX Corps' 29th Infantry Division had accordingly been attached to V Corps for the assault.[4]

Weather conditions at H hour were actually somewhat better than predicted, with fifteen-knot winds and eight-mile visibility. Heavy bombers struck coastal defenses on the British beaches and Utah Beach, but low clouds forced bombing on instruments at Omaha, which resulted in most ordnance being dropped to the rear. At 0550, the naval flotilla opened its bombardment of Omaha and Utah beach defenses. The battlewagons and cruisers fired until just before the troops hit the beaches, at which time rocket gunships and other close-support vessels took up the task.[5]

## THE GOOD NEWS: UTAH BEACH

Utah Beach offered advantages to the Germans, who had 110 emplacements with guns ranging from 75mm to 170mm. Immediately behind the beach was a stretch of sand dunes between 150 and 1,000 yards deep, and behind that the terrain had been flooded back to 1 to 2 miles, forcing all traffic onto causeways.[6]

Except for a standard military issue of screw-ups, such as putting troops ashore far away from their assigned landing spots, the Utah Beach assault went as planned. Invading troops encountered only light artillery fire, and by 1000 hours six infantry battalions were ashore.[7] The water was relatively calm when the 70th Tank Battalion DDs launched 1,500 yards offshore and puttered to the beach. All but five made it to the sand. Company C tanks, which were supposed to land after the DDs of companies A and B, actually hit the beach first, becoming the assault wave. The company lost four tanks on the way in, presumably because one LCT (landing craft, tank) was sunk. Little fighting occurred at the water's edge.[8] While Company C tanks took over the mission of suppressing defenses laterally to the left and right of the beach, the DD tanks landed and moved quickly inland. One Company B DD tank commander recalled later, "We dropped our screen and headed for the seawall. Engineers were carrying fifty pounds of TNT on their backs. It was in a block, about the size of a farmer's salt block. They made a pyramid of them against the seawall and set it off, blowing out a big hole. One of our dozers was there moving concrete around. . . . We went over chunks of concrete in the hole and onto a causeway that went through a flooded swamp."[9]

Tanks of the 70th pushed inland to link up with paratroopers of the 101st Airborne Division who had jumped the previous night. Tankers were "unprepared" for the hedgerow

terrain they encountered,[10] but initially faced little resistance
beyond shelling and mines.

Tanks of the 746th Tank Battalion hit Utah Beach late in the
morning in the second wave, although 1st Platoon of Company
A had landed more than two hours earlier in support of the 3d
Battalion, 22d Infantry, 4th Infantry Division. The unit history
describes the landing:

> The run in took a bit over two hours. As we drew nearer
> we became increasingly aware of the great battle taking
> place on the V Corps beach [Omaha] to the southeast. Our
> own beach, Utah, appeared ever more active as we drew
> closer. One half hour before grounding, tank and vehicu-
> lar engines were turned over, shackles removed, and per-
> sonnel readied to mount vehicles. As we drew to one
> thousand yards of the beach, we could see the 1st Platoon
> of Company A in action along the beach against concrete
> fortifications. The tank gunfire from this platoon was be-
> ing augmented by naval fire from vessels just offshore.
>       At 1140 hours the LCTs grounded in three and a half
> feet of water at the bow. The tanks landed on hard sand
> and started toward assembly position. . . .

On both beachheads in the first few days, an emerging
pattern of rapid resubordinations of tankers complicated early
efforts to grapple with the new experience of combat. The
746th, for example, had elements attached to both the 4th Infantry and the 82d Airborne divisions on D day.[11] Company C
was attached to the 82d Airborne Division from 6 to 11 June;
Company A was attached to the 101st Airborne Division on
7 and 8 June; and the remainder of the battalion was attached
to the 4th Infantry Division until 11 June, when the entire

746th was attached to the 90th Infantry Division. On 13 June, the battalion was attached to the 9th Infantry Division, with the exception of Company A, which went to the 82d Airborne Division.[12]

The AAR of the 746th Tank Battalion recorded some of the first hours of the war in Europe for the separate tank battalions:

> At 1750 after de-waterproofing their vehicles in the assembly area L, Company C moved out behind a reconnaissance platoon from the 82d Airborne Division [through] St. Marie du Mont to cross roads southeast of St. Mere Eglise. . . .
>
> With the reconnaissance elements leading, the company moved northwest along the road to St. Merc Eglise but was forced to hastily deploy before reaching the creek at 354943 [map coordinates] because of heavy AT [anti-tank] fire coming from the high ground across the creek and just south and southeast of the town. Lieutenant Mercer and 1st Platoon deployed to the left of the road engaging AT guns on the enemy's right flank. In this action three tanks were lost and Lieutenant Mercer [was] mortally wounded. [Under Lieutenant Plagge,] 3d Platoon deployed to the right of the road and approached the creek in an effort to flank the enemy positions from his left. The platoon was unable to cross the creek and one tank bogged. Sergeant Smith, the tank commander, remained in this position for four days with his crew and a staff sergeant from the 82d Airborne Division. During this time and after the action had passed them by, they engaged in firefights with bypassed enemy elements, killing a total of twenty and taking twelve prisoners.
>
> Lieutenant Shields of the 2d Platoon deployed along a narrow front immediately adjacent to the main road and

engaged the guns from these positions. Staff Sergeant Buza moved his tank forward and succeeded in crossing the creek and reaching the high ground. Although other tanks could not follow to support him, Staff Sergeant Buza succeeded in knocking out four AT guns and several vehicles, inflicting heavy casualties on enemy troops.

## THE BAD NEWS: OMAHA BEACH

Wayne Robinson describes the scene briefly in his history of the 743d: "Omaha Beach. 6th of June 1944. France. Six in the morning. Sunrise. Chill, wet wind. In the Channel, heavy weather. Angry waves churned and tossed by a day-old gale. . . . Before they banged close their hatches, tankmen on the invasion boats squinted their eyes against icy spray and tried to make out detail on the hazy horizon ahead of the plunging craft."

The landing beach was about seven thousand yards wide and flanked by cliffs. Defensive obstacles covered the beach. Next came a shingle shelf, which presented a problem for vehicles, and then either a seawall or sand dunes. After a flat, somewhat marshy stretch of ground, bluffs honeycombed with German defensive positions rose 170 feet. A mere four valleys offered exits from the beach.[13]

Off Omaha Beach, winds of ten to eighteen knots caused waves averaging four feet high in the transport area, with occasional waves up to six feet. Breakers were three to four feet.[14] The DD rigging provided about three feet of freeboard.

At approximately H plus 60, LCTs bearing DDs of companies B and C of the 741st Tank Battalion reached position about six thousand yards from shore. In view of the rough weather forecast for D day, the commanding general of Task Force O and the admiral commanding Force O Naval had agreed that the senior naval commander in each LCT flotilla carrying DD tanks would decide whether to launch them at sea or carry them to the beach; the senior DD tank unit commander was to advise the flotilla commander on the matter.[15] Captain James G. Thornton Jr., commanding Company B, was able to reach his counterpart from Company C, Capt. Charles Young, by radio. The two discussed the advisability of launching the DD Shermans in the extremely rough seas—much rougher than any they had tackled during preparatory training. Thornton was an extremely brave man; a product of The Citadel and deeply respected by his noncommissioned officers and men, he was always eager to take the lead.[16] The officers agreed that the advantage to be gained by launching the tanks justified the risk, and they issued orders for launching at approximately H plus 50.[17]

Soon, Thornton was standing atop his strange little armored boat. His head, more than ten feet above the deck, swung through wild arcs as the LCT pitched and yawed. The bow door opened, and it was action time. Thornton could see the beach four miles away and explosions from the naval bombardment churning the bluffs just beyond. Yellow launch flags went up, and Thornton ordered his driver, who could see nothing over the DD's canvas wall, to ease forward into the choppy water.

The tank following Thornton's off the LCT bow swamped immediately, as did the fourth Sherman to launch. Thornton's DD began to suffer damage after only a few yards; struts snapped and canvas tore, and water eventually flooded the engine compartment. He could see other tanks from his company and Company C suffering similar alarming problems, but he could do nothing for any of them. After sailing only a thousand yards, Thornton's tank foundered.[18] The beach—the object of Thornton's planning, training, speculation, and apprehension for months—still seemed so very far away. The crew scrambled to escape, and Thornton found himself bobbing amid the waves and bustle of assault landing craft headed for shore.

All but three of the Company B DD tanks launched, but only two of those survived the full distance to Omaha Beach. Three others landed after a wave sank the first DD to exit their craft and smashed the remaining tanks together, which damaged their screens. Sergeant Paul Ragan, the senior man present, convinced the skipper to take the remaining three Shermans all the way to the beach.[19] The doomed tanks of Company B and all of Company C sank at distances from one thousand to five thousand yards from shore.

Small craft maneuvered to rescue the freezing tankers, and Thornton and his crew were pulled aboard a small landing craft. The boat pointed its bow back toward the long line of transports. Once aboard ship, tankers gratefully changed into dry clothes. The crews were told that they would be evacuated to the United Kingdom.[20]

The tank-dozer platoon of four tanks and all but three tanks from Company A did make it to shore in the second wave. The tanks blazed away with their 75mm guns as they neared the beach, although the odds of hitting anything with aimed fire from a pitching landing craft were remote. Three Shermans went down with an LCT sunk by enemy fire. The LCT bearing Sergeant Holcombe's tank dozer was struck and caught fire but was able to unload its tanks.

In the 116th Regimental Combat Team's (RCT) zone, the officers in charge of the tank-loaded LCTs decided not to risk the conditions of the sea, so all thirty-two DDs of the 743d Tank Battalion were carried to the beach.[21] The unit's S-3 Journal recorded: "Company C landed on Dog White and Easy Green beaches at H-6. Upon approaching beach we were met with fire from individual weapons, 155mm, 88mm, and machine guns. . . . Air support missing." Company A tanks followed the DDs ashore as planned.

## Snafu on the Sand

Once landed, the tankers found themselves on a beach swept by hostile fire and, as the day wore on, cluttered with men and equipment unable to push beyond the seawall and take the bluffs and critical exits through the cliff face. The 1st Infantry Division assault had landed in the teeth of a defense mounted by eight battalions of the well-trained German 352d Infantry Division.[22] Wayne Robinson described the environment met by the tankers of the 743d:

> [A]bout the only type of direct fire that the enemy did not hurl at the tanks was bazookas [tankers applied this term to all German infantry antitank rocket launchers]. The bazookas were to be met later inland. The beachline was a maelstrom of shells ranged in by heavy artillery up to 155mm. Down from the cliffs came the direct fire of anti-tank guns. Mortar shells dropped down. Light and heavy machine guns spewed lead, and there was the crack of small arms, the spray from such automatic weapons as the German burp gun. While four of the five men in each tank crew were not immediately concerned with the hail of machine-gun and small-arms bullets, the fifth man—the tank commander with his head out of the turret—stood exposed to constant danger in the storm of splattering slugs and whistling shell fragments.[23]

The AAR of the 3d Armored Group, to which the 741st and 743d were attached, records the following:

The battle on the beach was hot and heavy. Exits from the beach were not established until the afternoon of D day, so the tanks were deprived of one of their chief tactical advantages: *movement*. In many cases, the tanks had a scant thirty to fifty yards from the water's edge to the seawall or hill in front of them to maneuver in; as one tank commander put it, "We could go straight ahead thirty yards or straight back twenty yards—that's *all*, brother!" Later all movement was impossible in practically all cases because of mines, other vehicles, and foot troops. Consequently, the tanks, making as much use of maneuver as possible but still usually fully exposed, "slugged it out" with the enemy, firing at pillboxes, machine-gun nests, sniper positions, and any other targets of opportunity that presented themselves while taking equal punishment in return. Tank fire was coordinated with infantry attack by verbal and visual instructions of infantry officers. Platoon leaders and company commanders of infantry units pinned down by enemy fire pointed out the sources of enemy fire and the tanks silenced enemy guns by 75mm, HE, and machine-gun fire. Searching tank machine-gun fire in the weeds and trees in the paths ahead of the foot troops helped greatly in clearing out snipers.

Staff Sergeant Fair commanded one of the Company A tanks in the 741st Tank Battalion that made it to the beach aboard an LCT, along with another Sherman and a tank dozer. Sergeant Fair reported his experience shortly after landing:

[We were] supposed to land at 0630 hours about two hundred yards right of Exit-3, but due to weather conditions and other landing craft we beached at Exit-1 near to 743d Tank Battalion. The ramp was dropped in pretty deep water and we left the craft. I was in No. 1 tank, Sergeant

Larsen No. 2 tank, and the dozer No. 3. The water was up
over our turret ring. We finally pulled up on the beach but
still stayed in the water enough for protection. Our bow
gunner and gunner started spraying the trees and hillside
with .30-cal. while, not helped by the snipers and shrapnel, we looked for antitank guns and pillboxes. It wasn't
long until we spotted one, which no doubt was a machine-
gun emplacement. I put my gunner on it and he fired. His
first shots went low, but after the correction was made the
next shots entered straight through the opening and put it
out of action.

We had to keep moving up with the tide, for it was
coming up pretty fast. All of a sudden hell broke loose in
front of us; they had made a hit on the boat obstacles on
which were Teller mines. We moved to a new position to
the left and began firing in the direction we thought it
came from. I noticed the tide was closing in on us and we
had no exit to escape from in case we had to move, for
there was a hill in front of us, a good tank obstacle, and
casualties were piling up all around us. I started down the
beach to look for our platoon leader, who was Lieutenant
Barcelona. The going was slow, for we had to weave in
and out among bodies and sometimes stop till the medics
cleared them from our path. On our way down, we accounted for two machine-gun nests that the infantry located for us. We finally located the 1st Platoon, so we got
in firing position, as we were firing at gun positions located below Exit-3. Sergeant Larsen's tank was hit by 57mm
*[sic, not used by defenders]* AP between the gun shield and
extra armor plate, wounding his gunner. It also smashed
the breach mechanism and recoil. Sergeant Larsen got a
few powder burns on the face. He gave orders to abandon tank.

About that time, Lieutenant McDonough came moving

up the beach. I was sitting crossways in his path so I
pulled up on the bank and got stuck in the pebbles. I heard
someone call me and I looked over the side. I saw Private
First Class Robinson of Company A, 741st Tank Battalion.
He was wounded. I couldn't hear what he was trying to tell
me, so I dismounted. He wanted a cigarette and told me
to give him morphine. I took him on up where Sergeant
Larsen's crew was and gave him morphine and covered
him up. Coming back I tried to unhook our trailer [holding
extra ammunition] so we could back up. It was in our way
all of the time. If I had known what an obstacle it was in
the first place I would have left it on the LCT. I finally got
it unhooked and we tried to get off the bank again, resulting in breaking about ten connectors and threw the track.
We were out of HE and all the heavy firing was about over
with so we dismounted and got behind our tank. All told
we fired, Sergeant Larsen and our tank, 450 HE and an
uncounted number of .30-cal.[24]

Corporal Steve Hoffer was a crewman in a Sherman commanded by Staff Sergeant Skiba that landed nearby. Hoffer
had to take command of his tank when the sergeant was
killed:

Second Section of 2d Platoon arrived on LCT at Easy Exit-1
at 0635 hours 6 June 1944. Staff Sergeant Skiba's tank was
first to debark followed by Sergeant Call at about fifty
yards. Staff Sergeant Skiba's tank drove around the obstacles to the left and Sergeant Call to the right, and took up
a defiladed position behind the bank approximately one
hundred yards apart. Encountered only machine-gun fire
up to that point. From our defiladed position Staff Sergeant
Skiba's tank fired on several machine-gun nests from which
fire was visible, then picked up a log emplacement located

at extreme top of hill on our right and fired several rounds of 75mm. A captain from the 16th Infantry came to the tank and directed fire on a concealed 88mm gun. Later this captain and a lieutenant colonel went up to the same position and captured twenty-one prisoners. In the meantime the captain directed fire on two other targets, which were knocked out, and the infantry was then able to advance. The enemy during this time was laying down heavy mortar fire around us, and several holes were noticed in around our [temporary exhaust] stacks. One shell landed quite close to the tank and Staff Sergeant Skiba was killed almost instantly (approximate time 1045 hours). The crew assisted in taking Staff Sergeant Skiba out of the tank and calling the medics to his aid. Captain King came with information first to move to Exit-3. Seeing Staff Sergeant Skiba had been killed, he gave Corporal Hoffer command of the tank. In backing out of defiladed position the tank threw a track. The crew then worked on track under mortar fire. Crew had to quit work several times to hunt cover.[25]

Sergeant Holcombe of the 741st, meanwhile, followed the tank dozer in front of him from the burning LCT. They were in water almost up to the Shermans' back decks. Suddenly, the first tank lurched to a halt after being struck by an 88mm shell. The men bailed out and clambered aboard Holcombe's tank, which carried them to the sand. By this point, however, Holcombe had had enough of his first time under fire and ordered his crew to abandon tank. Realizing that their sergeant was in shock, the crew refused. The bow gunner climbed into the turret, took command of the Sherman, and helped load the 75mm gun. Once ashore, the dozer began clearing obstacles and pushing sand into berms to shield the pinned-down infantry. The crew of Holcombe's tank decided to share blankets and food with the wounded and pulled the machine guns out of the tank for the infantry to use while the dozer went about its work.[26]

Meanwhile, because the command radio had been ruined by seawater, battalion command personnel had to move from tank to tank to direct fire and move vehicles into more advantageous positions. Both technical sergeants and the radio operator in the group were wounded and had to be evacuated.[27]

Offshore from the 743d Tank Battalion's beach, Sergeant Gerald Bolt's leg was shattered by a shell burst while he climbed into the turret as the landing craft headed for the beach. When he found that his leg would not support him while standing in the turret, he ordered his crew to strap his leg to the recoil guard on the 75mm gun. In another tank, Pvt. Irvin Reddish moved from the bog seat to take command of his tank dozer after the commander was hit, and he climbed out again under fire to release a stuck blade with a swift kick. Corporal Arthur Graves, meanwhile, climbed from his driver's seat in a burning tank dozer to replace a wounded gunner in another tank.

Casualties mounted in the 743d. Company A lost eight of sixteen tanks and six dozers; the confusion was such that, at the end of the day, the company commander was not sure how many men had been lost. Company B lost seven tanks with three officers and six enlisted men killed in action. Company C was luckier, suffering the loss of only one tank disabled and five men wounded.[28] The battalion commander, Lt. Col. John Upham—who had put the battalion together—directed operations from an LCT a few hundred yards offshore until he landed ninety minutes after the assault wave. Upham moved from tank to tank, directing fire and movement. Sometime during the morning, a sniper's slug destroyed his right shoulder, but he continued to exercise personal leadership until Green Beach was cleared. Only then did he finally allow medics to evacuate him—an action for which he was awarded the Distinguished Service Cross.[29]

The U.S. Army Center of Military History concluded that, regarding the importance of the tanks on the beach that day, "[t]heir achievement cannot be summed up in statistics; the best testimony in their favor is the casual mention in the records of many units, from all parts of the beach, of emplacements neutralized by the supporting fire of tanks. In an interview shortly after the battle, the commander of the 2d Battalion, 116th Infantry, who saw some of the worst fighting on the beach at Les Moulins, expressed as his opinion that the tanks 'saved the day. They shot the hell out of the Germans, and got the hell shot out of them.' " The history also notes an interesting by-product of the role the tanks played on the beach. In what was described as "silent cooperation," the destroyer *Carmick* did her best to help some tanks on Dog Green that had managed to reach the promenade road. The destroyer's observers watched for the tanks' fire to show targets on the bluff edge and then used the bursts as points of aim for the *Carmick*'s guns.[30]

The first tanks of the 741st crawled off Omaha Beach at about 1700 hours via exit Easy-1, having spent almost twelve hours on that steel-raked sand. At 2000 hours, four battalion tanks were still supporting the infantry against machine-gun nests in the vicinity of St. Laurent-sur-Mer. The battalion's first daily tank status report, submitted to V Corps at 2315 hours on 6 June, indicated that it had three battle-ready medium tanks, two tanks damaged but reparable, and forty-eight tanks reckoned destroyed.[31]

Nearby, the 743d began exiting the beach at about 2200 hours through exit Dog-1 and moved to a bivouac point about two hundred yards from Vierville-sur-Mer. The tankers continued to receive sniper and machine-gun fire until dark. The battalion lost sixteen tanks destroyed or disabled during the day.[32]

Meanwhile, engineers had cut several roads to the top of the bluffs, and landing schedules were adjusted to take advantage of this. The first tanks of the 745th landed on Fox Green about 1630 and made it to the high ground by 2000, with the loss of three Shermans to mines.[33] Because of the high losses suffered by the 741st, Maj. Gen. Leonard Gerow, commanding general of Task Force O, decided to commit the battalion to battle immediately.[34] (Only one company landed on 6 June, with two more coming ashore on 7 June.)[35] The arrival of the 745th raised to five the number of separate tank battalions in France by the end of D day. The 747th would disembark on Omaha at 0700 on 7 June,[36] and at the height of the Normandy campaign, twenty-one independent tank battalions were employed.[37]

The assault on Omaha had succeeded, but ground units there made less progress than planned. The beachhead was one and a half miles deep at its deepest point. At Utah Beach, in contrast, casualties had been low, and the 4th Infantry Division's 8th Infantry Regiment had advanced all the way to its D day objectives.[38]

## Normandy: The Big Picture

American and British beachheads linked up within days. While the Allies raced to build up supplies and reserves, American and British fighter aircraft and guerrillas of the French Resistance blocked movement of German reinforcements. On the ground, Allied troops besieged Cherbourg and struggled to expand southward through the entangling Norman hedgerows. Earthen embankments hundreds of years old matted with the roots of trees and shrubs, the hedgerows divided the countryside into thousands of tiny fields. The narrow roads, sunk beneath the level of the surrounding countryside, became deathtraps for tanks and vehicles. Crossroads villages were clusters of solidly built medieval stone buildings, ideal for defense. Small numbers of German infantry, dug into the embankments with machine guns and mortars and a tank or two or a few antitank guns for support, made advancing across each field costly.

With time short and no room to maneuver, the struggle to break out became a battle of attrition. Allied troops advanced with agonizing slowness from hedgerow to hedgerow, in a seemingly endless series of small battles. Advances were measured in hundreds of yards. Requirements for fire support far exceeded pre-invasion planning, resulting in a severe shortage of artillery shells. The British made several powerful attempts to break through to the open country beyond the town of Caen, but were stopped by the Germans, who concentrated most of their armor in this threatened area. By 18 July the U.S. First Army had clawed its way into St. Lô. . . .

*A Brief History of the U.S. Army in World War II,* Center of Military History, United States Army, Washington, D.C., 1992

# 3

# THE BOCAGE:
# A SCHOOL OF VERY HARD KNOCKS

The need for attaching a tank battalion to an infantry division became apparent in Normandy, and policy to that effect was established.

> The General Board, United States
> Forces, European Theater,
> *Organization, Equipment and
> Tactical Employment of Separate
> Tank Battalions.*

The hedgerow country, or bocage, of Normandy is much like the Gallic persona in general: quaint in its way, but a source of unending frustration for any outsider. The Tactical Study of Terrain in the Neptune package offered this anodyne description: "The eastern section, which is our immediate area of operation, is featured by rolling hills, more-or-less open fields, and wooded areas. Cultivated areas consist principally of rectangular fields and orchards bordered by hedges." It almost sounds nice.

Tankers knew that they would be fighting in hedgerow country, but men from more than one unit say that the reality came as a rude surprise to them upon landing in Normandy. The independent tank battalions would bloody themselves in this morass from 6 June until after the Operation Cobra breakout, starting 25 July. Wayne Robinson describes the bocage from the tanker's perspective:

The open sun-baked stretch of beach was bad; now it was the green hedgerows, and those were very bad, too.

The hedgerows divided the battlefront into hundreds of separate small boxes, each box a separate battle, a lone tactical problem on a checkerboard of fields, each in itself a single objective to be fought for, gained, or lost.

South of St. Jean de Daye, the hedgerows were spaced so close together that a man could sometimes run from one to another across an open stretch of field in four or five seconds—if nothing stopped him.

There was plenty to stop him.

The hedgerows were perfect field defenses for a holding army, and the Germans, never slothful in military matters, took every advantage of this tough terrain to build a defense in depth that, to break through, would take all the fighting spirit, and many of the lives, of "a soft generation," as German propaganda mistakenly plugged American youth.

Dirt embankments and deep natural ditches were standard accessories with every hedgerow. Those embankments and ditches gave the German fighter protection—ready-made trenches on all four sides of each field, so that parallel hedgerows covered each other, and one hedgerow linked with another to form a system of communicating trenches. . . .

Behind the leafy screens were such unseen targets as machine guns, big and little antitank guns, tanks, self-propelled guns on tank chassis, infantrymen equipped with bazookas—all waiting, playing a deadly cat-and-mouse game.

There was only one way to fight the hedgerows—one at a time, expecting the worst at each (and almost always finding it) and thinking of each row as a fortress from which the enemy must be routed, field by field. And that was how it was done.[1]

The German defenders did not simply sit still; they employed an active defense, launching many local counterattacks supported by tanks. Indeed, the Germans used their armor almost entirely for infantry support in a role similar to that of the American separate tank battalions. They also became increasingly aggressive in firing their artillery in battery and battalion volleys.[2]

By D plus 1, tankers were running into the full panoply of German assets: prepared strongpoints, mines, antitank guns, artillery, bazookas, and tanks. The next few days would add a few bombing runs by the largely absent Luftwaffe.

Generals Dwight Eisenhower, Bernard Montgomery, and Omar Bradley (supreme commander of the European Theater, commander of Allied ground forces, and commander of American ground forces, respectively) on D plus 1 agreed to adjust plans somewhat to put more emphasis on linking the beachheads. They feared that the isolated toeholds were vulnerable to German counterattack. Although the Germans had few reserves immediately available, this issue was not moot.[3]

On 7 June, the 746th Tank Battalion was called to St. Mere Eglise to support the 82d Airborne Division in driving off an armored counterattack; it destroyed two German tanks in the action for the loss of one Sherman.[4] (Another source asserts that seven German tanks were knocked out for the loss of two Shermans.)[5] Also on 7 June, Company C of the 743d encountered and destroyed its first enemy tank—a Mark IV—in Formigny, where its own tanks came under fire from friendly troops "who failed to recognize DDs as Shermans."[6] On 9 June, the 745th claimed that it had run into its first Tiger tank, which knocked out one Sherman.[7] Postwar research suggests that American troops faced no Tigers in Normandy; either the tankers were wrong (which is quite possible, as any tank probably looked like a Tiger to the green American tankers), or modern historians are.

The tankers and their infantry partners found they were unprepared to communicate and operate together effectively, just as pre-invasion exercises had foreshadowed. June and July witnessed repeated, often uncoordinated, efforts at the level of each battalion and infantry division to formulate through trial-and-error a new doctrine for resolving these problems. Ironically, considering the problems to come in tank-infantry communications, the infantry at Omaha beachhead relied heavily on tank radios to maintain contact with their own units and offshore naval assets during the first four days of fighting. The infantry had lost most of its radio gear getting to and fighting on the beach. On D day itself, the only working radio in the 116th RCT was that of the 743d's liaison officer. For days, a radioman from the 743d accompanied the commanding officer of the 116th RCT.[8]

Except for some veterans in the 70th Tank Battalion, which had fought in North Africa and Sicily, combat was new and confusing. Homer Wilkes of the 747th realized that on 8 June:

> The column . . . formed up at Vierville in terrain curiously free of hedgerows. We started out in column on the road with Company C leading. I know not what others thought, but I thought we were marching to the front. This impression was corrected minutes later by the appearance of an infantry skirmish line. Although it was my first taste of battle, I knew what that meant. . . .
>
> [One] strongpoint was Osmanville. And there on a clear day this village was attacked by a dozen British fighter-bombers.
>
> The Company C platoon leader of the advance guard was killed trying to display his identification panel. Other officers threw out smoke grenades.
>
> But the strike was pressed home until the pilots had

dropped all their bombs and expended all ammunition. As a result, thirty-two infantrymen were slain, plus our officer, and Company C lost an entire platoon of tanks. . . .

This seemed to paralyze the infantry command group, as well it might. Omaha was their first combat too. After sitting on the road a while we were notified to attend officers call in a field.

There we found Major General [Norman] Cota (the assistant commander [29th Infantry Division]), officers of the 175th [Infantry] Regiment and 747th Tank Battalion officers.

The general asked for a situation report upon which the regimental commander told him he could not get through the enemy line by any means, frontal or flank. He would have to wait for artillery support, which probably wasn't ashore.

The general replied, "All I can tell you, Colonel, is the commanding general told me this attack has to get moving."

He then addressed the 747th's commander. "Colonel Fries, can you get us through this strongpoint?"

To which the Colonel replied, "Yes, Sir."

"Who will be your leading officer?"

The colonel indicated the 3d Platoon, Company A [Wilkes's platoon] would be in the van, whereupon the general was introduced to the officer [Wilkes], who promptly received a pep talk.

"Is there a place for me in your tank?" asked Cota.

The reply was a crewmember would have to be dismounted. And if the general rode, it would be as assistant driver, which entailed handing ammunition up to the turret.

"I can do that. Which is your tank?" he replied. . . .

Cota's request (actually an order) made me nervous.

The general had to serve as a crewmember. Hence I as commander gave him several orders during the night, all of which he obeyed with alacrity. . . .

Before describing the attack, two things must be understood. First, we were then in the bocage. The macadam road was lined with hedgerows over which a tank could climb only at the expense of shaking all ammunition and other moveables loose. Second, by the time the attack started, dusk had fallen.

Now, the plan as [I outlined it to my] tank commanders was to drive along the road until targets were encountered (meaning buildings. We had found out the enemy would be in buildings). Then the first tank would ease left while the second tank, commanded by Lt. George P. Gale, then an enlisted man, would pull alongside. The commanders would engage targets on their respective sides of the road.

General Cota and Captain Stewart listened to the order but said nothing. After all, there wasn't much else one could do. The infantry was stymied. No one had told us about these hedgerows, and to sit still was to invite disaster.

The general took up the assistant driver's slot in the officer's tank and was furnished with crash helmet, headset, and microphone.

An infantry captain accompanied by a Browning Automatic Rifle-man came up to report that his company was attached to the platoon. The BAR-man was an alert, clear-eyed soldier, an encouraging sign under any circumstance. The captain said they would be right behind the lead tank any time [I] needed them.

At one hundred yards, the first buildings were successfully attacked. The advance continued.

No flank guards were visible, therefore after dark [I] commenced throwing hand grenades over the hedgerows.

After a while, the infantry captain requested this be stopped so he could put out flank guards. . . .

Coming upon a mined place, the point stopped. The division had not placed engineers forward with the advance guard. No one present knew how to remove the mines.

The infantry captain suggested firing the coaxial machine gun at them. This was done, but no mines exploded. Therefore it was thought the mines were inactive.

The march continued and the platoon sergeant's tank was blown up by the mines. . . .

[Lieutenant Colonel Fries] came forward on foot to be captured by American infantrymen who promptly stole his pistol (One reason this happened is that the 29th Division landed wearing olive drab uniforms. The 747th landed wearing gas impregnated fatigues that were nearly identical to German Army uniforms. Several tankers were almost shot before we could get a change of clothing).[9]

The 747th AAR reduced these events to this summary: "[The battalion proceeded] to Osmanville, which was taken at 1500 on 8 June, although strongly defended by automatic weapons and AT guns, thence to Isigny, which was taken at 0300, 9 June, encountering little opposition except for sniper fire." Regarding the capture of Isigny by the 747th, the unit diary adds an interesting vignette. Tanks entered Isigny ahead of the infantry and knocked out machine-gun and sniper nests. "Lt. Col. Fries upon order was the first foot trooper in the city—unarmed—the colonel had lost his pistol. Col. Fries walked the length of the city and then returned to the outskirts to inform the inf[antry] that the city was clear and ready to be occupied."

The 741st and 743d Tank battalions, meanwhile, moved

their remaining tanks behind the foot soldiers of the 1st, 2d, 29th, and 30th Infantry divisions and recovered what tanks they could from the surf. On the morning of 7 June, Capt. James Thornton strolled into the 741st transit area. Rather than return to England, he had hitched a ride to the beach, where he fell in with an infantry platoon heading inland. He eventually found someone who knew where the battalion had set up, and he parted ways; now he had a tank company to rebuild.

Just one week later, Wilkes's platoon in the 747th was attacking with the infantry through the hedgerows when his gunner called out, "What's that?" "That" was a 75mm German assault gun only one hundred feet away that opened up on the Sherman.

"Fire!" ordered Wilkes. The 75 roared, and the shell struck true. The round in the chamber was HE, however, and did no damage to the German tank.

"Shot rounds!" ordered Wilkes.

"Up," replied the gunner.

"Fire!" Rounds from the enemy gun were striking obliquely off the turret wall, sending sparks flying through the enclosed space.

"Fire!"

"The gun won't fire!"

"Abandon tank!"

Wilkes's Sherman was knocked out and every member of the crew wounded, two seriously. While his men headed for the aid station, Wilkes limped from tank to tank in his platoon and put them in the best position possible. About this time, the enemy counterattacked, and a sniper shot out the eye of Wilkes's platoon sergeant. Wilkes took over his tank and fought the rest of the day. Wilkes's company commander, meanwhile, took charge of the confused infantry, called in artillery fire, and prevented a German success.[10]

### The "American Luftwaffe"

Tankers quickly learned that they would have to fear their own air force. "Friendly" air attacks on the tank battalions started in Normandy and continued with some frequency until the final dash across Germany in 1945. On 24 June, for example, twenty Allied aircraft strafed the CP of the 746th Tank Battalion near Cherbourg, killing several American soldiers. On 28 June, personnel of the 747th Tank Battalion participated in an experiment to see whether the panels and smoke used by the tankers could be observed from ten thousand feet—something one might have thought the Army would have investigated before invading Europe. The results indicated that the large panels from the vehicle kits were visible but small panels and smoke were not.[11]

---

Replacement tanks and crews began to arrive (by 17 June for the 741st and 20 June for the 743d) but not in numbers adequate to make up losses. The 741st required so much work to recoup its strength that it established a forward command post (CP), under the command of the battalion operations staff (S-3) to control combat operations, and a rear CP to direct salvage and repair operations.[12]

About noon on 18 June, Capt. James Thornton was at his CP just south of the village of La Parque. Orders arrived from the 9th Infantry Regiment to deploy his company to support an effort by the 2d Battalion to recover two antitank guns that had become mired in mud. Thornton ordered Lieutenant Wilson to take Company B's seven Shermans on the mission. Thornton's outfit was still the size of a platoon, and its first operation was perhaps a bit disappointing, but Company B was back in business.

Finally, after nearly nonstop fighting, some of the tank battalions that first assaulted Normandy were given time to perform critical maintenance on their vehicles and to try to work out better ways to fight in the bocage. The 743d went into bivouac from 17 June to 7 July, the 747th from 18 June to 10 July, and the 741st from 20 to 30 June. Some other developments were encouraging. On 20 June, kitchen trucks served hot meals to the men of the 743d for the first time since the invasion.[13]

The assault battalions inland from Utah Beach encountered the enemy in strength and began to suffer heavy losses after their easy landing. During June, the focus of the American effort in Normandy was northward out of the beachhead with the goal of capturing the port of Cherbourg. The 70th (attached most of the time to the 4th Infantry Division) and 746th (attached by late June to the 9th Infantry Division) were committed to the drive on Cherbourg. From D day to 31 July, the 70th lost forty Shermans and six M5s.[14] By 9 June, Company C of the 746th assessed its combat efficiency at only 33 percent and reported that most tank machine guns were burned out from overuse and that many of the tank guns were ineffective. On 11 June, the company had only two officers, seventy enlisted men, and six tanks in action. As of 10 July, the battalion had lost half its tanks to enemy fire.[15]

The 746th Tank Battalion recorded two firsts during the attack on Cherbourg. On the outskirts of the city, tanks of the 746th lobbed 75mm rounds into the fortress, marking the first mass use of a tank battalion in its secondary role as artillery in the ETO. The tankers also were the first to help capture a major city. The battalion AAR records that "By the morning of the 27th [of June] all of the city was in our hands except the highly fortified arsenal. At 0600 the three platoons of Company B moved up to shell the arsenal before they would withdraw, allowing our air support to bomb the fort at 1000 hours. After the tanks fired but before time for the air bombing, the general in charge of the German fortifications said that he would surrender the fort only if we would show our forces. So Lt. Kegut's platoon of tanks moved up to the gates of the arsenal and actually stuck the tank guns into the doors of the fortifications. This convinced the general that we had force and he surrendered his entire command. [When the battalion pulled out, the] tankers, feeling very victorious and also some of them feeling the effects of the Cherbourg wine, brought with them a captured German command car and a liberated French tank."

---

### The Other Role: Mobile Artillery

In addition to supporting the doughs through direct fire, regular line tanks at times fired indirect fire-support missions. A study conducted by the General Board of U.S. Forces, ETO, at the end of the war, however, concluded that tank units found it increasingly difficult later in the conflict to use tanks in the indirect-fire role. The reason was that replacements for casualties almost never had received artillery training.[16]

---

After the capture of Cherbourg on 26 June, General Bradley tried to get an attack moving southward and inland. As of the beginning of July, Bradley's expanding forces included four corps headquarters and thirteen combat divisions: nine infantry, two armored, and two airborne. To the south, however, lay the heart of the bocage. And, on the Carentan plain, five large swamps and numerous slow-moving rivers and streams further broke up the terrain. Frequent rainfall turned fields to mud; indeed, the amount of cloud, wind, and rain in June and July was greater than that recorded at any time since 1900, and this cut air support in half.[17]

The going was horrendous for the infantry, particularly

the units tasting battle for the first time. Using twelve divisions over seventeen days in July, the First Army was able to advance only about seven miles in its western zone and little more than half that in its eastern zone. It suffered forty thousand casualties during July, most of them infantrymen.[18]

New tank battalions were thrown into the fray. Inland from Omaha, the 737th, committed to battle on 14 July in support of the 35th Infantry Division, lost eleven Shermans on its first day and another twelve—plus an assault gun—on the second day of action.[19] Inland from Utah, the 6th Armored Group—which had landed at Utah along with the 70th and 746th Tank battalions—also controlled the 712th and 749th by 28 June.[20] And despite the hard lessons being learned in action, the green battalions still were being committed without meaningful training in tank-infantry cooperation in the bocage.[21] It was left to the armored group headquarters ashore to arrange a briefing by commanders from battalions already on the line and perhaps a few days of demonstrations and training, but that was not always possible.

The key lessons being learned included how to meld the infantry and tanks into a more effective combat team and how to fight in the hellish physical environment of the bocage.

---

### A Week in the Life: AAR, 743d Tank Battalion

9 July 1944: Company A held in reserve in vicinity of 467737. Called up to give support and repulsed violent enemy counterattack. Enemy armor encountered in strength.

Company B moved to attack in support of the 2d Battalion, 120th Infantry, 1,200 yards southeast of La Desert with the 1st and 2d platoons in the assault and the 3d in reserve. Stiff opposition encountered by enemy AT guns and tanks. Staff Sergeant Benson's tank received a direct hit killing Sergeant Benson, Corporal Riffle, Technician 4th Grade Rogers, Private Pierce, and Private First Class

Robinson. Two other tanks were hit, the crews with the exception of Private First Class Chestnut escaped. After all infantry support had withdrawn, orders were received to abandon disabled tanks. On leaving their vehicles, Private Alexander, Technician 4th Grade Homme, and Private Kirk were wounded. Corporal Ferish mashed his foot while traversing and was pulled from the tank by Staff Sergeant Mosey.

Company C left bivouac and was joined by Lieutenant Williams and the 3d Platoon, moved to 463738 for reorganization of the company. Heavy artillery, machine-gun, and sniper fire during the afternoon, did not engage the enemy. One man wounded by shrapnel.

Company D, 2d and 3d platoons, which had been operating with Company C, joined the company. At 1300 hours, company moved up to repulse enemy counterattack. Advanced to 462727 and remained there until 2000 hours. Bivouacked in the vicinity of 468756.

Mortar Platoon with two staff tanks took up a new position at 498748 in support of Company G, 120th Infantry. Position under enemy artillery, machine-gun, and sniper fire during enemy counterattack.

Assault guns fired on Hill 32 from position 467739. Service Company trains had difficulty in reaching forward elements due to intense enemy artillery fire.


10 July 1944: Company A moved out to engage enemy at 0910. Dozer out of action due to engine trouble. Flamethrower used against the hedges. Enemy counterattack repulsed. Artillery fire and bazooka fire encountered. Lieutenant Jones, company commander, wounded and evacuated. Lieutenant Oliver took over command. Company relieved at 2030 hours and placed in regimental reserve.

Lieutenant Williams took over command of Company B. Bivouacked near St. Jean De Daye.

Company C left bivouac to engage the enemy at 461723. Little resistance, only small arms fire encountered. Continued to advance to 467411. Engaged enemy until 2130, remained all night at 467411.

Company D moved up with the 2d Battalion, 120th Infantry, to 463729. At 2100 hours, moved up and joined 1st Battalion, 120th Infantry, at 456712. Extremely heavy enemy artillery fire was encountered at this point.

Mortar Platoon in support for Company C fired seven missions from 467411. The assault gun platoon in support of Company A fired from battery position at 466737.

Service Company's T2, while looking for knocked out tanks, hit a mine; damage repaired. Supply trains went forward as usual.

11 July 1944: Company A remained in bivouac for maintenance and repair. Captain Miller took over command. One officer wounded when shell fell in area. One enlisted man NBC [non-battle casualty], seven enlisted men listed as missing in action.

Company B in reserve. Lieutenant Williams reorganizing the company. Lieutenant Macht replaced Lieutenant Mittendorf.

Company C left bivouac at 0740, engaged the enemy throughout the morning, fierce resistance. Knocked out enemy AT gun and tank (Mark IV), also several machine-gun nests. Captain Elder killed in action. Lieutenant Hansen took over command. Lieutenant Fitzgibons and Lieutenant Hunter wounded. Seven enlisted men wounded, one returned to duty. Bivouacked at 2100 hours at 463710.

Company D moved to join the other forward elements at 463709 and bivouacked there for the night. . . .

12 July 1944: Company A engaged the enemy at 450693 at about 0900 hours. Remained in this vicinity all day repulsing several enemy counterattacks. Returned to 450670 for the night at 2100 hours. Two enlisted men wounded, Technician 5th Grade McMichael and Private First Class Larson. Four enlisted men MIA.

Company B attached to the 3d Battalion, 117th Infantry. Heavy mortar and artillery fire fell all day. One enlisted man killed in action. Four enlisted men seriously injured in action. Moved to a position in bivouac at 463710 for reorganization and maintenance.

Company D with the 2d Battalion, 117th Infantry, moved to 456712. Attacked at 2045; little opposition, only small arms fire; advanced to 452798. Drew back for the night to 456712 at 2300 hours. Mortar and Assault Gun platoons attached to Company D fired nine missions during the day.

Service Company trains as usual. Drivers reported increase in artillery fire from screaming meemies [German multibarrel rocket launchers].

13 July 1944: Company A remained in area 450670 in defensive position. Subjected to heavy enemy artillery and mortar fire all day.

Company B remained in alerted defensive positions south of Hautes Vents. Heavy artillery fire, no casualties, but the infantry suffered heavily.

Company C in defensive position south of Hautes Vents. Corporal Reynolds and Corporal Rusech seriously wounded by shrapnel. Remained in this position through the night.

Company D took up position at 452708 repulsed several enemy counterattacks.

Mortar Platoon fired in support of companies B, C, and D. Technician 5th Grade Hembre wounded in the arms and legs by shrapnel, not evacuated. Assault Gun Platoon fired ten missions indirect fire.

Service Company trains went forward without too much difficulty.

14 July 1944: Company A moved out at 1900 hours to 461721, where it engaged the enemy until 2300 hours. Levegue seriously wounded and evacuated. Went into bivouac at 461721 at 2300 hours.

Company B in battalion reserve. Reorganizing company, difficult problem as all platoon sergeants and lieutenants have become casualties. New crews have to be established and trained.

Company C dozer and one tank returned to the company without crews. Alerted and moved out at 2230 to position at 451190.

Company D was shelled at 0100, Technician 4th Grade Kolf wounded by shrapnel. At 0745, Company D attacked and advanced to bridge 443705 and secured position with the infantry. At 2000 hours moved in support of the 3d Battalion, 117th Infantry.

HQ Company Mortar Platoon fired fifty rounds at La Viqosrie. Assault Gun Platoon fired on road net south of the Battalion CP at 467722.

Battalion rear CP moved eleven miles from 430813 to new area three-quarter miles north of St. Jean De Daye.

Supply trains went forward to service the line companies, and returned as safely.

15 July 1944: Company A, Captain Miller transferred to HQ Company as S-3A [assistant operations] officer. Lieutenant Aas took over command of Company A. Lieutenant Tichnor assigned and joined. Remained in bivouac to reorganize.

Company B continued program of training and reorganization. Company C remained in position 456690 acting as a roadblock. Captain Bulkan took over command of Company C.

Company D received heavy artillery fire, two men seriously wounded, privates O'Neil and Wandzala. Lieutenant Korrison took over command and the company went forward to relieve Company C at 456690.

HQ Company Assault Gun and Mortar platoons remained in bivouac area 458719.

Service Company usual trains and activities.

---

## WORKING WITH THE DOUGHS

In the first hours after the troops moved inland, operational planning was scant, and commanders on the scene often made up their plans as they went. As had been the case on the beach, communications between the infantry and the tank initially were of the mouth-to-ear variety. This method had one major drawback: It was insanely dangerous because tank commanders had to expose themselves under fire to talk to the doughs. The degree of danger meant that often communication simply did not occur when things got hot. The AAR for Company A of the 746th records for 12 June: "Coordination in the effort was very poor due to heavy concentrations of mortar and artillery fire, which pinned down the infantry." Oral communication was also rather haphazard, in part because tank crews could not see well through their periscopes, and the infantry had to get the crew's attention amidst the roar of battle and the tank's engine. Riflemen guiding tanks sometimes had to get in front and jump up and down to get the crew's attention.[22] Tankers eventually figured out that the doughs often did not understand how blind they were when buttoned up and tried to teach them.[23]

Life was already dangerous enough for tank commanders, who frequently entered battle with their heads stuck out of the turret nine feet above the relative anonymity of the ground. This was the only way to overcome the restricted view of the battlefield afforded by the tank's periscopes. The large number of tank commanders reported shot in the head indicates that they were priority targets for German snipers. Moreover, as tankers learned that they could not trust the infantry's notion of what constituted passable terrain for a tank, commanders began to expose themselves during frequent foot-reconnaissance forays.

Wayne Robinson encapsulated how tank-infantry cooperation was supposed to work in describing the attack on Caumont by 743d tankers and 1st Infantry Division doughs on 12 June:

> An occasional house or a bush or a position suspected of harboring undesirable tenants was given a treatment of lead by trigger-happy machine gunners and riflemen.

Tanks joined the spraying parties whenever the infantry
called for it. In working with infantry, a separate tank battalion learns not to shoot at everything in sight. It might
turn out to be a platoon of friendly infantry. Tank-infantry
coordination is a difficult operation. . . .

As the evening wore along both companies [B and C]
began receiving heavy concentrations of artillery fire
mixed in with customary mortars. Direct fire from antitank guns worried tank commanders. Machine-gun fire
pinned down the doughboys. The attack, however, kept
moving in toward the objective. It was slow and cautious
work. The tank-infantry coordination of the 26th Infantry
Regiment, veterans of the proud and battle-hardened (in
Africa and Sicily) 1st Division, remained extremely good
on this attack as strongpoint after strongpoint was reduced and overrun with the minimum of casualties to the
doughs. The infantry efficiently infiltrated antitank gun positions; a tank cannot bull its way past an antitank gun
without somebody getting hurt—a sorry lesson learned
in Africa by Armored Force men. Machine-gun positions,
deadly to the doughs, were another story to tanks. A few
rounds of HE (high explosive) from the 75mm fired into
the laps of the crews usually was all that was required.
An antitank gun was almost always protected by flank-
ing machine-gun nests. Each was a tactical problem to be
worked out by infantry and tankers.[24]

The 743d had the good fortune to be working with the
only combat-tested American division to land in Normandy.
Generally speaking, tactical planning remained largely an *ad
hoc* affair for weeks, worked out on the spot between the infantry and tank commanders; tanks and infantry decided their
actions autonomously once the action began. This is not to say
that solving problems on the fly could not be quite effective.

On 11 July, for example, Lieutenant Colonel Norris, commanding the 2d Battalion, 38th Infantry, 2d Infantry Division, told Capt. James Thornton of the 741st Tank Battalion that his unit was receiving fire from a camouflaged position south of a junction on the St. Lô road. Thornton considered the problem. There was obviously at least one high-velocity gun in the German position. He ordered Lt. John Bruck, leader of the Assault Gun Platoon, to take out the position by direct fire. Bruck maneuvered one of his Shermans behind a house that sat at the intersection facing the enemy position. He picked a spot from which he could fire through the rear and front doors of the house directly into the German position. The crew unleashed several rounds from the 105mm howitzer, and flames and smoke spouted up from the target. Infantry patrols later reported that the position contained a Mark III assault gun and an antitank gun, both of which were completely demolished by the smashing impact of the projectiles.[25]

Tankers were particularly concerned about coordination with the doughs on those nights when tanks remained in forward positions and were vulnerable to attack by infiltrating German infantry. Tank gunners could see nothing whatsoever through their sights at night. Tanker complaints on the subject started early and recurred throughout the war. Company C of the 743d, for example, reported on 15 June, "Infantry left us without protection and under fire of enemy in darkness."[26]

The dough, of course, had his own point of view about all this. For one thing, tanks drew enemy fire, both direct and indirect.[27] And not only the doughs on the line worried about this fact. Two platoon leaders from the 741st who attempted to find out how their tanks would be used in one day's attack, for example, found that "the infantry commanders were very vague about the situation, and confessed a reluctance to use the tanks at all, because of tanks drawing artillery fire."[28] For another thing, the infantry concluded that the poor-sighted friendly tanks could sometimes be just as dangerous as the enemy. One 6th Armored Group liaison officer reported, "1st Division troops do not like to precede tanks. Claim our tanks shoot them. Prefer to go alongside or behind our tanks."[29] But when the fighting got heavy, the infantry usually wanted as many tanks around as possible. A report filed by the 746th Tank Battalion in late July captured this moth-and-flame dilemma of the infantry: "9th Inf[antry] Div[ision] still says tanks are no good but won't allow them back for rest or training."[30]

The infantrymen also resented the fact that the tanks usually withdrew at night for maintenance, and they stewed over false images of tankers getting a comfortable night's sleep while they crouched in foxholes.[31] What the dogface in his foxhole did not understand was that nighttime servicing was critical to keeping the tanks in running condition. Whenever possible, the tank companies withdrew to a bivouac where the tanks could set up a perimeter defense, each tank covering a field of fire. Often under shellfire, exhausted tankers gassed up their vehicles, restocked shells, and then shared the watch through the night.[32]

All this took place in an environment that was extremely fluid, because frontlines often meant little in hedgerow country. The 746th, for example, recorded in its AAR, "CP installations were not what one would naturally consider even relatively free from [enemy] activity. The very heavy shelling of our entire forward and rear areas coupled with the enemy infiltration through the frequently disorganized front lines brought the 'front' to the 'rear' and frequently vice versa. . . . [I]t was not uncommon for troops or commanders to experience as much and at times more difficulty in moving from the rear to the front or front to rear as in fighting forward to new positions."[33]

Staff Sergeant Vernon D. Skaggs, a tough and popular tank commander in the 743d Tank Battalion, took his Sherman to the "rear" on a routine supply mission one evening. On the way, a platoon of German infantry ambushed his tank. Skaggs grabbed his tommygun and began shooting at point-blank range. The Germans were driven off, leaving their dead behind.[34]

## First Fixes

One of the first field solutions to improve communications between tanks and infantry was the installation of a standard field telephone, at first ensconced in an empty ammo box hung under the Sherman's rear deck overhang, which was wired into the intercom system of the tank. Infantrymen could simply lift the phone to reach the tank commander. Installation of such rigs began by about 20 June and became standard operating procedure in most, if not all, independent tank battalions. Despite the demonstrated usefulness of the installation of the phones on the tanks, battalions were not so outfitted before being committed to combat. The 749th, for example, did not install the boxes until 22 or 23 July, three weeks after having entered battle.[35]

Corporal Jack Boardman from Capt. James Thornton's Company B, 741st Tank Battalion, recalled in the unofficial unit history some hedgerow action that illustrated the contribution to tactical success made by the field telephone:

[W]e rolled through the opening with both our machine guns blasting at the enemy hedge. The squad of doughs scrambled and tore their way through the jungle-like shrubbery on the high bank and desperately ran down the field to gain the shelter of the opposite bank. . . . Suddenly the doughboy I could see in front of me dropped to the ground. I strained my eyes into the gunsight and traversed the turret back and forth trying to pick up the gun that was firing on them. The doughs' squad leader began yelling over the telephone on the back of the tank, "We're getting heavy fire from the left corner! Hit 'em, hit 'em!" I snapped the turret to the left and put an HE on delay into the corner of the hedge. It passed through the bank and exploded in the middle of a machine gun nest. The Jerry gun that had been pointed through a small slot on the bottom of the hedge fired no more.[36]

This solution had several problems associated with it. First, the foot soldier still had to expose himself to talk to the tank commander. Second, the boxes were vulnerable to being knocked off by small arms fire and shrapnel.[37] Third, the system proved to be a drain on the tank's battery.[38]

Other, less successful, experiments were carried out. One unit tried to use a waterproofing intake tube for communication with the infantry. The tube ran out of the tank turret and over the rear deck, so that anyone wishing to get the tank commander's attention would walk up behind the tank and call through the tube.[39]

Experiments were also undertaken to provide a direct radio link between the tanks and infantry, initially very indirectly. On 12 June, for example, the 747th Tank Battalion kept two company command tanks at the regimental CP to provide radio liaison with the platoons in action. The company commanders relied on "peeps" (the famous Jeep in tanker parlance) to make quick personal trips to visit his tanks.[40]

Some battalions used light tanks for liaison with infantry command posts because they could tie into the tankers' radio net and were less useful than Shermans in combat. The 749th, for example, on 9 July sent one light tank to the CP of each of the three infantry battalions the unit was supporting that day.[41] The 747th also used light tanks in this capacity.[42]

The first efforts to get radios into the hands of the infantry that could link directly to tanks began by July. On 18 July, the 3d Armored Group ordered all attached battalions to supply their partner infantry battalion CP with a peep carrying an SCR-510 tank radio, as well as peeps carrying the similar SCR-509 to work with the infantry platoons.[43]

The idea to establish a communications presence at the infantry battalion CP evidently was deemed successful and gradually came into wide use. It would be some time after American forces broke out of Normandy, however, before tankers and infantry hit upon a more or less satisfactory solution to radio communications at the platoon level. On 16 July, the 745th Tank Battalion received a message from the U.S. First Army foreshadowing what months later would become the standardized solution: The battalion would receive four extra SCR-509 radios for tank-infantry communications on a loan basis, which would eventually be replaced by the "300 series tank set." The infantry's standard radio was the SCR-300 walkie-talkie. The official U.S. Army history asserts that signal companies in Normandy installed infantry-type radios in the tanks, but the battalion records suggest that such installations did not take place in any numbers—if at all—until the autumn.[44]

These tactical experiments demonstrated that coordination with the infantry and control of the tanks were interrelated issues that could involve tradeoffs. By late July and early August, some battalions turned to direct personal contact between tanks and infantry down to the lowest level. In the 745th, tank platoon commanders were actually walking with infantry battalion COs during operations.[45] The 747th tried a similar system, but platoon commander Homer Wilkes quickly realized he and his buddies had a problem:

> [O]ne platoon of tanks would be assigned each battalion of a committed regiment. Second, the company commander would go to regimental headquarters where he would be briefed on the mission for his company. Afterward, he would stay at Regiment, serving as an armor staff officer. Third, infantry jeeps would call for the tank platoon leaders at the assembly area, taking them plus a sergeant to the various battalion command posts. (This sergeant was to return for the tanks when they were needed.)
>
> No one in the division seemed to realize that not only did this dilute armor to the point of non-effectiveness, but it also removed all commissioned leadership from company control group forward plus the enlisted commanders of three additional tanks. Stated another way, seven of the complement of seventeen tanks would be minus their commanders.[46]

Wilkes's opinion did not improve after he was intercepted one day by German infantry while being driven to the infantry command post. He and the other men in the peep had to run for their lives under machine-pistol fire.[47]

## Best Fixes

Communications issues aside, the record suggests that the only means for working out a solid partnership between the doughs and the tankers was for them to spend time together taking the same classes at the school of hard knocks. The stream of units flowing into France made lasting attachments rare. For the tank battalions that landed early, this meant that now veteran tankers sometimes had to teach new infantry outfits the ropes, or die trying. The 746th Tank Battalion, for example, was attached to the virgin 83d Infantry Division on 5 July. That division was badly mauled over the next several days, and tank-infantry cooperation was especially bad. The infantry accused the tankers of refusing to fight at night and of disobeying orders, and one infantry commander threatened to shoot a tank officer for refusing to advance in support. One tank commander, meanwhile, threatened to shoot infantrymen who appeared ready to bolt and abandon the tanks.[48] The July AAR for Headquarters Company, 746th, groused, "The employment of tanks in a profitable and successful manner at a time when green infantry needed encouragement and strong reinforcement was the chief concern of the battalion CO, especially as the tank commitment in this situation tended toward expenditure of armor without maximum results. . . ."

When an enduring partnership could take hold, tankers grew to respect infantry commanders who learned how to use their tanks effectively. In some cases battalions came to be treated as members of the infantry division to which they were attached for months. Reattachment of a battalion to another division generally provoked anxiety. Men of the 70th Tank Battalion, for example, landed with the 4th Infantry Division, wore the division's "ivy leaf" patch, and viewed the partnership in the most positive terms.[49] In contrast, after being briefly attached to the unfamiliar 4th Infantry Division, Homer Wilkes of the 747th commented, "I personally viewed this command with distaste."[50] Wilkes's commander, Lt. Col. Stuart Fries, recommended in his AAR for July, "In future training programs, a tank battalion should be an integral part of an infantry division at its activation. This would enable both units to learn the limitations and capabilities of each other."

The tankers tried to encourage the development of life-saving familiarity at the tactical level. In the 737th, for example, standard procedure when assigning tanks to support infantry operations gave first priority to sending the company best suited to the mission in view of its current strength. But whenever possible, the battalion sent the same company to the same infantry combat team to improve mutual understanding.[51] Similarly, Lt. Col. Wallace J. Nichols, CO of the 745th (who would be fortunate enough to have his outfit attached to the 1st Infantry Division from D day until the war's end) recorded in his AAR for July, "Through the practice of attaching each company of this battalion to one infantry regiment continuously, a more thorough understanding and closer cooperation has developed between infantry and tank personnel."

---

### No Consistent Army Policy on Attachments

Over the course of the fighting in Europe, tank battalions experienced the extremes of shared time with infantry divisions, and everything in between. Enjoying a continuity similar to that experienced by the 745th and 1st Infantry Division, the 70th Tank Battalion spent most of the campaign attached to the 4th Infantry Division. The 90th Infantry Division considered the 712th a virtually organic component.

The 761st, in contrast, rarely spent more than a few weeks attached to any one unit, a circumstance that forced it to fight under the least advantageous circumstances for most of the war. The modern observer may be drawn to the conclusion—perhaps unfairly—that the nearly all-Black 761st had to fight under such ultimately dangerous circumstances because of racist distrust within the still segregated Army. The records of the 3d Armored Group for March 1945, for example, leave one with the strong impression that—

shortly after the 761st was attached—infantry and armor agreed on the desirability of pushing the battalion elsewhere, which they did.

The 740th or its companies at one time or another were attached to seven different infantry divisions. Because at peak there were only twenty-eight standard separate tank battalions and two light tank battalions available for attachment to forty-two infantry divisions in the ETO, most battalions operated at some time with more than one division despite efforts to pair battalions and divisions for long periods.[52] The shortfall was made up for by the attachment of combat commands from armored divisions or even British Commonwealth units to infantry divisions when appropriate.

## TACKLING THE BOCAGE

At Omaha, hedgerows reached to the bluffs above the beach.[53] At Utah, the hedgerows began just beyond the inundated area behind the beach.[54] There were, on average, fourteen hedgerows per kilometer in Normandy.[55]

Incredibly, the invading forces had no tactics worked out for dealing with the terrain nor equipment tailored to the situation. The hedgerows were not wholly impenetrable to tanks, but in the first few days they often enough channeled armor onto narrow roads where defenders could focus their antitank and artillery pieces. The first Sherman of the 737th that tried to ram through a hedgerow was flipped onto its back and lay there like an upended turtle.[56] The infantry had to attack across fields, however, which meant that tank battalions had to figure out a way to move their tanks to places where the infantry needed support. There was one benefit, at least, although it probably did not seem so at the time. The bocage provided terrain relatively advantageous to the Shermans in the sense that few engagements occurred at the long ranges that maximized the advantages held by German armor. Tanks generally engaged at ranges between 150 and 400 yards.[57] On 7 July, a Sherman from Company C of the 749th knocked out a "Tiger" (at least a tank of some sort) with one round of AP and one round of HE from a range of only twenty yards!

Thus began a period of trial-and-error progress. As the 737th's CO, Lt. Col. James Hamilton Jr., put it, "We've spent years studying the book and practicing, and then in our first action we had to throw away the book, and everything we learned in practice was no good to us at all."[58]

## Dozer Wars

The first alternative to trying to ram tanks through the hedges was to have a tank dozer punch a hole through them, which the tanks would pass through in support of the infantry. This occurred to tankers as soon as they saw the hedges.[59] Experience eventually showed that dozers were capable of breaching about 50 percent of hedgerows.[60] Tank dozers were also used for combat tasks, such as burying enemy infantry on the far side of hedgerows.[61]

Homer Wilkes in the 747th described one such attack during fighting in early July near St. Lô:

As the infantry moved forward, I called Sergeant Castignoli and told him to cut a hole [using his tank-dozer] in the middle of the platoon line. He did this, then backed away to provide support as we went through the hedge.

I led out, zigzagging all the way to the next hedge. The entire platoon followed without loss. . . .

[T]he infantry company had been decimated. There was no one on the hedge with us as we went into action again. We could only hope more infantry would come up.

A German threw a smoke grenade down the hatch of the tank on my left. The crew jumped out, the driver first

putting the transmission in reverse. The vehicle ran back-
ward until it stalled in a shell hole.

On the right, Sgt. Herman Deaver [in his first battle]
saw an antitank SP go into action and fire one round at my
tank. Deaver knocked it out before a second round could
be fired. He was a veteran from that time on.

Another company of infantry came into the line. The
officer commanding . . . and his NCOs knew the drill, and
we started taking fields with alacrity.[62]

The main drawback to the dozer approach was that the
Germans quickly figured out the procedure; when a tank
dozer created a gap, tanks were likely to follow. The Germans
sighted their antitank guns on the hole and waited.

Symptomatic of the sporadic sharing of lessons among the
tank battalions was the fact that some newly arrived outfits
were left without even the tank dozer approach. In the 749th,
six tanks were temporarily put out of action after becoming
stuck in hedgerows from the time of the battalion's debut on
3 July until 10 July, when it obtained its first dozer with which
to attack those barriers.[63]

## The Poke-and-Blow Method

The next ad hoc solution relied on infantry, tank, and engineer
elements. Several locally developed variants of this scheme
were employed. The 741st began training in rear areas on
20 June using the following plan, according to the AAR:

[A]ttach a tank to an infantry squad, together with four engineers. . . . Since the tank would encounter great difficulty in negotiating the hedgerows, the engineer group
would blow a hole in the hedge of sufficient size to enable
the tank to get through. The team play of this group was to

be as follows: The squad leader of the infantry would form
a base of fire with his squad along the hedgerow to be
used as a line of departure. The tank would take up a firing position along the same hedgerow with the engineer
personnel near the tank, the explosives to be carried on
the rear deck of the tank where the engineers could obtain them. Since sufficient personnel were not available to
cover all the fields within the zone of advance, the fields
on either flank of the field covered by a team had to be
covered by fire, in some cases this fire was furnished by
light or heavy machine gun, emplaced in the corner of the
field at the line of departure to sweep the adjacent fields.
A reserve tank would be directly behind the assault tank
for over-watching purposes and to provide a reserve tank
in case the assault tank became stuck or was knocked out.
After the base of fire neutralized the enemy fire in the first
hedgerow past the line of departure, the squad leader
would send the scouts of the squad forward along the
hedgerows parallel with the line of advance on each side
of the field. Then the BAR-man and the tommygunner
would move forward. In short, the infantry squad infiltrated to the next hedgerow. The squad leader, when he
went forward, would pick a spot suitable for the tank to
secure a fire position and would signal the tank forward. If
necessary, the hedge at the point of departure would be
blown. In some cases, the tank was able to push through
the hedge. . . .

When the tank moved forward, the engineer group
went with it to protect the tank from the fire of bazookas
and antitank grenades. Upon reaching the next hedgerow,
the tank would again go into firing position, the squad
would form a base of fire with the tank, and the entire
process of advance would be repeated. . . .[64]

The 743d began practicing hedgerow tactics on 2 July.[65] In that battalion's approach, engineers blew three holes simultaneously in a hedgerow. At a signal from a tank's siren, everybody in the operation rushed through the openings simultaneously, thus preventing German gunners from picking tanks off one by one. In the 737th, teams also relied on the rush tactic. Engineers blew holes in the hedgerow using twenty-second fuses, and then tanks, infantry, engineers, and any other assault elements would pelt through before the dust settled and the Germans could sight their antitank guns on the gaps.[66]

This method involved an extra risk for the tank crews, however. The S-3 Journal of the 741st records that on the morning of 11 July, "One tank had turret blown off when TNT [on the deck] was hit by direct mortar fire." The technique was ruled impractical by late July because the demolition packs could be detonated by artillery, mortar, or bazooka rounds.[67]

The 747th tried a somewhat different approach. The battalion welded two prongs made of six and one-quarter-inch iron pipe cut four and one-half feet long to the final drive housing at the nose of thirteen battalion Shermans. The tank poked holes in the hedgerow, into which engineers placed prepared TNT charges and then blew a gap.[68] When the battalion practiced this tactic with the infantry and engineers during late July, company-level officers concluded it would not work and briefed the tank dozer commanders to stand by; the backup plan was needed the first time the technique was tried in combat. Meanwhile, at the tactical level, tankers and infantry worked out the following drill: Using HE shells with fuse delay, tanks blew out the corners of the opposite hedgerow where the Germans often put their machine guns. The tanks then skipped fuse-delay shells above the hedgerow, causing airbursts, and fired machine guns. The infantry advanced under this protection to the next hedgerow, over which they would throw hand grenades.[69]

Higher commands tried to help. On 25 June, the 29th Infantry Division sponsored a conference on coordination of tanks, infantry, and engineers in the assault, and it published a memorandum entitled "Infantry Coordination of Tanks, Infantry & Engineers in Hedgerow Tactics." Two days later, a booklet arrived at the front, courtesy of the XIX Corps, entitled, "The Tank and Infantry Team."[70] If these publications had anything helpful to say, it had doubtless come from the guys on the ground painfully working it out.

Commanders also learned that patience and preparation, rather than the audacity of armored cavalry, generally paid off in bocage fighting. The 741st Tank Battalion, for example, conducted extensive reconnaissance with the infantry, and the engineers drew up extremely detailed maps at 1:10,000 scale showing every hedgerow, sunken road, building, trail, and crossroads, and a coded number assigned to every field.[71] The use of numbered fields enabled the tank battalion to control the action by radio once the attack had started, facilitated the use of supporting artillery fire, and expedited the recovery of damaged tanks.[72]

## Hedge Cutters

The last tactical innovation in the bocage was the invention of the "Culin hedgerow device." Designed by Sgt. Curtis G. Culin of the 102d Cavalry Reconnaissance Squadron, the contraption (the 3d Armored Group referred to them as "Rube Goldbergs") was made of steel girders from German beach defenses. It amounted to a set of steel teeth protruding from the nose of the tank, and it could be mounted on M4s and M5s. The teeth allowed the vehicle to grip and plow through a hedgerow with hardly any loss of speed.[73] A similar device that looked more like a blade was referred to as the "green dozer." Tanks outfitted with the Culin device were called "Rhinos." Tank battalions hurriedly installed the devices during the second half of July in preparation for Operation Cobra, the planned breakout from Normandy. By the time Cobra began, 60 percent of the tanks involved had been fitted with Culin devices.[74] The invention gave American tanks a decisive edge in mobility over German armor during the final phase of the Normandy campaign. In fact, the use of the Rhino in combat was barred until the launch of Cobra in order to maintain tactical surprise.[75] Some evidence indicates, however, that continued use of tanks equipped with prongs for planting explosives in hedgerows was permitted.[76]

## Extra Credit

It took the tankers a surprisingly long time to learn the importance of camouflaging their tanks. In late July, engineers finally began painting tanks of several battalions in camouflage patterns, described in one case as a combination of green and gray-black. Some battalions also began to attach chicken wire to their tanks to hold leafy branches, which further broke up the sharp outline of the armored vehicle.[77]

Tankers learned that they faced one last problem: The infantry divisions they supported typically rotated the units doing the actual fighting, with two regiments in combat and one held in reserve. The tank battalions, in contrast, remained on the line for weeks at a time, supporting whichever infantry units happened to be engaged on a given day. This was extremely hard on both machines and men.

### *Breakout: The Big Picture*

By 18 July the U.S. First Army had clawed its way into St. Lô and, on 25 July, launched Operation Cobra. As heavy and medium bombers from England pummeled German frontline positions, infantry and armor finally punched through the defenses. Pouring through the gap, American troops advanced forty miles within a week.

Rejecting his generals' advice, Hitler ordered a counterattack against the widening breakout by Germany's last available mobile forces in France. U.S. First Army forces stopped the Germans and joined Canadian, British, and Polish troops in catching the enemy in a giant pocket around the town of Falaise. Allied fighter-bombers and artillery now aided a massive destruction of twenty enemy divisions. Suddenly, it seemed the Allies might end the war before winter. Calling off a planned halt and logistical buildup, Eisenhower ordered the Allied forces to drive all-out for the German frontier.

With enemy forces in full retreat, French and American troops rolled into Paris on 25 August 1944. Meanwhile, veteran U.S. and French divisions, pulled out of Italy, landed on the beaches of the French Riviera. While French forces liberated the ports, the U.S. Seventh Army drove northward in an effort to cut off withdrawing German troops. Moving rapidly through the cities of Lyon and Besançon, they joined up with Allied forces advancing from Normandy on 11 September.

Victory seemed to be at hand. But by mid-September Allied communications were strained. Combat troops had outrun their supplies. British and Canadian forces advanced into the Netherlands, and American troops crossed Belgium and Luxembourg and entered German territory. Then both met strong resistance. Bad weather curtailed unloading of supplies directly across the Normandy invasion beaches, while the ports on the North Sea and the Mediterranean were in ruins. As logistical problems piled up, Eisenhower . . . sanction[ed] one last bold gamble: Operation Market-Garden. Two U.S. and one British airborne division were to open the way for a British armored thrust to seize a bridge across the Lower Rhine at Arnhem in the Netherlands. The airborne troops took most of their objectives, but German resistance was much stronger than expected, and the operation failed to gain a bridgehead. . . .

*A Brief History of the U.S. Army in World War II*, Center of Military History, United States Army, Washington, D.C., 1992

# OPEN-FIELD RUNNING

Now we began to roll—long marches and shorter bivouacs.
This was the happier type of fighting, the blitzkrieg style.
No endless days of sweating out a battle within earshot of
the enemy, although we were often less than six hours behind them. It meant more work, and less sleep, but everyone knew he was getting somewhere.

Al Heintzleman,
*We'll Never Go Over-Seas*

Operation Cobra, which ripped the threadbare German defenses in Normandy, unleashed the kind of fluid campaign
tankers dream about, one that even the dirt-grimed infantry
tankers could enjoy. The attrition in the bocage had hurt the
Germans badly. In all of Normandy between 6 June and 9 July
(including the British sector), the Germans lost 2,000 officers
and 85,000 men and received only 5,210 replacements. They
also lost 150 Mark IVs, 85 Panthers, 15 Tigers, 167 75mm assault guns and antitank guns, and almost 30 88mm guns.[1]

General Bradley conceived Cobra as a way to end the
bloody hedgerow war with a major breakthrough on a narrow
front west of St. Lô.[2] He planned a massive air attack by strategic bombers and fighter-bombers to crack the German line. As
eventually formulated by VII Corps, three infantry divisions—
the 30th, 9th, and 4th—and their supporting tank battalions—
the 70th attached to the 4th, the 743d attached to the 30th,
and the 746th attached to the 9th—were to punch a hole in the
defenses. The 2d and 3d Armored divisions and 1st Infantry

Division (motorized) were to provide the initial exploitation forces.

Cobra experienced an inauspicious false start on 24 July. Bad weather forced commanders to cancel the air operation, but the word did not reach some of the heavy bombers already in flight. American troops had withdrawn 1,200 yards from the bomb zone, but some bombers released their loads early and hit soldiers of the 30th Infantry Division some 2,000 yards north of the Periers–St. Lô highway "no-bomb" line. Twenty-five American soldiers were killed and 131 wounded. Cobra was postponed for twenty-four hours, although some American units trying to reoccupy their lines spent the day fighting Germans who had infiltrated behind them when they withdrew prior to the airstrike.

American forces tried again on 25 July, and once more the initial signs were inauspicious. Flying north to south over American and then German lines despite the previous day's mishap, 1,500 B-17 and B-24 heavy bombers from the U.S. Eighth Air Force dropped more than 3,300 tons of bombs, while some 380 B-26 medium bombers unloaded more than 650 tons of high-explosive and fragmentation bombs. Theoretically the only aircraft attacking in the zone closest to American ground troops, more than 550 fighter-bombers from the IX Tactical Air Command (TAC) dropped more than 200 tons of bombs and a large amount of napalm.

Roughly 75 of the bombers dropped their loads within American lines due to various errors, killing 111 troops and wounding 490. This time, tankers were under the bombs, too. One officer in the 746th Tank Battalion was seriously wounded. Medics of the 743d Tank Battalion raced among burning fuel trucks to help doughs hit or buried by the bombs.[3] Lieutenant General Lesley McNair, Army Ground Forces commanding general and father of the separate tank battalions, was killed while observing the attack. So was the entire command group of the 47th Infantry Regiment except the CO, and many soldiers were in deep shock.

There would be no more delays. Assault elements were ordered forward.

The bombing had dealt German units in the assault zone a shocking and crippling blow, although that was not immediately apparent to the tankers. The German commander, General Fritz Bayerlein, had organized a tank defense in depth and thought his position strong; he had not reckoned, however, on being carpet-bombed. The Panzer Lehr armored division—already badly depleted—and small attached elements from Kampfgruppe Heinz and a fallschirmjäger regiment were shattered. About one-third of the combat effectives manning the main line of defense and the immediate reserve line were killed or wounded, and the remainder left in a daze. Forced to throw their remaining armor reserves into the line to stop Operation Goodwood, launched by Montgomery in the British sector a week before Cobra, the German command had almost nothing with which to fill the gap. Feldmarschall Günther von Kluge, the German theater commander who had recently replaced Gerd von Rundstedt, by that evening had to conclude, "As of this moment, the front has . . . burst."[4]

Advancing American troops, however, were surprised to find groups of enemy soldiers fighting stubbornly despite the saturation bombing. The 9th Infantry Division, attacking toward Marigny, generally fell short of its initial objectives.[5] The 746th Tank Battalion encountered stiff resistance through 29 July as the doughs advanced. Beginning 1 August, however, the division pushed through to St. Pois, and the 746th's AAR records that "The operation was characterized by more open hilly terrain with increased visibility and faster movement from high ground to high ground. The operation was one of mopping up heavy centers of resistance and fighting delaying actions accompanied by local counterattacks. Losses were considerably lighter than in the previous period. Employment of tanks with the 9th Infantry Division during this period was generally good."

The 4th Infantry Division had ongoing trouble maintaining contact with supporting tanks. Nevertheless, each time resistance brought the advance to a halt, Shermans of the 70th Tank Battalion eventually showed up and hammered a way through.[6] At the end of the first day, the battalion had advanced only two thousand yards but—despite what it considered stubborn opposition—had lost no tanks. The next day the 70th advanced rapidly, and by 2 August, it was at Villedieu, about twenty-five miles from St. Lô.[7] Major General Raymond Barton, 4th Infantry Division CG, told his commanders, "We face a defeated enemy, an enemy terribly low in morale, terribly confused. I want you in the next advance to throw caution to the winds . . . destroying, capturing, or bypassing the enemy, and pressing recklessly on to the objective." His troops did just that.[8]

The 30th Infantry Division, attacking generally toward St. Gilles, immediately ran into a roadblock built around three Panther tanks that knocked out three Shermans from the 743d Tank Battalion. Wayne Robinson's history of the 743d records, "It did not seem like the battle was getting any place in that welter of confusion, with the attack beginning under the ill-starred bombing, with the roads heavily mined, with direct-fire weapons hidden in the hedgerows, with the enemy shells falling constantly, and with the infantry disorganized. It did not seem that anybody was getting anywhere."[9] Excellent tank-infantry cooperation eventually enabled the attacking troops to destroy a dozen armored vehicles and punch through the German defenses.[10] Transferred to XIX Corps control on 28 July, the 30th Infantry Division turned toward Tessy-sur-Vire, where it ran into the lead elements of the 2d Panzer Division, with which von Kluge was attempting to plug the gaping hole in his line.[11] Finally, after some of the toughest hedgerow fighting experienced so far, resistance in front of the 743d collapsed on 31 July.[12]

During the initial phase of the attack, the tankers finally were permitted to exploit the mobility afforded by their Rhino attachments. Some outfits used them to better execute standard hedgerow tactics. The 709th Tank Battalion, attached to the 8th Infantry Division in the VIII Corps' zone, for example, was able to support the infantry by sideslipping German positions and by putting enfilade fire on hedgerow defenses.[13]

The 741st Tank Battalion nevertheless seized the opportunity to write a new chapter on tactics with the 2d Infantry Division, which formed part of the V Corps' attack east of the main Cobra operation. The 741st's AAR recorded:

> With the new [Rhino] device, it was felt that the unit would be enabled to operate with more freedom, as the hedges were much less an obstacle than they had been before. . . .
>
> The commanding general, 2d Infantry Division, after conferring with Lieutenant Colonel Skaggs, conceived a plan for the use of tanks in the next attack that would very nearly approximate the manner of using tanks in open country suited for tank combat. This plan, which came to be called a sortie, involved the maximum number of tanks, equipped with the Rhino device, that could be brought into position, allowing for the variation of the terrain. In most cases the full number of tanks could be used. The tanks would be placed in position at the LD and the infantry elements withdrawn several hundred yards in rear, for safety purposes. At H hour a barrage of timed fire would be laid

down over an area from three hundred to five hundred
yards in depth past the LD. The tanks would advance
rapidly under the airbursts, smashing hedges and uproot-
ing enemy emplacements in the zone of action, at the
same time placing a maximum amount of direct cannon
and machine-gun fire on the enemy. After breaking the
enemy defenses the tanks would return to the LD, establish contact with supporting infantry, and resume the attack with the infantry-tank team.

On 26 July, 1944, at 0600, this battalion attacked in
support of the 38th and 23d Infantry regiments, with the
LD south of the St. Lô–Berigny road. . . .

With companies A and B, both reinforced, attached
to the 38th Infantry, and Company C attached to the 23d
Infantry, the attack started on schedule and the tanks
smashed through the hedges on the tank sortie. With their
cannons blasting and machine guns stuttering, the tanks
were an awe-inspiring spectacle as they churned their
way through the enemy positions after a crashing barrage
of timed fire. The enemy was obviously stunned by the fe-
rocity of the attack, as not a single tank was lost on the initial sortie. Hundreds of German infantrymen were killed
as they lay in their foxholes, and then ground under the
tracks of the onrushing tanks. Machine-gun emplacements were ripped out of the hedges by the impact of the
Rhino devices, and the enemy lines, to a distance of three
hundred to five hundred yards, were a shambles.

At H plus 20 [minutes] the tanks returned from the
sortie, joined the infantry half of the team and resumed
the onslaught at H plus 30.[14]


The battalion continued to use the sortie technique with
great effect through at least August.

Tank battalions that did not directly support attacking infantry in some cases contributed their guns in the form of artillery support. On 26 July, Company A of the 749th alone fired 1,600 rounds indirectly.[15]

For all the work that had gone into perfecting tactics during the hedgerow fighting, the tankers' effectiveness and survival still depended on the insight or folly of even seasoned commanders. Despite nearly two months in the field, the 743d on 26 July complained to 6th Armored Group headquarters:

Colonel Edward Sutherland, [CO] of 119th Infantry Regiment, has consistently demanded tanks precede infantry. For example: At 2200 26 [July], Colonel Sutherland ordered Major Phillips (through Captain Miller) to send tanks ahead of infantry approximately one and one-half miles to occupy objective without regard to darkness. . . . Major Phillips refused and called Lieutenant Colonel Duncan. Lieutenant Colonel Duncan talked Colonel Sutherland out of the idea and it was finally abandoned.[16]

That same day, Captain Thornton also had problems working with the doughs as the 741st Tank Battalion went into battle with the 2d Infantry Division. The morning had been marvelous as the battalion carried out its crushing first sortie. By midafternoon, however, Company B found itself low on ammo and under artillery and mortar fire so heavy that Thornton could not maintain contact with the pinned-down infantry. He radioed his tank commanders to advance anyway. As Company B's Shermans crawled carefully forward alone, football-sized metal objects rocketed from the hedgerows, joined suddenly by high-velocity rounds from a hidden antitank gun. In quick succession, four tanks were hit, and Lieutenant Wilson, seriously wounded by a bazooka round, was among the

casualties. Thornton in frustration realized he would get no-
where that day without the doughs alongside. The attack
would stand down until the German artillery fire lifted.[17]


On 26 July, the VII Corps commander, Maj. Gen. J. Lawton
Collins, decided to commit the 2d and 3d Armored divisions
and the motorized 1st Infantry Division despite the initial slow
progress by the assault elements. By 27 July, it was clear to
American commanders that they had broken open the German defenses.[18] This was not to say that resistance in front of
the leading units disappeared. On 28 July, advance vehicles
of the 745th Tank Battalion, which was attached to the 1st
Infantry Division during the drive on Coutances, ran into artillery, tank, and antitank defenses outside Cambernon; Company A reported that the artillery and mortar fire was the
heaviest experienced since D day.[19]

General Patton and his U.S. Third Army followed. On 28
July, Bradley temporarily named Patton deputy army group
commander and gave him charge of VIII Corps on Collins's
right flank. Patton immediately threw the 4th and 6th Armored divisions and the already attacking 8th and 79th Infantry divisions against the Germans, who by now were trying
to "advance to the rear" to avoid complete encirclement. This
advance passed through Avranche at the base of the Cotentin
Peninsula on 1 August. That same day, Patton's Third Army officially became operational. The doorway to France was ajar.
Said Patton, "Those troops know their business. We'll keep
right on going, full speed ahead."[20] On 2 August, the 749th
Tank Battalion, attached to the 79th Infantry Division, pushed
forward more than thirty-three miles, and on 7 August it advanced forty miles.[21] Patton's spearhead first cut right into
Brittany. The next wave—XV Corps, composed at this time

of the 5th Armored Division and the 83d and 90th Infantry divisions—hooked eastward toward Paris and Germany.

The breakout ended the bloodiest chapter in the history of the separate tank battalions. Attrition in the bocage had been grim. The 747th, for example, lost eight men killed and thirty-four wounded between 7 and 17 June alone. In late July the 741st suffered sixteen men killed and sixty-four wounded, more than 10 percent of its strength, in just over two weeks. The 743rd in June and July lost at least 25 officers and men killed in action and another 116 wounded—nearly 20 percent.

For the separate tank battalions, once clear of the bocage, breaking out offered a rare opportunity to act like armored divisions in slashing maneuver. The main difference was that, whereas the armored-infantry battalions and motorized-infantry divisions had organic transportation, the tanks carried the infantry to whom they were attached. The infantry divisions "motorized themselves," using not only tanks but mortar carriers, artillery prime movers, fuel and ammunition trucks, and anything else that would roll. The doughs loved it.[22]

After starting slowly because of congested roads, advancing troops broke into open ground, and hastily organized task forces (TFs) formed spearheads that struck toward distant objectives. Ad hoc by nature, TFs could vary substantially in size. In the 5th Infantry Division, for example, TF Thackery, commanded by the division intelligence officer, consisted of the reconnaissance troop, one infantry company, one light tank platoon from the 735th Tank Battalion, an engineer platoon, and medics. On 7 August this small band was ordered to race roughly one hundred miles to Angers at the base of the Brittany Peninsula to capture the bridge there intact and prevent German movement into or out of the region. Unfortunately, the bridge had been blown.[23] At the larger end of the spectrum, TF Taylor, activated on 1 September by the 4th Infantry Division to drive for Brussels, consisted of the 22d Infantry Regiment, the entire 747th Tank Battalion, Company C of the 893d Tank Destroyer Battalion, a company of engineers, the 44th Field Artillery Battalion, and the division antitank company.[24]

As American forces broke free, combat tended to consist of short, often sharp, engagements against delaying forces and strong points. This was a new style of warfare for the tankers for which, again, they and the doughs had not trained. Adaptation came easily, however, because an entire village often posed no greater challenge than had a well-defended hedgerow. This account from the AAR of 741st is typical:

> Company D, with Company A, 1st Battalion, 23d Infantry, [2d Infantry Division,] mounted on the tanks' decks . . . by 0250, 1 August, had reached the village of St. Amand without encountering resistance. By 0430, this company had penetrated still further on, to the railroad station near Les Bessardierre. At this point the advance was halted to await the coming of daylight.
>
> At 0730, the advance was continued, with the infantry still riding the tanks until, at 0900 near the village of Cour de Precuire, a bazooka projectile slammed into the lead tank of the 1st Platoon, and the fight was on. Withdrawing slightly to permit the attack to be organized, the tanks and infantry attacked before noon, facing a concentration of artillery and mortar fire in addition to fire from machine guns and rifles. The attack pressed on steadily, in spite of steady opposition, and at last reached the village of Lovdier, where the action ceased at 2030.

American air and ground commanders were aware that they needed to find ways to minimize attacks on friendly ground units by Allied fighter-bombers, particularly given the uncertainty that a rapid advance would introduce. Just before Cobra, Maj. Gen. Elwood Quesada, commander of the IX TAC, had high-frequency radios installed in the tanks that were to lead armored-division assault columns, allowing tankers and pilots to talk to each other.[25] Unfortunately for the separate tank battalions, the Army does not appear to have provided them with similar capabilities, which meant that the old problems of coordination with fighter-bombers would continue for the infantry-support tankers.[26]

Pilots had plenty of trouble figuring out who was who on the ground, a situation that armored units did not always help to rectify. On 8 August, the U.S. First Army issued orders to advancing forces: "Pilots report some tanks, tank destroyers, and armored vehicles not displaying fluorescent panels. Requisition for shortage or redistribution within units to cover losses should be expedited. As necessary repaint white star markings." Less than a month later, the 747th Tank Battalion received the following message: "Pilots report increasing difficulty identifying vehicles due to fluid situation. Urgent! All vehicles display available vehicular panels prominently. All Allied white star markings must be clean and visible to prevent attack by friendly planes."[27]

Whatever the cause, separate tank battalions continued to lose men and tanks to "friendly" aircraft. On 6 August, for example, a platoon leader in the 746th was killed in an Allied strafing attack.[28]

## BRITTANY: PERSISTENT PORTS

Patton's VIII Corps overran Brittany in only one week after turning the corner at Avranche on 1 August, bottling up the German troops into port fortresses: Brest, Lorient, St. Malo, and St. Nazaire. Possessing facilities potentially important to

Allied logistics as well as U-boat pens, the ports had been high priorities in pre-invasion planning. Hitler ordered the garrisons defended to the last man.

The attack into Brittany would accomplish little beyond tying down American troops. The 4th Armored Division reached Brest, at the tip of the peninsula two hundred miles from Avranche, on 7 August and attacked at once to no effect. Brest would not fall until 18 September following a ten-day assault by three infantry divisions.[29] St. Nazaire and Lorient held out until the end of the war.[30] The 83d Infantry Division, backed by the 709th Tank Battalion, captured the seemingly indestructible citadel in St. Malo after a two-week assault, but only because the German commander surrendered after his outer defenses were breached.[31]

The experience at the Breton fortresses offered one lesson it would have behooved Patton and other commanders to remember when their troops ran into fortresses around Metz and even the comparatively puny casements of the Siegfried Line: Tanks are not particularly good weapons for attacking such fortifications. For old fortresses that shrugged off strikes by heavy bombers, rounds from a Sherman's 75mm were of modest value.

The troops fighting around Brest in August and September were back in hedgerow country. The hedgerow cutters once again proved to be an important asset for maneuvering tankers.[32]

## MORTAIN AND FALAISE:
## HITLER STICKS HIS PAW IN THE HONEY JAR

After American forces broke out of Normandy, only one major battle stood between them and the German frontier: Mortain.

With German defenses in an obvious state of collapse, Allied planners sensed an opportunity to strike boldly eastward instead of sticking to Overlord's plan to concentrate first on the capture of the Breton ports. On 4 August, Montgomery ordered the first major change to the invasion plan: Patton was told to use minimum force to clear Brittany and to throw most of his troops eastward, with an initial objective of the Mayenne River. The U.S. First Army would continue to attack in the Vire-Mortain area, making a tighter wheeling movement. Anglo-Canadian forces, meanwhile, would pivot toward Falaise and Argentan. The goal was to encircle German forces west of the Seine River or, barring that, to trap them against the river and destroy them. Mortain was the pivot point for all Allied movement.[33]

With Patton's forces racing eastward, Feldmarschall Günther von Kluge decided to strike with the panzer divisions (1st SS, 2d SS, 2d, and 116th) and battle groups that he could quickly bring into play to cut off the American spearheads.[34] Hitler, who wanted to attack with eight panzer divisions, reluctantly agreed. The available divisions, however, were already weakened by attrition and had no more than 250 tanks among them—less than the authorized equipment of two full-strength panzer divisions.[35] The entire 2d SS Panzer Division had only thirty operational tanks remaining, and the 116th Panzer Division only twenty-five. The 1st SS Panzer Division, meanwhile, was strung out on the roads from Normandy.[36] The attack nevertheless would begin at Mortain the night of 6 August.

Late to the line of departure, short of equipment, and lacking air cover from German fighters that had trouble penetrating Allied air support, the German forces ran into trouble immediately. The 2d Panzer Division accomplished a minor penetration but was stopped by the reserve armored force of the 3d Armored Division. The 2d SS Panzer Division, meanwhile, captured Mortain but could not push the 30th Infantry Division off high ground west and northwest of town.[37]

Allied air reconnaissance and the top secret British Ultra code-breaking system detected the scope of the German build-up, and Bradley reacted. He deployed five infantry divisions, backed by two armored combat commands, along eighteen miles of front between Mortain and Vire, and held three of Patton's divisions to anchor the right flank to the west of Mortain. He also increased pressure at Vire on the assembling German forces. Patton moved to swing behind the Germans with the rest of his divisions.

Battered by Allied fighter-bombers and facing stiff resistance, the German armored columns ground to a halt and the attack broke down within five days, having advanced to a depth of between three and seven miles.[38]

On the ground, where the armored fist struck the American defenses, the picture did not look nearly so cheery at first. For one thing, the German attack achieved tactical surprise.[39] Second, at the local level the first effects appeared to be catastrophic: The 2d SS Panzer Division overran the CP of the 2d Battalion, 122d Infantry Regiment, in Mortain and isolated the battalion on the heights of Hill 317 east of town. (The proper designation is Hill 314—the official Army history is in error—but Hill 317 has worked its way into the common literature and is retained here.) Third, the 30th Infantry Division had just moved into positions vacated by the 1st Infantry Division, so it was poorly oriented, lacked decent maps, and had inherited a tangled telephone wire net.[40]

On 7 August, the 743d Tank Battalion, attached to the 30th Infantry Division, deployed Company C to protect the division's left flank and deployed the Mortar, Assault Gun, and Reconnaissance platoons to defend the right flank. By evening, things were so tight that the rear echelon went on alert and established roadblocks with a few bazooka teams. On 8 August, Company A fought a German armored column. Its first losses at Mortain came not at enemy hands, however, but from British Typhoon fighter-bombers that struck two Shermans, knocking one out for good. (Another source indicates that the Typhoon attack actually occurred on 7 August.)[41] Beginning 10 August, the assault guns were used to fire smoke shells filled with medical supplies to the isolated battalion on Hill 317. On 12 August, after five days of heavy German attacks and generally ineffective American counterattacks, Company B finally reentered Mortain in the face of only sniper fire. On 16 August, the Assault Gun Platoon was able to report that it had fired on *retreating* enemy infantry and armor through the day. The fighting cost the battalion seven men killed and twenty-three wounded, roughly its losses during all of June after D day and more than it would suffer in the Battle of the Bulge.[42]

Also on 10 August, the 737th Tank Battalion, attached to the 35th Infantry Division on the right flank of the 30th Infantry Division, received hurried oral orders to support a drive by the 320th Infantry Regiment to relieve the troops trapped on Hill 317. All medium tanks were to attack in column, and all tanks but the first five were to carry five doughs each. Tankers were ordered to bypass any tanks knocked out and not to leave the road. Starting with fifty-three of their own Shermans and fifteen light tanks from the 3d Armored Division, the battalion was soon in the thick of the fighting. The 737th AAR recorded:

Tanks moved north on road as planned. . . . They came under heavy MG [machine gun], mortar, artillery, and AT fire at Phase Line C, at which time the infantry jumped off the tanks and dug in. The tanks continued on mission in spite of heavy fire, even though ten tanks were knocked out before objective was reached. . . . After arriving on objective [a crossroads near Hill 317], tanks held, waiting for infantry aid; at 2100 none had arrived and tanks were ordered to take up positions in adjacent fields and set up all-around defense. At 0300, 11 Aug 1944, one battalion of infantry arrived at Phase Line C to aid tanks. One company of 1st Battalion had bypassed tanks and started north toward Hill 317. Shortly after dawn, the battalion, which had arrived at 0300, moved forward. The tanks could move no farther due to unfavorable terrain and enemy counterattacks. . . . During the entire period that these tanks were in action they were under heavy enemy fire from artillery, AT guns, mortars, bazookas, rifle grenades, and small arms. They had no infantry support.[43]

The infantry of the 320th Regiment say that this account is inaccurate and that, in point of fact, Able Company of the 737th abandoned *them* at 1800 hours on 10 August.[44]

The 70th Tank Battalion, meanwhile, was as usual attached to the 4th Infantry Division, which protected the left flank of the 30th Infantry Division. Only Company B was committed (with the 12th Infantry Regiment), although Company D manned some roadblocks.[45] The Company B tanks were held in the line for three days and nights under frequent shelling; it helped to plug holes and beat back German attacks. The company nonetheless lost only one Sherman.[46]

One day after the Germans attacked at Mortain, the Canadian First Army, near Caen, launched a massive attack southeast toward Falaise, about thirty miles behind and west-northwest of the German spearhead. On 10 August, Patton ordered XV Corps, which had captured Le Mans seventy miles to the rear and southeast of the enemy's Mortain line, to attack north across the German rear toward Argentan and Falaise.[47] The entire

German Seventh Army was in danger of encirclement even as it pressed its faltering attack toward Avranche. As the situation became clear, Hitler finally agreed that the Seventh Army must withdraw.

Punching through desperate German resistance at Alencon on 11 August, the French 2d and U.S. 5th Armored divisions, followed closely by the U.S. 79th and 90th Infantry divisions, reached Argentan. Patrols reached Falaise. But on 13 August, SHAEF ordered the 90th Infantry and French 2d Armored divisions to stop in Argentan and wait for Montgomery's troops, who were pushing south to close the gap; the rest of XV Corps was ordered to turn east toward Paris. Unfortunately, the Canadian attack stalled halfway to the objective, and Montgomery's troops did not close the trap until 19 August, which allowed perhaps one-third of the German troops to escape.[48] The collapse of the Falaise pocket was nonetheless a disaster for the German army. It left behind fifty thousand prisoners, ten thousand dead, as many as five hundred tanks and assault guns destroyed or captured, and most of the transportation and artillery of the troops who fled.[49]

Those who did escape did so under withering attack from the air and fire from the American units holding the southern edge of their route. In his oral history of the 712th Tank Battalion, which was attached to the 90th Infantry Division, Aaron Elson records tank commander Jim Gifford's recollection of the immense scene of chaos and slaughter as the pincers closed:

The next morning, it was just daylight, I took my field glasses and went up the hill so I could see out over this valley. . . . I see all these little sparkles, little sparkles all over the valley, what the hell is that? I looked through the field glasses and I'm telling you, I couldn't believe the sight I saw. It was thousands of bayonets flashing in the early morning sun. These guys, these infantry guys, were walking toward us, now they're about three miles away up that valley, and they're dispersed among hundreds of tanks moving along. Holy shit, I saw this, this was coming toward us, this is it. So I ran down, I got on the radio and I started hollering over the radio what's coming. And it wasn't twenty minutes later a bunch of our P-47 Thunderbolts were flying towards them, at treetop level, those guys were our saviors, they were our angels up there, they were there all the time so we felt secure. They used to run in groups of four, and they came flying in one group after another. They'd go and the next thing there'd be more of them coming, they were knocking the shit out of them, and shells started flying over us, big shells. . . .

Well, these poor bastards out there three miles away, they were catching bloody hell, I'll tell you, they were getting it. We were firing at them from a mile or two away. . . . companies A and B were spread out across the valley [with] the 773d Antitank Battalion. . . . And this monolith, whatever you want to call it, was slowly rolling, with all the destruction that was going on, it was coming right along by us—and Jesus, it wasn't stopping—and we were hitting everything. They had hundreds of horses drawing artillery. And instead of turning and coming up the hill toward us, they continued to head toward the gap with our [companies] A, B, and 773d Antitank Battalion dispersed there, and those two companies were catching hell because the Germans started rolling through them. And when they hit these two companies plus the 773d they started piling up, and the next thing they turned and started to go back and started running into themselves.

By two o'clock in the afternoon, airplanes had been flying over dropping leaflets . . . saying surrender, wave the leaflet, you'll be okay. We got orders, they kept coming over the radio, stop firing at two o'clock. . . . Then at two o'clock it stopped, and they started coming up, out of the gap. Their equipment was burning all over the place, as far as you could see. . . . I looked down from the tank, and these guys were all dusty, dirty and filthy, and tired. They were a bedraggled army, it was a defeated army. They were just so goddamn glad to just be alive.[50]

The S-3 of the 702d Tank Battalion, attached to the 80th Infantry Division, on 22 August recorded the scene and yet one more field solution to improving communications with the doughs: "S-2 sergeant out to Argentan Gap—saw scenes of utter destruction reaped by German Seventh Army in their desperate attempts to break through gap. Countless numbers of burned out vehicles in the fields, guns, tanks, equipment and dead strewn all over a concentrated area. The stench of putrid dead horses and German dead was something awful. We garnered much signal equipment for use of Infantry-Tank communication, phones (field) (radio)."

## PARIS AND BEYOND: THE PURSUIT

After Mortain and the closure of the Falaise gap, the road race eastward truly began. On 19 August, Eisenhower made another major adjustment to the plan. Instead of stopping at the Seine River for three months in order to build up supplies, open ports, and build airfields, he decided to pursue the retreating Germans relentlessly on a broad front.[51] The U.S. First and Third armies would charge ahead. Eisenhower's decision to advance on a broad front led to months of friction with Monty, who wanted to stage a single thrust in the north all the way into Germany and cut off the Roer industrial basin.

The official U.S. Army history describes this period almost entirely as a series of movements rather than clashes. Contact with the enemy, whose forces were in disarray, was sporadic. The Germans tried to make a stand in only a few instances, usually at river crossings. Otherwise, American units faced scattered roadblocks or small rear-guard actions that rarely lasted even a few hours. Many bridges were captured intact, and the Germans defended few towns and villages.[52] Only the armored division spearheads ran into serious fighting—and even then highly localized—once the race began.

For the separate tank battalions, the action was essentially one of rapid pursuit of the enemy, who threw up defenses in the form of mined roadblocks, demolitions, and mobile strong points consisting of infantry, tanks, and self-propelled artillery.[53] After slugging it out in Mortain, for example, the 743d Tank Battalion raced 123 miles between 19 and 20 August.[54] At one time, the battalion's point was only eight minutes behind the enemy rear guard. The retreating column was frequently shelled, and the highway was littered with knocked-out vehicles and abandoned equipment. So fast was the advance that the Germans had no time to lay mines or do more than construct the simplest roadblocks.[55]

Homer Wilkes advanced across northern France with the 747th Tank Battalion, which formed part of TF Taylor. Blown bridges on most days posed greater obstacles than did the Germans. Near Landrecies the tankers encountered members of the French Resistance, who told them that yet another bridge ahead was wired for demolition. Five tanks charged the bridge, but it exploded just as the first Sherman was about to drive onto it. Scouts found a railroad bridge intact, however, and the task force crossed late that evening.

The next morning, TF Taylor pushed into Landrecies, where Company C, the advance guard, ran into antitank, small-arms, mortar, and bazooka fire. Infantry support was brought up, and the tanks and doughs worked their way forward. They benefited from direct air support strafing an enemy column on the road to the immediate front—one of the few such cases mentioned in separate tank battalion records in northern France. In no more than a few hours, the Americans broke the German resistance at the cost of three tanks knocked out by bazooka fire but no casualties among the crews.

Shortly thereafter, the task force reached Pommereuil. Company C tanks, with one company of infantry, were ordered to clear the northern fringe of Bois L'Eveque. Here the crews tried a different tactic. By riding two or three hundred yards at a time and stopping to shout in chorus, *"Kammen sie hier kammerades!"* (vaguely reminiscent of "Come out and surrender!" in German), they induced 218 dispirited defenders to give up.[56]

Aside from such occasional run-ins with German troops, the race eastward was a triumphant experience for the tankers. Locals mobbed them in every village, eager to greet their liberators with flowers, cheers, wine, and kisses from the girls. For once, fear was far away. Homer Wilkes recalled that on one occasion, none of the gunners in another 747th platoon were able to hit an escaping Tiger tank in full view because they were all inebriated.[57]

Paris fell on 25 August. Eisenhower had hoped to bypass and surround the city, but the French Resistance launched a rebellion that quickly got into trouble. They called for help. Free French leader Gen. Charles de Gaulle insisted on intervention, and he and the French 2d Armored Division commander, Maj. Gen. Jacque Leclerc, gave every indication that French troops under U.S. First Army command would disobey orders not to take the city. Eisenhower gave in.[58] For evident political reasons, the French 2d Armored Division was officially the first unit to enter Paris; Patton's Third Army had been poised to move earlier, but it had been ordered to stay to the south. Simultaneously, the 4th Infantry Division moved into the French capital, providing the 70th Tank Battalion with the unmatched opportunity to perform two days of "guard" duty in the center of a joyous and momentarily generous Parisian public. The tankers enjoyed the time—a lot.[59]

The 741st also got to Paris, and Capt. James Thornton and his men had great expectations when the word went around. "Paris was on everyone's lips," recalled Sgt. Bill Merk. "Paris, the ambition of any vacationer, playboy, or fashion expert!"[60] The tankers reached the city at 1015 on 29 August, where they formed up to participate in a parade through the city center. Along with doughs of the 28th Infantry Division, they rolled four tanks abreast down the Champs Elysée—and straight out the other end of Paris! They had orders to attack at 0730 the next day.[61]

The 70th Tank Battalion, meanwhile, sadly left the City of Light and was fully recommitted to battle on 27 August, a day it suffered one of its highest loss rates of the war: seven Shermans. Perhaps hangovers played a role.[62]

On 8 September, the 712th Tank Battalion was in bivouac around Mairy, a village near Landres, when it experienced the only real tank battle in the separate tank battalion annals during the race through France. At 0200 hours, about thirty-five Panthers and Mark IVs of the 106th Panzer Brigade, accompanied by halftracks, stumbled into the bivouac area. George Bussel, who was standing guard near his Sherman, watched in amazement as the column appeared out of the dark and the commander in the first German panzer leaned over the turret to read the sign pointing toward the 90th Infantry Division artillery CP.

Shooting broke out at once. At least one Sherman exploded in flames, and a confused exchange flared until daybreak. At 1000 hours, two Panthers broke past the American tanks and headed for the battalion CP. Guns from many directions turned on the panzers and knocked them out. Captured German crewmen said that by this time they were trying to break out, not in.

About noon, two German tanks advanced on the glade where Service Company was repairing tanks. As men scattered, maintenance officer Forrest Dixon and another man clambered into one of the Shermans. Doubting that the sights and main gun were aligned, Forrest waited until the lead German tank was only fifty yards away. The enemy's turret began to turn in his direction, so Forrest let him have it and called for help over the radio. The assault guns soon rolled up in support, and German soldiers began to surrender.

By the time the fighting finally died down, the 712th had knocked out 20 German tanks and several halftracks, and had captured 10 tanks, at least 50 halftracks, and 764 enemy soldiers. The battalion AAR does not record the 712th's own losses that day, but they appear to have totaled only a handful of men and Shermans.[63]

The rapid advance across France took a tremendous toll on the equipment of the tank battalions despite the Sherman's remarkable durability. On 10 September, for example, the 749th Tank Battalion, advancing with the 8th Infantry Division, could muster only a composite platoon of five operational Shermans; all its other tanks were out of action for maintenance reasons. The battalion that day dispatched thirty trucks to Utah Beach or Cherbourg to find tank tracks, engines, and other needed spares. On 12 September, one of the 749th's five tanks hit a mine and a second broke down.[64] U.S. First Army reacted to the shortage of tanks throughout armored formations by adopting a provisional table of organization and equipment that reduced the size of armored divisions and the separate tank battalions, in the latter case to fifty medium tanks.[65]

But while steel suffered, for a change human flesh did not to any great degree, except perhaps for those portions that sat in bouncing tank seats for hundreds of miles. During the entire race across France after the battle at Mortain, for example, the 743rd Tank Battalion lost only one man killed and two wounded.[66] The 741st suffered only one man lightly wounded in action in the first two weeks of September.

The race across northern France ended by mid-September. Patton's advance elements reached Metz on 1 September,[67] but Eisenhower's decision in August to throw most of the available logistic support behind Monty's advance along the coast starved the Third Army of fuel and other necessities, and the tanks ground to a halt. Patton improvised a bit by using captured German fuel. Farther north, American columns had similar supply problems. The 743d Tank Battalion—whose tanks were the first to enter Belgium and the Netherlands—by early September was rationing tank fuel and sending supply trucks far to the rear in search of more; on 12 September, the point halted because it had no more gas.[68] The 702d Tank Battalion noted in mid-September that the distance to its various supply points ranged from one hundred to five hundred miles.[69] That any fuel at all was reaching the advance elements was due to the tireless efforts of the famous Red Ball Express, which moved gasoline forward in five-gallon jerry cans on quartermaster trucks. By September, however, the Red Ball was approaching the point at which it burned more gas to reach the front than the trucks could carry.[70]

In any event, U.S. First Army elements reached prepared defensive positions in the Netherlands and the Siegfried Line along the German border by 11 September. There they slowed or stopped in the face of reemergent German resistance.[71]

## OPERATION DRAGOON: THE OTHER SHOE DROPS

On 15 August, forces of the U.S. Seventh Army drawn from the Italian campaign landed on the southern coast of France in an operation arguably pointless by then. The British certainly argued that position, and with great vigor. German forces in southern France, almost stripped of effective armored units and many of the best infantry divisions to help hold the line in Normandy, already confronted an untenable position as Patton raced across their rear toward the German border. Faced with the deteriorating situation in northern France, Hitler by 16 August had settled on a withdrawal from southern France except, as in Brittany, for the ports of Marseilles and Toulon.

American forces faced virtually no opposition as they came ashore near St. Tropez.[72] Three infantry divisions of VI Corps—the 3d, the 36th, and the 45th—made up the invasion force, which was to be followed by four French divisions. Three tank battalions—the 191st, 753d, and 756th—were each equipped with the rough equivalent of one company of DD Shermans for the invasion. On D day, all three of the 191st DD platoons puttered to shore safely, although an entire platoon was immobilized by mines on Blue Beach after landing. Three DDs were total losses, and the platoon drew standard replacement tanks. In the 753d, the Company A DDs were floated four thousand yards offshore and lost only one temporarily when its screen was punctured by an antitank round, which flooded the engine as the tank neared the beach.[73]

The need for effective tank-infantry communications apparently had filtered south by August. Each company commander's tank in the 191st went ashore with an infantry SCR-300 radio installed in an armored box behind the turret. A shortage of such radios, however, prevented their use in platoon leaders' tanks. The battalion, meanwhile, gave the infantry regiments to which it was attached SCR-509 radios as a backup. The records of the 753d and 756th Tank battalions provide no evidence that they adopted the same system.

American forces pushed aggressively west and then hooked north to the east of the Rhone River. French troops advanced west of the Rhone behind the French 1st Armored Division. German forces fought delaying actions to enable as many troops as possible to escape from France. They launched two major actions. The first was by the 11th Panzer Division and an infantry division at Montelimar from 22 to 25 August, and the second was a spoiling thrust at the 45th Infantry Division east of Lyon on 1 September. Tankers from the 753d Tank Battalion had a run-in with the panzers just after the main action at Montelimar, as recorded in the AAR:

[On 27 August] a German attack of infantry and three tanks of the Mark V or VI type was working its way around our north flank. Having the protection of the north ridge our artillery was unable to stop it. Our tanks in the houses east of town were also not in a position to fire on them. A platoon of tanks was placed on the ridge north of the Condillac road. When the German tanks appeared they were taken under fire at a range of eight hundred yards by our M4s. Unfortunately our shells just bounced off and caused no damage. A tank destroyer was maneuvered around the German right flank. This tank destroyer succeeded in knocking out one German tank but was itself knocked out by the remaining two. . . .

At about 1300, and while the tank company commander was still on reconnaissance, German tanks and infantry again attacked our north flank. This was again broken up and dispersed. In the tank fight our tanks succeeded in breaking the track of one of the Mark Vs or VIs. This fixed the German tank for the kill. Two of our M4s at a range of six hundred yards fired altogether fourteen rounds before they succeeded in penetrating the German armor and setting it on fire.[74]

On 11 September, French tanks linked up with Patton's Third Army north of Dijon, and the two fast-moving fronts became one. On 14 September, tankers from Company C of the 753d Tank Battalion were supporting the infantry near Allencourt and pressing the retreating Germans hard. The battalion AAR recorded just how hard:

First Section [of the 1st Platoon] . . . had run into numerous enemy withdrawing. In fact so close to the enemy and so many, [that] one tank moving down the road to St. Sauver from Allençourt was given a stop sign by an enemy MP [military policeman] to allow enemy vehicles to continue along the road perpendicular to the advance of the troops. A tank destroyer advancing parallel to the tank moving along the road was pulling onto [the] road perpendicular to advance when [an] enemy bus loaded with withdrawing enemy ran into [the] gun tube of tank destroyer and stripped [the] traversing mechanism within the vehicle.[75]

This was war, and the tankers shot up the enemy column.

On 12 September 1944, Lt. Raymond Zussman of the 756th Tank Battalion was in command of two tanks operating with an infantry company in the attack on enemy forces occupying the town of Noroy le Bourg, France. At 1900 hours, his command tank bogged down. Throughout the ensuing action, armed only with a carbine, he reconnoitered alone on foot far

in advance of his remaining tank and the infantry. Returning
only from time to time to designate targets, he directed the
action of the tank and turned over to the infantry the many
German soldiers he captured. He located a roadblock and
directed his tank to destroy it. Fully exposed to fire from
enemy positions only fifty yards distant, he stood by his tank
and directed its fire. Three Germans were killed and eight
surrendered. Again he walked before his tank, leading it
against a group of enemy-held houses while machine-gun and
small-arms fire kicked up dust at his feet. The tank fire broke
the resistance and twenty enemy soldiers surrendered. Again
going forward alone, Zussman passed a house from which
Germans fired on him and threw grenades in his path. After a
brief firefight, he signaled his tank to come up and fire on the
house. Eleven German soldiers were killed and fifteen surrendered. Going on alone, he disappeared around a street corner.
The fire of his carbine could be heard and in a few minutes he
reappeared driving thirty prisoners before him. Under Lieutenant Zussman's heroic and inspiring leadership, eighteen
enemy soldiers were killed and ninety-two captured. He received the Congressional Medal of Honor for his actions.


The "Champagne Campaign," as critics called it, cost the U.S.
Seventh Army 2,733 men killed, wounded, or captured to
reach Lyon on 2 September. Casualties in the tank battalions
were correspondingly low despite an assault landing and five-
hundred-mile advance. The 756th Tank Battalion, for example, lost twenty-five men killed and thirty-seven wounded
between 15 August and 15 September.

    On 20 September, VI Corps set out to force the Moselle
River but found that Jerry was no longer running. The Germans now held VI Corps, dangling at the end of a long supply

line, before the Belfort Gap in the Vosges Mountains west of
the German border.[76] The 756th Tank Battalion AAR noted in
September, "Enemy defended approaches to Belfort Gap. Contact gained near La Fied on 4 September. As enemy moved
back into the hills, he began using considerable numbers of
antitank mines. Enemy used few tanks, but employed considerable numbers of AT and SP guns. Enemy resistance stiffened
as the terrain grew more favorable for defense, and artillery
fire increased in intensity."[77]

Weather and terrain aided the Germans. The 191st Tank
Battalion AAR recorded in October, "Continued rainfall rendered the surrounding territory unfit for cross-country maneuver. In addition, much of the action took place in densely
wooded areas, where the employment of tanks was extremely
dangerous."[78]

Physically isolated from the tank battalions in northern France,
the outfits in the south evolved separately at first. On the one
hand, this meant learning hard lessons already learned in
Normandy. For example, the CO of the 191st concluded after
operations in September, "For infantry close-support battalions, a liaison set-up similar to that employed by the artillery
is needed. That is, a liaison officer with radio and vehicle
should be lent to each regiment and assault battalion."[79]

Tankers in southern France also experienced some of the
same frustrations inherent in the Army's standard attachment
policy. The 191st Tank Battalion commander's narrative for
September 1944, for example, complained:

Sufficient time must be allowed for maintenance of equipment during sustained operations. Tanks cannot continue
to pass thru [*sic*] infantry battalion after battalion, leading

the attack day after day. Three days of sustained operation has been found to be the maximum time without maintenance. After three days, efficiency is greatly reduced due to breakdown. . . .

Coupled with maintenance on vehicles, tank crews must be allowed some time to rest. It must be realized that tank crews usually must reservice after dark. Radio watches must be continually maintained. Therefore, tank crews do not get as much rest as infantry troops. If these factors are not considered, battle exhaustion will take a high toll of good tank officers and men. During the past month, eight tank platoon leaders were evacuated for battle exhaustion. This could have been practically eliminated had crews been given a day's rest after three or four days' operation.

On the other hand, the southern tank battalions learned some things that their counterparts would not learn for weeks. For example, by September, the 191st had installed one of its radios in the division artillery observer Piper Cub airplane, and a battalion officer flew along to provide air observation in support of tank operations. The 191st, fighting in heavy forest along the Swiss border, also discovered some lessons about working in those conditions that could have helped battalions entering forests along the German frontier.[80]

The rapidly advancing troops experienced many of the same problems as their counterparts farther north. Air support proved a mixed blessing during the rapid advance. On 19 August, Task Force Felber (including elements of the 753d Tank Battalion) was strafed by six Spitfires. On 27 August, six more Allied aircraft pounced on and disrupted an attack that 36th Infantry Division troops, supported by the 753d, were just getting under way; they set two Shermans on fire and wounded a company commander despite the use of yellow identification smoke.[81]

On 1 September, the 191st expressed concern that long road marches and shortages of spares were forcing the battalion to continue using worn-out tank tracks.[82] By the second week of September, fuel shortages were hampering the advance.[83] The 753d also reported near-critical shortages of tracks, support rollers, bogie wheels, and tank engines during September. On 6 September, the battalion CO warned the commanding general of the 36th Infantry Division that his tanks would not be operational after two more days of movement unless parts could be obtained. At mid-month Company C had only three tanks that would run.[84]

As German resistance toughened, the 753d in September was hit by another shortage that soon would hit tank battalions farther north: qualified replacement personnel. Since the Dragoon landing through September, the battalion lost sixteen tank commanders and seventeen drivers; these positions required crucial skills, and the battalion had shifted its surviving veterans to fill them after heavy losses in Italy during May and June. The battalion in September had to "deadline" operational tanks because of crew shortages.[85]

## Hitting the West Wall: The Big Picture

There was to be no early end to the war. Despite its recent defeats, the German Army remained a dangerous foe, fighting for its life in prepared defenses. Furthermore, as the Allies approached the frontiers of the Reich, they encountered a series of formidable terrain obstacles—major rivers, mountains, and forests—and the worst weather in over thirty years. Yet Eisenhower, believing that unremitting pressure against the enemy would shorten the war, called for the offensive to continue.

*A Brief History of the U.S. Army in World War II,* Center of Military History, United States Army, Washington, D.C., 1992

# 5

# HITTING THE WEST WALL

The reality of war was grimly present once more. Along the
Meuse (Maas) River, the Germans showed a frantic—and
fanatical—determination to throw up some semblance of a
line from Maastricht to Charleyville after vacating Charleroi,
Mons and Tournai. The Meuse thus was the German army's
first defense line to confront the First U.S. Army after the
Seine crossing. There were remnants of four infantry and
seven panzer divisions dug in there. By 12 September, the
First Army's sustained drive had been stopped. The war settled down to a foot-soldier's walk again. Ahead was some of
the bitterest fighting of the war.

> Wayne Robinson,
> *Move Out, Verify*

The officially recognized U.S. Army campaigns in northern
and southern France, characterized by rapid movement and
isolated pockets of German defense, ended on 14 September
1944; on 15 September, the Rhineland Campaign began, a
slugfest that dragged on by official count until 21 March of the
next year.

The First Army's three corps butted up against the Siegfried
Line between 13 and 19 September. General William Simpson's Ninth Army, shifted from Brittany, took over command of
part of this sector in late September.

In the Third Army's zone, Patton's troops had just breached
the Moselle River line by 14 September but faced a looming
cutoff of most supplies and an order to go onto the defensive
as of 25 September. Patton nevertheless was determined to

knock through the fortifications around Metz that stood between him and the Siegfried Line.[1]

On Patton's right flank, Seventh Army troops were stuck in
the rough, forested terrain of the Vosges Mountains.

From north to south, the separate tank battalions faced
broadly similar challenges in the next phase of the conflict.

Tanks were committed against prepared—and often
fortified—German positions where, lacking room for maneuver and heavy punch, they were at their least effective.

Infantry and tankers had no training to deal with this and
found themselves enrolled in another school of hard knocks.

The weather was horrible, which magnified most other
problems. The fall and winter of 1944 produced weather of
near-record severity, first in the form of mud-producing rain
and then snow and unusually harsh temperatures.[2]

Instead of fighting a hedgerow-by-hedgerow battle, the
doughs and their supporting tankers found themselves embroiled
in a fortification-by-fortification, strongpoint-by-strongpoint
struggle. Having experienced—and mastered—the first type of
warfare, however, they showed quick adaptability to the new
circumstances. Moreover, a more tightly integrated and effective combined-arms team was emerging in units that had spent
time together in battle; the team integrated infantry, tanks, artillery, tank destroyers, and airpower into a package that could
bore through the defenses. For example, with ever greater
frequency AARs show tanks and tank destroyers working together (a great rarity in Normandy) and even the occasional
creation of provisional platoons that combined the two types
of armor for specific missions. More battalions began to put
officers in artillery liaison planes from which they could spot
German tanks, guns, and other elements and coordinate action on the ground.[3] And a tank battalion could now expect to
have its CO at the front and officers equipped with tank radios
at the infantry's battalion, regiment, and division headquarters.

The worst experiences occurred in circumstances, such as the dense Hürtgen Forest, where the entire package could not come into play simultaneously.

The U.S. Army's official history goes too far, however, in describing the infantry-tank-artillery teams at this time as "close-knit families, into which had been adopted the fighter-bomber," that possessed an "almost reflexive knowledge of how to fight this kind of war."[4] American troops were frequently shot up by their own planes.[5] Disconnects between infantry and tanks continued to occur, and infantry commanders still sometimes made bad calls on the use of tanks. Homer Wilkes had another hair-tearing experience with an infantry officer as the 747th first reached the Siegfried Line on 14 September:

> After dark, a liaison officer from the commanding general, 4th Infantry Division, came up. This gentleman relayed the personal order from the general to the platoon leader for 3d Platoon, Company A, to attack the Siegfried Line at first light, going as far as possible before all the tanks were knocked out.
>
> [I] asked about supporting troops such as reconnaissance, infantry, engineers, and especially artillery and air. [I] was told there would be no artillery preparation, no air, and no other support of any kind, not even a medical aid man (which the platoon did not have).
>
> Since the general had ignored the chain of command, bypassing all intermediate headquarters and officers to include Company A's commander, this liaison officer was informed he could tell the general his orders would not be obeyed on the grounds it was not a field order but a demand [that] twenty-four men and one officer commit suicide. . . . A few minutes later Captain Stewart's jeep driver arrived with orders to revert to battalion control. This was executed with alacrity.[6]

Units had to work at keeping the team functioning because there was no reflexive knowledge. In the midst of bitter
fighting in the Rötgen Forest, for example, the CO of the 746th
felt compelled to confront the 60th Infantry Regiment commander over tank tactics, and during a break in the action late
in the month the infantry and tanks conducted joint exercises.[7] The 747th Tank Battalion, upon attachment to the 29th
Infantry Division, conducted fifteen days of daily tank-infantry
exercises with the doughs while in division reserve.[8] This
time, the partners experimented with putting the infantry platoon commander inside the tank in the bog seat, which proved
a poor idea as he could no longer control his troops, and the
tank lost a valuable crew member.[9] Despite the training efforts, the battalion judged that several of its tank losses during
the first weeks fighting together would have been prevented
by better infantry support.[10] The main change from Normandy
days was that both infantry and tankers better understood that
they had to work out solutions together in order to survive
and win.

## THE SIEGFRIED LINE

The West Wall, construction of which began in 1936, ran
nearly four hundred miles from north of Aachen along the
German frontier to the Swiss border. The Germans had ne-
glected the defenses after 1940, so Hitler now worked furiously to put together a scratch force of 135,000 men to
partially rebuild and man the line as the Allies approached the
border. The strongest portion faced Patton along the Saar
River between the Moselle and the Rhine. The second most
formidable section was a double band of defenses protecting
the Aachen gap, with the city of Aachen lying between the
two. Immediately behind the West Wall in this sector was the

Roer River, which gave the Germans a backstop that they could flood from the dams farther south near Schmidt.[11]

Pillboxes in the West Wall typically had reinforced concrete walls and roofs three to eight feet thick and were generally twenty to thirty feet wide, forty to fifty feet deep, and twenty to twenty-five feet high, with at least half the structure underground. In some areas, rows of "dragon's teeth"—reinforced concrete pyramids—acted as antitank obstacles. In other areas, defenses relied on natural features—rivers, lakes, forests, defiles, and so on—to provide passive antitank protection.[12] Wayne Robinson gave a tanker's perspective:

> So much has been written about the complex fortifications of the Siegfried Line that a stranger to it might suppose it was nothing but one pillbox after the other with bands of steel and concrete jutting out of the earth. This is a false impression. Much of the Siegfried looked deceptively like normal countryside. The massive barriers, a favorite subject for war photographers, were only a part of it. There were long stretches of green countryside . . . with sleepy, normal-looking villages spotted through it. There was nothing sleepy and nothing normal about [them]. . . .
>
> [E]very village was part of the fortress system. The countryside might appear normal because the pillboxes built by the hundreds into its woods and contours were carefully concealed and camouflaged. Some of them were built so as to hide in the ground—when they went into action, they rose out of the ground, and then after firing sank back into the ground, out of sight again. Every house seemed to have its quota of snipers and gunmen. . . .[13]

## TRY AND TRY AGAIN

On 11 September, U.S. First Army authorized V and VII corps to conduct a "reconnaissance in force" with the aim of breaching the Siegfried Line before the Germans could fully prepare their defenses. The V Corps' operation committed three divisions, the 28th and 4th Infantry and 5th Armored, that were spread out over a wide front and feeling the effects of the long advance across France. They faced rough terrain with the Schnee Eifel, a thickly forested highland, in the center. On the left, VII Corps threw the 1st Infantry and 3d Armored divisions, backed by the 9th Infantry Division, against Aachen from the south in anticipation of an eventual pincer move from the north by XIX Corps.[14]

Another unwelcome learning experience began. American tankers had never trained to assault fortifications before actually seeing them, although the attacks on the fortress ports in Brittany had provided a foretaste to a few. The tankers discovered that their cannons were unable to knock out most bunkers. Even the 105mm howitzers of the assault guns proved unable to knock out the pillboxes.[15] After trying, they soon realized that their main contribution was to keep the defenders down by firing at embrasures and using tank dozers to cover up the doors and embrasures of captured pillboxes. Here was another puzzle to be solved along with the doughs, the tank destroyers, and the artillery. Air support would prove practically worthless.

In the 28th Infantry Division's sector, the attack from 14 to 16 September painfully poked a pencil-like hole through the West Wall at the cost of 1,500 casualties, losses so high that they precluded exploitation.[16] Supporting tanks had a great deal of trouble maneuvering off the roads because of the torrential rains that had fallen.[17]

The attached 741st Tank Battalion participated in one of the first assaults on the West Wall. On 14 September at 0930 hours, Capt. James Thornton ordered two platoons of Company B into motion to support the 2d Battalion, 109th Infantry. His goal, the high ground southeast of Harsfelt, lay 1,500 yards ahead. Thornton deployed one platoon on each side of the road ahead, knowing that it was sure to be mined. Heavy fire from pillboxes and two sturdy houses that appeared to hold enemy troops swept the area. His crews advanced methodically, taking each strongpoint under fire. Then came an unexpected setback: An antitank ditch barred the way. Thornton radioed for one of the tank dozers to fill in a space wide enough for his Shermans to cross. This was soon accomplished. Thornton, looking around, realized that the enemy fire had become so heavy that the infantry had gone to ground. To hell. He ordered the Company B tankers to press ahead alone. Soon, the high ground was his, and the infantry was able to join the Shermans on the objective.

At 1600 hours, Thornton's radio crackled to life. Regiment wanted him to lead a platoon of tanks to support his 3d Platoon in the neighboring battalion's sector, where his boys had already lost two Shermans. Thornton quickly decided that the quickest route lay through the German defenses, so he set off to shoot his way past. His gamble cost him two tanks and three men, but Thornton made it. The ranking infantry officer ordered Thornton to lead an attack over the next hill. Thornton took the point and ordered his tanks to advance once again. The Shermans crested the rise. Suddenly, Thornton's tank rocked under a massive blow, followed by two more in quick succession. Fragments of the antitank shells and armor ricocheted like angry hornets inside the tank. Thornton was

blown from the turret and badly injured. An infantry captain—
an old friend and classmate from The Citadel—saw Thornton,
pulled him away from the burning tank, and left two men to
protect him. The Germans counterattacked, however, and that
was the last Thornton was seen alive.[18] Only one crewman,
the gunner, would make it back to American lines.

Not too far away, 2d Lt. Joseph H. Dew, commanding 1st Platoon, Company C, 741st Tank Battalion, led his Shermans
toward the staggered rows of dragon's teeth. The bocage
fighting had claimed every one of the company platoon leaders; Dew—a tall, straightforward man—was one of the replacements. Dew recorded his first major engagement in an AAR:

> On 14 September, [we] moved into position at 0840 hours
> southeast of Groskampenberg. The 1st Platoon moved up
> on the right side of the road to the edge of the dragon's
> teeth and placed direct AP and HE fire on two pillboxes at
> four hundred yards. We then placed a few HE on a small
> clump of trees just over the dragon's teeth and then placed
> fire on three pillboxes to the left front at ranges from 700
> to 1,200 yards.
>
> We waited until 0915 for the engineers to come up and
> blow a way through the dragon's teeth, and when they
> failed to arrive my tank pulled within a few feet of the con-
> crete pillars and fired AP point-blank at them. About 0925
> my tank went through and the rest of my platoon followed.
> We moved up to the pillboxes and fired AP and HE at
> them, point-blank. Then we moved ahead and over the
> hill. There were two pillboxes on our right at about two
> o'clock, and we fired on them. I heard AP whistle around
> the tank and then saw an antitank gun directly ahead of us
> by a building about eight hundred yards away. We blew

that one up and swung towards the town. We saw another antitank gun by the corner of the building and blew the corner off the building firing at it, but I'm sure we didn't hit the gun for I saw it pull back. Then Captain Young called me and said an antitank gun had knocked out one of my tanks behind me, so we pulled back to get him. The gun that got the tank was in the woods to the right and we put three rounds of HE at it at four hundred yards and blew it up. We covered the wounded until they were dragged behind the pillbox where they were temporarily safe. One of my tanks pulled back across the dragon's teeth to get a round out of his 75mm gun, and my tank sat by one pillbox and the other tank of [my] platoon sat by the other one. We waited until 1230 for the infantry to come up and take the pillboxes, because they were full of Heinies. But the infantry didn't come and it finally got so hot with AP that Captain Young pulled us out of there. Before we pulled out, Lieutenant Covington came up and removed the wounded men on his tank. Then we took up positions back of the dragon's teeth and didn't do much except sit there and sweat out enemy artillery from the woods about two thousand yards to our left flank. We were out of HE in my tank and had just a few AP left. About 1700 we pulled into a better position about three hundred yards to our left rear and waited until 2200 when we were relieved.

The following account from the 3d Armored Group AAR for September captures the nature of the battle and the attempts on both sides to adapt to it:

On 15 September this headquarters with two tank battalions, the 741st and 747th, was attached to the 28th Infantry Division and on 17 September, with the support of the 110th Infantry and Division engineers, was designated as

Task Force M and given the mission of widening the gap forced in the Siegfried Line between Heckhuscheid and Groskampenberg, Germany; the 108th Field Artillery Battalion provided artillery support. Due to the reduced strength of the infantry at this time the bulk of the force was to be composed of tanks, with one infantry company (at very reduced strength) in support of each tank battalion. Each of the tank battalions had an average of thirty-five medium tanks. Each was formed into composite companies. To these assault companies in each battalion were attached the tank dozers, and all available assault guns were placed in support in direct-fire position.

The general plan of attack was for the tanks to assault a position and, as soon as the fire superiority had been gained, the infantry would move out and occupy the position until a tank dozer had covered the embrasures and entrances to the pillbox. An artillery observer from the 108th Field Artillery Battalion accompanied the group commander and group S-3 to the forward OP [observation post] in the Siegfried Line in order to direct supporting artillery fire; it had been found that direct radio communication between the forward OP and fire control headquarters was unreliable, so one of the three SCR-508s at the group CP acted as a relay station. . . .

The enemy had all the advantages that go with a well-planned defensive line: terrain favorable to the defenders, direct observation, thick concrete pillboxes, and underground telephone communications. The mutual support provided by enemy pillboxes was particularly effective against the attacking troops. Yet, notwithstanding the many important disadvantages it faced, Task Force M made progress, and reduced the enemy line pillbox by pillbox.

The first day's operation, on 19 September, resulted in

the capture of twenty-nine enemy pillboxes. Very heavy accurate enemy mortar and artillery concentrations were received by the attacking units throughout the day; it was evident that the enemy had direct observation and excellent communications between pillboxes. The captured pillboxes were either blown up by engineer demolition squads or locked and covered up with dirt by tank dozers to prevent the enemy from reoccupying them should he reinfiltrate the position.

On 20 September, twelve enemy pillboxes were captured and rendered unusable; heavy enemy mortar and artillery fire again caused trouble. On 21 September, Company I, 110th Infantry Regiment, replaced Company L; during the day's operations ten pillboxes were captured, under extremely heavy mortar and artillery concentrations, which pinned down the attacking infantry time after time. Dive-bombers supported Task Force M on 22 September, but poor visibility caused the results to be unsatisfactory; the first strike missed the pillbox targets by at least one thousand yards, and two near-hits on the second strike did not damage the pillboxes at all. Although hindered by antitank mines and the usual heavy, accurate enemy mortar and artillery fire, the task force succeeded in capturing and sealing five pillboxes.

In four days of operation this task force covered forty-nine pillboxes, sixteen of which were either unoccupied or previously taken and located in the area held by the infantry, and the remainder of which were captured by the task force and destroyed by the engineers. The bulk of these were captured during the first two days of combat for, as objectives were limited, the enemy grasped our method of operations and stationed men armed with bazookas in foxholes in the vicinity and on top of pillboxes.

Lieutenant Homer Wilkes of the 747th participated in these operations. He recorded one day's action:

> Third Platoon had to go, with Company B's dozer attached, and cover the apertures [of a pillbox]. Woljlechowski was the dozer commander's name. This sergeant was an efficient, intelligent man; highly respected in the command.
>
> As the platoon supported him with machine-gun fire from two tanks and the remainder fired other directions to keep the foe's heads down, the sergeant approached the pillbox.
>
> As the blade[-full] of earth came within about five feet of the first aperture, a bazooka was fired from the pillbox.
>
> Immediately, flames shot five feet high from the turret and all knew there were no survivors.
>
> Its mission completed, 3d Platoon started a shooting withdrawal. . . . The platoon was out and clear but still machine gunning the woods when the battalion commander called to say a man was following us. With two tanks in close support, [I] turned about and went to the man's side.
>
> Getting out of the tank, [I] discovered heavy machine-gun fire coming from the wood. [I] tossed the man up on deck, then lowered him through the commander's hatch and continued the withdrawal.
>
> It was Sergeant Woljlechowski, who had somehow survived the inferno. And though blinded, his head and hands burned black, he had followed us. . . .[19]

The sergeant did not live long.

Bunker-busting was dangerous work. During the fighting between 23 and 25 September described by Wilkes, the 747th lost probably ten men killed (crew members in tanks that burned were often listed as missing in action because they left no remains) and four wounded. After losing only one man during the last two weeks of the race across France, the 741st suffered the loss of probably eighteen men killed and twenty men wounded during the first two weeks on the Siegfried Line.

South of the 28th Infantry Division's sector, the 4th Infantry and 5th Armored divisions rolled through the West Wall in areas that were either weakly held or undefended by German units that were, in some cases, just arriving at the front. Both thrusts pulled up, however, because the rough and forested terrain and the villages behind the fortifications offered nearly as good a position to the gradually jelling German resistance—and because the still-critical logistic situation compelled First Army and V Corps to call a halt. On 22 September V Corps went over to the defensive. The relative inactivity that followed lasted until mid-December.[20]

## A HOT IDEA

The U.S. Army had put some thought into equipment that might make tanks more effective against the fortified line that loomed ahead. Presumably inspired by the British Crocodile flamethrower tanks mounted on the Churchill chassis, the Army decided to install flamethrowers in tanks already in combat with the line battalions. It had first investigated the idea during the Normandy fighting, but delays put the concept on hold.[21] U.S. Headquarters, ETO, in fact had received four Crocodile-style Shermans built for it by the British in early 1944; eventually, these were deployed by the 739th MX Tank Battalion (mine exploder), but the project had been dropped by August.[22]

The Sherman Crocodile used a large-capacity tube mounted on the side to ignite and deliver the fuel, which was carried in a four-hundred-gallon trailer. The E4-5 equipment selected for use by most outfits instead put a nozzle in the place of the hull machine gun, and the storage tanks containing compressed air and fifty gallons of the fuel sat behind the bog, who operated the weapon.[23] This system was capable of using crankcase oil mixed with gasoline, Napaline mixed with gasoline, or British fuel.[24]

On orders from Maj. Gen. J. Lawton Collins of V Corps, the 3d Armored Group recommended on 4 September that the 70th Tank Battalion serve as the test bed for the new flamethrowers.[25] The 70th received its first four units on 11 September, and the hardware spread gradually through other outfits.[26] By 15 September, the 741st Tank Battalion had two flame tanks.[27] In November, according to battalion records, the 709th and 774th each installed six flamethrowers, the 747th nine (three per medium tank company), and the 743d began installing a flamethrower in the tank of each platoon leader. Men from the 707th, 709th, and 750th received flamethrower training at this time, which suggests that those units also received the equipment.

Tankers were divided over the utility of the American-style flamethrowers, which an AAR of the 743d described as "calculated to make the enemy burn with more than embarrassment."

One tanker who fielded the hardware in the 70th recalls having used it to good effect against pillboxes.[28] The AAR for the 741st Tank Battalion, however, records for 18–19 September, "A flamethrower tank was used on one pillbox, but flamethrower had to approach within twenty yards of the box, and even then the flame was very unsatisfactory." Tankers in the 747th realized that the flamethrower and the German bazooka had similar ranges, which made them loath to use the gear in battle against strongpoints. Another drawback of

M5 crews from the 761st Tank Battalion, one of two in the ETO with black enlisted men, somewhere in England before shipping to the Continent. *(NARA, Signal Corps photo)*

Infantry and tanks advance through a French village in Normandy. *(NARA, Signal Corps photo)*

Doughs hold a captured Panzerschreck, 8 July 1944.
This German bazooka was more powerful than its
American counterpart, on which it was based.
*(NARA, Signal Corps photo)*

Sherman of the 743d Tank Battalion passes
knocked-out Mark IV tanks in the vicinity of St. Lô,
9 July 1944. *(NARA, Signal Corps photo)*

A Duplex Drive (DD or "Donald Duck") Sherman of the
756th Tank Battalion crosses the landing beach during
Operation Dragoon on 15 August 1944. The crew has
already collapsed the skirt that converted the vehicle
into an armored boat. *(NARA, Signal Corps photo)*

Remains of a Sherman struck at 100 yards by the
much-feared 88 near Rians, France, on 20 August 1944.
*(NARA, Signal Corps photo)*

LEFT: Tanks and infantrymen find it difficult to make their way through the hilarious throng while passing through a French town, August 1944. *(NARA, Signal Corps photo)*

RIGHT: U.S. tanks participate in the big parade through Paris on 29 August 1944. Wartime censors have blocked out the unit markings, but these probably are tanks of the 741st Tank Battalion, which proceeded from the end of the parade route into combat. *(NARA, Signal Corps photo)*

LEFT: Doughs and tankers of an unidentified unit encounter a pocket of resistance near the Marne River on 31 August 1944. *(NARA, Signal Corps photo)*

Sherman from an unidentified tank battalion rolls through northern France in early September 1944. Note the Culin hedgerow device and extra gas can on the front of the tank. *(NARA, Signal Corps photo)*

Sherman from an unidentified battalion tests a newly installed flamethrower, intended for use against Siegfried Line fortifications, in September 1944. *(NARA, Signal Corps photo)*

M4 of the 191st Tank Battalion crosses the Moselle River in support of the 3d Battalion, 179th Regiment, 45th Infantry Division, on 22 September 1944. (*NARA, Signal Corps photo*)

Tankers applied the description "self-propelled gun" to a range of German armored vehicles, including assault guns such as this, dedicated turretless tank killers, and mobile artillery mounted on a tracked chassis. This Sturmgeschütz III was knocked out near Luneville, France, in late September 1944. (*NARA, Signal Corps photo*)

RIGHT: A Sherman—possibly from the 745th Tank Battalion—and an M36 tank destroyer work in tandem during street fighting in Aachen in October 1944. *(NARA, Signal Corps photo)*

LEFT: The incredibly useful tank dozer, pictured in October mud. *(NARA, Signal Corps photo)*

RIGHT: Doughs of the 95th Division, supported by a Sherman of either the 735th or 778th Tank Battalion, move out near Metz on 18 November 1944. *(NARA, Signal Corps photo)*

Doughs of the 9th Infantry Division shelter behind a
746th Tank Battalion Sherman in Geich, Germany, on
11 December 1944. Note the ammo box containing a
field telephone for use by the infantry to talk to the
buttoned-up tank crew. *(NARA, Signal Corps photo)*

"It's as big as a house!" The Mark VI Tiger (this one knocked
out in Italy) had thick armor and the deadly 88mm gun.
The 741st Tank Battalion fought and destroyed many of
these in Rocherath, Belgium, during the Battle of the Bulge.
*(NARA, Signal Corps photo)*

A German Royal Tiger captured by American troops, December 1944. This panzer had even thicker, better-sloped armor than the Tiger, as well as the 88mm cannon. (*NARA, Signal Corps photo*)

A Jagdpanzer IV SP gun advances during the Bulge, 17 December 1944. Note the thick fog. (*NARA, captured German photo in the Signal Corps collection*)

LEFT: A Jumbo assault tank of the 737th Tank Battalion moves forward, probably near the Sauer River in January 1945. *(NARA, 737th Tank Battalion records)*

RIGHT: Tankers of the 750th support doughs of the 75th Infantry Division near St. Vith during the fight to eliminate the Bulge in January 1945. This M4 has a layer of concrete poured on the glacis between the steel bars welded along the edges. *(NARA, Signal Corps photo)*

LEFT: A column of tanks from the 709th Tank Battalion advances with the infantry during the reduction of the Colmar Pocket, 1 February 1945. The lead tank has a 76mm gun. *(NARA, Signal Corps photo)*

Doughs from the 78th Infantry Division get a lift courtesy of the 741st Tank Battalion during the drive to the Rhine River in early March 1945. The nearest tank shows the substantial increase in track width provided by the attachment of "duck bills" or grousers. *(NARA, Signal Corps photo)*

Tanks from an unidentified battalion cross the Ludendorff Bridge across the Rhine at Remagen on 11 March 1945. *(NARA, Signal Corps photo)*

Germany's awesome medium tank, the Mark V Panther. Note the well-sloped front armor, high-velocity 75mm gun, and wide tracks. This one was knocked out or abandoned at Kelberg, Germany, in March 1945. *(NARA, Signal Corps photo)*

Inspecting the dreaded Panzerfaust, March 1945.
The warhead, which fitted onto a short tubelike launcher,
was fully capable of disabling a Sherman. *(NARA, Signal
Corps photo)*

A heavily sandbagged "Easy 8" of the 781st Tank
Battalion rolls into Bitche, France, on 16 March 1945.
*(NARA, Signal Corps photo)*

Shermans of Company B, 702d Tank Battalion, fire rockets at targets near the Siegfried line in support of the 80th Infantry Division, 17 March 1945. *(NARA, Signal Corps photo)*

A Water Buffalo, probably manned by a crew from the 747th Tank Battalion, supports the assault crossing of the Rhine by the 30th Infantry Division, 24 March 1945. *(NARA, Signal Corps photo)*

A DD Sherman of the 748th Tank Battalion with its screen raised enters the Rhine River at Nierstein, Germany, 23 March 1945. *(NARA, Signal Corps photo)*

Waving white flags and guarded by doughs, German crews drive mammoth Jagdtiger tank killers into Iserlohn, Germany, after the surrender of the Ruhr Pocket, 16 April 1945. This photo offers some size comparison to the Sherman. *(NARA, Signal Corps photo)*

The new M24 (left) and the M5 that it replaced, both of the 744th Tank Battalion. *(NARA, Signal Corps photo, records of the 744th Tank Battalion)*

The graceful but deadly Jagdpanther tank hunter carried the 88mm cannon on a Panther chassis. *(Photo by Ed Heasley, Curator, U.S. Army Ordnance Museum, Aberdeen Proving Ground, MD)*

the system was that the equipment eliminated the cannon ammunition rack behind the assistant driver.[29]

The Army finally conceded that there was virtually no evidence that the E4-5 had rendered a contribution in combat that could not have been achieved with the bow machine gun or a white phosphorous round.[30] Nevertheless, battalions continued to be issued flamethrowers for months.

## Two Grim Months:
### The Big Picture

Battles of attrition followed throughout October and November, all along the front.

Canadian and British soldiers trudged through the frozen mud and water of the flooded tidal lowlands in the Netherlands to free the great Belgian port of Antwerp. The U.S. First Army took the German city of Aachen on 21 October. The drive of General Patton's Third Army toward the German border halted on 25 September due to shortages of gasoline and other critical supplies. Resuming the offensive in November, Patton's men fought for two bloody weeks around the fortress town of Metz, ultimately winning bridgeheads over the Saar River and probing the Siegfried Line. In the south the U.S. Seventh Army and the First French Army fought their way through the freezing rain and snow of the Vosges Mountains to break out onto the Alsatian plain around Strasbourg, becoming the only Allied armies to reach the Rhine in 1944. But there were no strategic objectives directly east of Strasbourg, and a pocket of tough German troops remained on the west bank, dug in around the old city of Colmar.

The attacks by the U.S. First and Ninth armies toward the Roer River were extremely difficult. The Hürtgen Forest through which they moved was thickly wooded, cut by steep defiles, fire breaks, and trails. The Germans built deep, artillery-proof log bunkers, surrounded by fighting positions. They placed thousands of mines in the forest. In addition, they felled trees across the roads and wired, mined, and booby-trapped them; and registered their artillery, mortars, and machine guns on the roadblocks. Tree-high artillery bursts, spewing thousands of lethal splinters, made movement on the forest floor difficult. Armor had no room to maneuver. Two months of bloody, close-quarters fighting in mud, snow, and cold was devastating to morale. Parts of at least three U.S. divisions, pushed beyond all human limits, experienced breakdowns of cohesion and discipline.

*A Brief History of the U.S. Army in World War II,* Center of Military History, United States Army, Washington, D.C., 1992

# 6

# TWO GRIM MONTHS

To put it candidly, my plan to smash through to the Rhine
and encircle the Ruhr failed.

General Omar Bradley,
*A General's Life*

October marked the beginning of a bitter war of attrition that
would characterize the fighting in Europe until mid-December.
General Omar Bradley focused on two priorities: pushing the
U.S. First Army forward near Aachen, Germany, with the goal
of reaching the Rhine River at Cologne; and using the U.S.
Third Army to reduce the fortifications at Metz, France.[1]

## PAINFUL AACHEN

Aachen would be the first major German city to fall to the Allies. The VII Corps attacked from the south, while the XIX Corps
formed the other jaw of a pincer to the north.

In the VII Corps zone, the 3d Armored Division led the
attack, with the 1st Infantry Division (745th Tank Battalion attached) on the left oriented to envelop Aachen from
the south, and the 9th Infantry Division (746th Tank Battalion attached) on the right flank. These assault units had
initially penetrated the Siegfried Line fortifications in September, but they were unable to exploit the gap because of logistic problems, mounting losses, poor weather, and German
reinforcements and counterattacks. Seeking to regain mo-
mentum, the 1st Infantry Division launched its drive into
Aachen on 8 October. Hitler ordered the defenders to hold the

historic city—the seat of Charlemagne's First Reich—at all costs.

Unfortunately, the records of the 745th Tank Battalion for the fighting in Aachen offer little feel for the battle from the tanker's perspective. The battalion commander, Lt. Col. Wallace J. Nichols, noted vaguely, "The use of tanks in support of infantry in street fighting in Aachen proved very effective." He also observed that indirect fire by his Shermans had been accurate and effective.[2] The U.S. Army's history records that the fighting quickly fell into a pattern. A tank or tank destroyer went into action beside every infantry platoon. The armor would keep each successive building under fire until the riflemen moved in to assault it.[3] The tanks also punched holes in buildings through which the infantry could attack.

Initial resistance was light, but by the time the tanks and doughs reached the city center, it had stiffened, and the battle grew desperate. Tank guns proved useless against the massive old buildings.[4] At this stage, the advance was aided by the use of heavy 155mm guns in direct-fire roles against the toughest structures.


To the north, in the XIX Corps sector, the attack to break through the Siegfried Line and envelope Aachen kicked off on 2 October, spearheaded by the 30th Infantry Division and the attached 743d Tank Battalion. The 2d Armored Division stood by as the exploitation force. Other corps elements were almost simultaneously becoming bogged down in an attack to clear the Peel Marshes adjacent to and even inside the British zone and were therefore unavailable for the Aachen operation.[5] Tankers of the 743d prepared for the attack by studying photos and maps of the Siegfried Line and surrounding terrain and by conducting foot reconnaissance beyond the American front lines. At 0900 on 2 October, a pre-attack airstrike began, reviving memories in the 30th and 743d of the fiasco prior to St. Lô. No bombs fell on American lines this time, although medium bombers accidentally struck a Belgian town twenty-eight miles to the west, killing thirty-four civilians. Few bombs fell in the target area; most dropped to the north and the southwest. The doughs moved forward and easily penetrated the fortifications. The 743d's tanks, however, sank into mud just across the narrow Würm River—which they crossed using a culvert-type hasty bridge designed by the battalion's own Captain Miller and the engineers—and it was not until nightfall that the Shermans were able to close with the infantry. By 7 October, the division had carved out a bridgehead beyond the West Wall that was four and a half miles deep and six miles wide.[6]

The good news ended there, and the struggle around Aachen became the bloodiest experienced by the 743d after the battle of the hedgerows in Normandy. German resistance became ferocious as reinforcements arrived. Nine more days of heavy fighting were necessary before a 30th Infantry Division patrol hooked up with 1st Infantry Division troops on Ravels Hill, completing the encirclement of Aachen.[7] During October, the 743d Tank Battalion lost twenty of its Shermans, one light tank, and one assault gun while destroying three Tigers, eleven Panthers, five Mark IVs, twenty antitank guns, two armored cars, and two heavy artillery pieces. The battalion suffered thirteen officers and sixty-two enlisted men wounded in action, twenty enlisted men killed in action, and seven enlisted men missing in action during the period— nearly all from the medium tank companies.[8]

---

### AAR, 743d Tank Battalion

20 October: The medics were informed that because of the dampness and continuous confinement in the tanks, colds were breaking out among the crews.

21 October: Training of Company D personnel in medium tanks as crews [to make up for heavy losses among Sherman crews].

24 October: Big event of the day was showers—*hot* showers—the first the men had been able to get under since 25 September 1944! This was also the first opportunity in more than six weeks for personnel to launder their clothes. . . . Company officer reported the morale of the crews was remarkably high considering the month of battle conditions in which the men had been living and fighting in their vehicles.

---

Aachen's defenders surrendered at 1205, 21 October.[9] The German commander observed, "When the Americans start using 155s as sniper weapons, it is time to give up."[10] Of this struggle, historian Stephen Ambrose concluded, "The Battle of Aachen benefited no one. The Americans never should have attacked. The Germans never should have defended. Neither side had a choice. This was war at its worst, wanton destruction for no purpose."[11]

## BLOODY HÜRTGEN

The 9th Infantry Division on VII Corps' right was the first of several American divisions to sink into the evil horror of the Hürtgen Forest, which commanders concluded had to be cleared in order to protect the flank of the anticipated advance to the Rhine.[12] The attached 746th Tank Battalion recorded in its AAR, "Operations during the period up to 27 October were in very rugged terrain, consisting of hilly, heavily wooded ground, principally the Rötgen and Hürtgen Forests, not suited to normal tank operation. Offensive activities consisted of closely coordinated tank-infantry teams employed against concrete and field fortifications within the forests in the Siegfried Line. Replacements in personnel were green and due to the tactical situation had to be put into tanks without the benefit of prior orientation in the unit."[13]

The informal history of the 70th Tank Battalion, which followed the 746th into gloomy evergreen woods, offers a pithier description:

> No soldier who was there will ever forget Hürtgen Forest— it was simply hell. The 70th moved into the Hürtgen in mid-November. The air was damp and bitter cold, especially inside of a moving tank. Snow covered most of the ground but underneath was soft, slippery mud that hampered a tank's every move. There was danger everywhere: danger of bogging down, danger of ambush in the dense woods, and danger of moving along the mined roads. Enemy artillery and mortar fire was almost incessant. Great tall trees were stripped and chewed to shreds by the continuous pounding of artillery from both sides. Every time a shell burst among the trees, the explosion sent a deafening roar echoing throughout the forest. Tanks entering the thick woods were road-bound and extremely vulnerable to mines and bazooka fire. Oftentimes infantrymen were not available to lead them through, so tankers had to advance alone, sweating it out every inch of the way.
>
> The 70th fought twenty-four separate engagements with the enemy in the Hürtgen death trap from 16 November to 12 December 1944. The tanks were used both offensively and defensively, depending on the situation, which at the time was most unpredictable. The Jerries counterattacked every night in an attempt to regain the ground they had lost during the day. . . . The entire Hürtgen fighting cost the 70th a total of ninety battle casualties and twenty-four tanks (twelve of which were later repaired).[14]

General Omar Bradley, who ultimately bears some responsibility for the fact that the battle took place at all, years later conceded, "What followed . . . was some of the most brutal and difficult fighting of the war. The battle . . . was sheer butchery on both sides."[15]

Indeed, the fighting was bitter for the doughs and tankers. During the period 6–25 October, the 9th Infantry Division suffered 4,500 casualties for the gain of a mere 3,000 yards. The 746th Tank Battalion, meanwhile, lost 10 Shermans, 1 Jumbo, and 1 light tank while knocking out 2 Mark IVs, 4 Panthers, 2 Tigers, 11 antitank guns, 16 large bazookas and rocket guns, 50 pillboxes with machine guns, 35 pillboxes without machine guns, and 134 machine guns in open emplacements.[16] The following entry from the 746th's S-3 journal gives some flavor for a typical day in action during the period:

October 12: Battalion, less service and combat elements, in position northeast of Zweifall (K965383). Service elements in position at (K930316). Battalion maintenance in position Vicht at (K962399). Assault Gun Platoon of three two-gun sections attached to each of three regimental combat teams in close support with indirect-fire missions. Mortar Platoon attached to 298th Engineer Battalion in support of road blocks between the 60th and 39th Infantry combat teams. Mortars wearing out and replacements difficult to secure. One mortar (81mm) unserviceable after 750 rounds. Division is reducing allotment of mortar ammunition. Company A, attached to 47th Infantry Combat Team, continues to hold its position in the Schevenhutte area, continuing to absorb mortar and artillery concentrations. At 0615 1st Platoon, Company A, moved from 47th sector to 39th sector with Company C for contemplated attack with Company C on Vossenock (F0332). Company B, attached to 60th Infantry Combat Team, supported attack to southwest on Vossenock. First Platoon reduced to three tanks, of which one is inoperative mechanically, in a very sensitive position at (F011304). Supply and maintenance of this platoon very difficult. Lieutenant Hayden returned from hospital and took over his platoon at 1000. Was again evacuated at 1400. After procuring some personnel replacements (one sergeant and two crewmen), the two tanks of the platoon and two TDs plus one platoon infantry assaulted from the flank the three pillboxes closely opposing them. One pillbox taken and the position improved somewhat.

Second Platoon held up by mined tank blocking the road. Retriever from company headquarters cleared road at 1500. By that time tanks had found way around. Crewmen from one tank of this platoon that was isolated from rest of the tanks fought off the enemy by dismounted [Thompson submachine gun] action. Machine guns of tank could not be brought to bear because vehicle had been mined. By 1630 other three tanks of platoon had joined it. Third Platoon of three tanks with Company I, 60th Infantry, at (F019324) were cut off for most of the day by counterattack. Two tanks of this platoon lost previously to mines. Company B drew four new thirty-nine-ton tanks (Ford engines and heavier armor) [Jumbos]. Personnel losses in Company B heavy due to both casualties and illness. One officer and five enlisted men evacuated. Company C plus one platoon Company A in position preparatory to launch massed tank attack on Vossenock. Before this could be accomplished, the 39th Regimental Combat Team's positions one thousand yards north of Germeter were strongly counterattacked by two companies of infantry reinforced with observed fire from SP artillery and mortars. Communication lines to the platoons attached to battalions of 39th severed. Lieutenant Heinemann, SWA and evacuated. One platoon leader left in Company C at close of period. Third Battalion of 39th, with tank platoon, had withdrawn from positions north of Vossenock and east of Germeter to positions north of Germeter. One platoon tank plus one infantry company secured Germeter. Two tanks in Company C lost. Company D, attached to 9th Infantry Division Reconnaissance Troop, maintained one platoon at division CP as guard. This platoon alerted at approximately 0930 for possible use against counterattack in 39th sector. Use did not materialize. One platoon dismounted on the left flank of the 39th Combat Team in a defensive position was overrun by the attacking enemy. Later reassembled and reestablished its lines. One platoon remained in support of roadblocks in 298th Engineer sector. Weather fair to good, visibility fair to good. Light air activity on both sides.

The M4A3E2 Jumbos referred to in this report were among the first to arrive in the separate tank battalions. The 746th drew fifteen in October, and the 743d received five. In November, the 70th, 735th, and 737th received allotments of various but smaller quantities. In December, the 774th obtained five.[17]

### Joining the Infantry Radio Net

In late October, a large-scale program to install SCR-300 radio sets in infantry-support tanks finally kicked off. In November, the 3d Armored Group recorded that "higher headquarters" had decided that twenty-eight tanks in each battalion should be fitted with the sets, but that they were in short supply.[18] The individual battalions, as in so many things, appear to have decided on their own how they would distribute the radio sets within the command. The records of the 743d, for example, indicate that sets were installed only in the tanks of the company commanders and the platoon commanders and sergeants.

The Army judged that these radios achieved "relatively efficient" radio contact between tanks and infantry.[19] Some battalions viewed the radio link as a godsend. The 781st Tank Battalion, for example, recorded that "There are two SCR-300 radios in each platoon of tanks, and the importance of making SCR-300s available to any infantry unit, no matter how small, that has a mission with tanks, cannot be overestimated."[20] Other tank officers saw the improved communications as a mixed blessing, because infantry officers could issue orders directly to individual tanks, thereby undermining control by the battalion's command structure.[21]

## CHAOS AT KOMMERSCHEIDT[22]

First Army commanding general Courtney Hodges ordered the 28th Infantry Division to replace the battered 9th on 26 October and to push eastward through the Hürtgen Forest toward Schmidt. Thus began an ill-conceived operation that would end in the mauling of the division, particularly its 112th Infantry Regiment and the supporting 707th Tank Battalion. From the German perspective, an attack in the direction of Schmidt could mean nothing but an effort to seize the Roer River dams on which the defenders depended to block an assault across the river downstream. American success would also menace plans underway for a counteroffensive in the Ardennes. American commanders, however, were thinking primarily in terms of flank protection and did not commit the resources that would be necessary to handle the likely German response to a threat to the dams.

The division attacked in bad weather on 2 November, and the 112th Infantry seized the first objective, Vossenock, with little difficulty. The battalions on the north and south flanks, however, became embroiled in confused and bloody fighting in the thick forest and made little progress. On 3 November, the 3d Battalion, 112th Infantry, pushed up the Kall Trail, little more than a cart track across the Kall River gorge and thence over rough, forested terrain to high ground. At the far end, the doughs first reached the village of Kommerscheidt and then Schmidt just beyond, meeting little resistance.

One hour before dawn on 4 November, a platoon of 707th Tank Battalion Shermans commanded by 1st Lt. Raymond Fleig warmed up their engines and made ready to attempt the Kall Trail to reach the doughs. Fleig's tank entered the trail and immediately struck a mine. Using a winch, Fleig and his men carefully maneuvered their four remaining tanks past the blockage. Taking command of the point Sherman, Fleig pressed on, his left track chewing the edge of the trail above a sharp drop into the forest. Near the bottom of the gorge, the last Sherman became stuck in mud and threw a track. After a heart-pounding journey over the precarious trail, the Shermans reached Kommerscheidt. To the rear, more tanks entered the path after daylight only to experience similar difficulties, made all the worse by the two crippled Shermans and the damage caused to the surface by each passing tank. Three more would slide off the path entirely.

The Germans counterattacked on 4 November with a regiment of the 89th Infantry Division that happened to be passing through the vicinity of Schmidt when American forces took the town. Twenty to thirty tanks of the 116th Panzer Division supported the regiment. The Germans quickly recaptured Schmidt, but, bolstered by Fleig's three Shermans and supported by P-47s, American troops held on to Kommerscheidt.

Fleig's crews maneuvered fearlessly. The lieutenant spotted a Panther overrunning positions in an orchard and ordered his driver in that direction. He told his gunner to fire the round already in the main gun, which unfortunately was HE and failed to harm the panzer. Even worse, all of the AP rounds were in the hull sponson racks, and Fleig had to turn his turret away from the target in order for the crew to pass the ammo up. As he did so, the Panther's high-velocity 75mm roared, but the first shot missed. Working feverishly, the American tankers slammed an AP round into the chamber as they spun the turret back into line. The gunner fired. His first shot cut the barrel of the Panther's main gun. Fleig pumped three more rounds into the side of the Mark V, which brewed up. The Germans pulled back at 1600 hours, leaving five knocked-out Panthers and Mark IVs behind—three of them accounted for by 707th tankers.

On 5 November, the Germans struck shortly after dawn. The records of the 707th indicate that Fleig and his men knocked out two tanks that day. The Germans pulled back again, but their tanks took up positions on high ground near Schmidt and began firing into Kommerscheidt from long range. Six more Shermans and nine tank destroyers that had finally made it across the trail joined Fleig during the day. But under the German pounding, two-thirds of the tanks and TDs were knocked out by midday on 6 November. The exhausted doughs huddled miserably in their foxholes and in ruined buildings.

By 6 November, moreover, German infantry began to interdict the nearly undefended trail. To the rear, American troops near Vossenock, pounded by artillery, panicked and broke.

On 7 November German tanks and infantry overran Kommerscheidt. The panzers knocked out two of the five remaining Shermans and three TDs. American infantry began to bolt for the trail. Facing an untenable situation, the surviving tanks and TDs withdrew toward the wood line as well, but two of the Shermans threw tracks and had to be abandoned. That afternoon, Maj. Gen. Norman Cota, commanding the 28th Infantry Division, obtained permission to withdraw his troops behind the Kall. The crew of the last Sherman destroyed its vehicle and pulled back with the doughs.

The 707th's records, skimpy in the wake of the disaster, do not record the losses in men suffered during the action other than to note the combat death of Company B's commanding officer. Lieutenant Fleig survived. By 8 November, the 707th had only nine operational tanks. An inspector from the 3d Armored Group who visited the front that same day recommended to V Corps that the 707th be given time to rest and reorganize. The battalion was withdrawn with the 28th Infantry Division to Luxembourg on 20 November for intensive rehabilitation.[23]

## DRIVE ON THE ROER

With Aachen taken and penetrations achieved through the Siegfried Line, American forces—including four divisions each of the U.S. Ninth and First armies—renewed their drive toward the Roer River in mid-November. The Germans, however, had taken advantage of the delay caused by the Aachen fighting to build a new defensive line east of the city. This ran from the Hürtgen Forest in the south into a region of factories and coal mines around Stolberg and then across open fields to the Siegfried Line proper at Geilenkirchen. Parts of the line incorporated fortifications, and in open areas the sturdily built village houses provided strong points. Minefields were ubiquitous, some with new models mounted in wood or glass containers that were invisible to electronic mine detectors. By mid-November, the sector was the most strongly defended area of the entire front. Headquarters, German Fifteenth

Army—disguised as the Fifth Panzer Army, which it secretly replaced on 15 November in preparation for the Ardennes offensive—had five infantry divisions in the line backed by two panzer divisions and two panzergrenadier divisions. The German formations were understrength but well supported by artillery and mortars.[24]

On 8 November, the first snow of winter in Germany fell in the Siegfried Line area occupied by the 70th Tank Battalion, but the main story along the front was rain.[25] Downpours turned fields to quagmires and contributed to repeated postponements of the main thrust.

## Eight Tough Miles

The First Army launched its main attack toward the Roer on 16 November after a powerful artillery bombardment and an elaborately planned aerial bombardment by nearly 2,500 American and British heavy bombers, which dropped more than 9,400 tons of bombs on forward positions and reserve areas.[26] Attacking troops quickly discovered that the German defenders had not been softened up much, if at all.

On the American right, the VII Corps' operations through the northern edge of the Hürtgen Forest, Stolberg Corridor, and rough terrain to the north constituted the main effort of the offensive.

The 4th Infantry Division, supported by the 70th Tank Battalion, drew the unenviable assignment of trying again to clear the heart of the Hürtgen Forest. On 22 November, Company C of the 709th Tank Battalion was also attached. Once more, tanks were largely limited to operating in muddy and mined fire breaks, and losses were high for the tankers and doughs. Some infantry companies had run through three or four commanders in the first thirteen days of the fighting.

Sergeants commanded most platoons, and most squad leaders were inexperienced privates.[27] Company C, 70th Tank Battalion, lost ten of its seventeen Shermans and all of its officers except one newly arrived lieutenant in the course of a few days. Cecil Nash, a platoon commander in Company C, remembered the events of 25 November as the doughs and tankers finally reached the edge of the forest at one point near the Cologne Plain:

> I could see the Germans walking around in a patch of woods beyond the forest about two thousand yards ahead and to our right. It had all the earmarks of a trap, of them trying to draw us out. In hindsight, we could have plastered that patch with phosphorous and smoked them out, but we didn't. We had been told not to use it, as Germans claimed it was gaseous and hence in violation of the Geneva Convention.
>
> [The platoon moved out, and the first tank was hit immediately.] Al Orner, my driver, stopped, but I told him to go around it. We did, and got about one hundred yards into open country when they got us. There was a blinding flash, and my legs folded under me. Ralph Planck, my gunner, was hit in his rear end, and the loader, Al Kieltyka, in the back. . . . Orner and the assistant driver were not wounded and helped us get to the ground and away from the burning tank before it exploded. . . . As it happened, the rest of our platoon was also knocked out and needed help, and the same with the TDs who were with us.[28]

Nash counted fourteen vehicles burning.

Beginning 3 December, the exhausted 4th Infantry Division was replaced by the 83d Infantry Division and withdrew to the quiet Ardennes sector just in time for the German offensive there. So, too, did the 70th Tank Battalion.[29]

*   *   *

On the American left, the 1st Infantry Division, supported by the 745th Tank Battalion, faced the task of fighting through the northern fringe of the Hürtgen morass; it gained only two miles during the first four days of fighting. Infantry and tanks became embroiled in a battle to take and then hold the village of Hamich, which they accomplished after a dash through heavy artillery fire on 18 November followed by tough house-to-house fighting.[30] In general, however, the tanks were unable to offer much support to the doughs fighting from strongpoint to strongpoint through dense forest, and concentrated heavy artillery fire often was substituted for tank support. Beginning 5 December, the returning 9th Infantry Division began to replace the spent Big Red One, which still stood three miles short of the Roer River.[31]

North of the Stolberg Corridor, the nearly untried 104th Infantry Division, with the untested 750th Tank Battalion attached, battered itself against tenacious and fortified defenses, particularly on the commanding heights of the Donnerberg.[32] In the first three days of helping the infantry rout the enemy from numerous pillboxes and fortified basements, the 750th lost seventeen tanks. On 20 November, the tankers of 2d Platoon, Company B, enabled the infantry to enter Volkenrath by dashing alone across a thousand-yard open field and laying down enough suppressing fire for the doughs to move forward. The tanks and infantry were virtually cut off for two days, however, and fierce fighting claimed another six Shermans and two assault guns. Moving onto the Roer Plain, the 104th was able to make much more rapid progress than the divisions bogged down in the Hürtgen Forest. But the fighting was hard. On 5 December in Lucherberg, for example, tanks, tank destroyers, and doughs fought off a fierce counterattack supported by Tigers, Panthers, and assault guns.[33]

* * *

As these actions were unfolding, First Army on 19 November
decided to shift the boundary between VII Corps and V Corps
one mile northward. This move shortened the 4th Infantry Division's line, thereby allowing greater concentration of force
and permitting the newly arrived 8th Infantry Division (re-
placing the battered 28th Infantry Division) in V Corps to
launch a supporting attack toward the town of Hürtgen. The
8th Infantry Division had attached to it not only the 709th
Tank Battalion but also CCR of the 5th Armored Division. The
infantry suffered the same bruising that others had in the
gloomy forest. But during 27 and 28 November, Shermans of
the 709th and the doughs finally moved into and cleared Hürtgen. This opened the door for a quick assault on Kleinhau by
CCR, which established firm American control over a key road
net in the path to the Roer. The 8th Infantry Division pushed
on toward that destination, working with the tanks of CCR and
the 709th, and finally reached the river on 9 December.[34]

The Ninth Army's XIX Corps, meanwhile, attacked directly
onto the Roer Plain on 16 November and fought a battle of
control over successive village strongpoints, seldom more
than one to three miles apart. Dug-in infantry supported by
artillery defended each village. The 29th Infantry Division—
with the 747th Tank Battalion attached—made the main effort
in the center of the corps zone, supported on the right by the
30th Infantry Division, to which 743d Tank Battalion was attached. The 104th Infantry Division operated to the corps'
right.[35]

    This was antitank country. German gunners had long
fields of fire that maximized the advantages of their excellent
optics and high-velocity weapons. The tankers found they

were attending yet another class in the school of hard knocks. Lessons that they and infantry thought they had figured out sometimes required adjustment. After initial fighting in November, for example, the 747th had concluded in its battle lessons that "Smoking of the flanks in a limited objective operation is the only feasible way of protecting advancing infantry and tanks from long-range enfilade, direct antitank, and machine-gun fire. . . . In attacking across open ground, the infantry should move out ahead of the tanks rapidly, with the tanks in support to prevent remaining too long in open country."[36] A few weeks more of experience, however, led the tankers to a different conclusion:

In open country, particularly in flat plains between the Roer and the Rhine, the tanks should habitually lead the attack. When a town is to be an objective to be attacked, the plan for supporting fires should be carefully laid on, the battlefield should be isolated, and the tanks, used in company strength or greater should move against the town, take full advantage of their speed to move into the edge of the town under artillery fire, and silence the outlying enemy machine guns around the perimeter enabling the infantry to move quickly into the town and commence clearing it up systematically. . . . The infantry cannot walk into grazing machine-gun fire, so the tanks should take them out by moving ahead. . . . The tanks and infantry should not go together because the tanks will be slowed down and the artillery fire that will fall on the tanks would cause casualties, and the infantry may be able to approach the objective from a direction unsuitable for tanks to take advantage of defilade.[37]

Indeed, the 29th Division ran into a buzz saw as it tried to penetrate the main German defenses around Jülich, and it made virtually no progress during daylight on D day. But determined infantry accompanied by close tank support and covered by mortar and artillery fire soon began to produce results, albeit slowly and painfully.[38] During November, the already battle-scarred 747th lost eighteen Shermans to enemy action and had nineteen additional tanks deadlined by mechanical failures, leaving the battalion with only nine operational medium tanks as of 24 November.[39]

---

### Rashomon *at Schleiden: Three Views of What Happened*

Charles MacDonald, *The Siegfried Line Campaign,* Office of the Chief of Military History, Department of the Army:

Of all these attacks [on the Roer Plain], none was more typical of the successful application of the techniques developed for assaulting the village strong points than was the 175th Infantry's conquest of Schleiden on 19 November. . . . The 175th Infantry's 3d Battalion under Lt. Col. William O. Blanford made the attack. Until the advance masked their fires, all the regiment's heavy machine guns and 81mm mortars delivered support from nearby villages. A forward observer accompanying the leading infantry companies maintained artillery concentrations on the objective until the troops were within three hundred yards of the westernmost buildings. Until the artillery was lifted, not a bullet or a round of German fire struck the infantry.

The infantry advance began in a skirmish formation just at dawn on 19 November. At the same time a platoon of medium tanks from the 747th Tank Battalion paralleled the infantry some 350 yards to the north so that shelling attracted by the tanks would not fall upon the infantry. The tankers maintained constant machine-gun fire into German trenches and foxholes on the periphery of Schleiden and occasionally fired their 75s into the village. When the forward observer lifted the supporting artillery, the tankers quickly shifted their 75mm fire to the trenches. It was only a question of time before the infantry gained the first houses and mop-up began. By 1430 Schleiden was clear of Germans.

AAR, 747th Tank Battalion:

The attack on Schleiden began at 0730 on 19 November 1944. The 3d Battalion of the 175th Infantry Regiment attacked from the vicinity of Hongen and Company A of this battalion (less one platoon) attacked from Bettendorf. At 1000 hours, the infantry was pinned down by artillery fire, and our tanks, having lost communication, were waiting for the infantry to move up in a defiladed position five hundred yards southwest of the objective. After about an hour of firing from this position, Captain Bulvin, commanding officer of Company A, proceeded east, where he joined the infantry with his tank company. He then placed one platoon east of the Hongen-Schleiden road and one west of the road. The attack was quickly resumed with the tanks and infantry moving abreast of each other. The main defenses of the town were located on the southwestern edge and were shattered by the arrival of the tanks. Numerous prisoners were taken from dug-in positions. The tanks gave supporting fire from the edge of town as the infantry moved in to eliminate the remaining resistance.

Homer Wilkes, 747th Tank Battalion:

On the 19th Company A, less one platoon, supported the 175th Infantry in an attack on Schleiden beginning at 0730.

At 1000 hours, when halfway to the objective, the infantry near Sergeant Deaver's tank suddenly started digging in. Since this was open, flat terrain, the sergeant became perturbed.

Dismounting from his tank, Deaver commenced getting the men on their feet and moving forward. It was then that he noticed a first lieutenant among them (he had thought the men were halted because their officers had become casualties). Pretending he didn't know the party was an officer, the NCO continued leading the infantry toward Schleiden.

Eventually, their own officers and NCOs took over and the unit took the objective in fine order.

The assistant division commander, General Watson, saw the entire thing from an observation post. He told his aide, "Get me that man's name. He gets a Silver Star." [He did.]

By dusk all enemy defenses had been overcome and the tanks returned to company forward for resupply.

(In defense of the infantry during the Schleiden attack, it must be said that the division used no preparatory artillery barrage and therefore enemy defenses were intact. And a forward observer was forbidden to call for fire unless he could identify a target, which on the battlefield is hard to do.)

---

Despite thick minefields and "enemy mud," the 30th Infantry Division, for its part, made fairly rapid progress through the urban strongpoints of Mariadorf and Wurselen. One 743d tank commander reported, "The battleground off the roads is so muddy that there seems to be no bottom to it." By 22 November, moreover, resistance stiffened considerably.

The tankers and infantry commanders in some divisions learned that night attacks were an effective solution to the challenges of fighting over open and flat ground. On 24 November, Company B, 743d, participated in such a night attack on Altdorf rather than advance across two thousand yards of open field in broad daylight in the sights of German AT defenses.

After tough fighting, the advance reached the edge of the Roer, and offensive operations halted on 30 November. The battalion paid in blood for its gains, losing eighteen tankers KIA and eleven more WIA.[40]

During the advance, tankers of the 743d encountered the new Jagdpanther tank killers—superbly armored SP guns on the Mark V chassis mounting the 88mm cannon. The battalion AAR recorded:

[On 19 November, Company A] tanks were in assault position at Aldenhoven, Germany. Here orders for the attack on Pattern, Germany, were awaited. At 1245 hours, orders came. Eleven batteries of artillery fired twenty minutes on objective from H hour. Infantry jumped off at H hour and Company A tanks moved out in support at H plus 20. For us, this meant a dash down the Aldenhoven-Pattern road with the tanks driven wide open. The terrain was level and open, but it was impossible to maneuver the mediums on the soft ground. As the leading tank led this racing column at twenty-five miles an hour, it sighted a minefield across the road about five hundred yards out of Pattern. There was nothing to do but stop. The entire column then "sweated it out" for fifteen minutes as direct enemy fire came to our left, until a pioneer platoon, which had been sweeping the road to our rear, caught up and cleared a path of safety through the mines.

Elements of Company B were in position on a hilltop commanding Pattern to the west and southwest. From this location direct fire was put on the enemy—a diversion which developed into a mousetrap, two of the new [Jagdpanther] enemy tanks being the mice. For as Capt. David W. Korrison . . . led Company A tanks into the town, the sights of his 75mm gun were crossed by two of these newest type of enemy armor, attracted by Company B's fire. Captain Korrison celebrated Thanksgiving by knocking out both tanks at a range of less than fifty yards. . . . A third Panzerjager Panther was claimed after we first blasted holes in a building in order to reach the vehicle at less than one hundred yards. It was knocked out by laying our fire through this aerated building.

The tankers in the 743d and 747th actually had it better than their counterparts in the 2d Armored Division, which attacked to the left of the 29th Infantry Division. On 17 November, the Germans threw their armored reserve—including a battalion of Tiger tanks—against Combat Command B (CCB), which was cut to ribbons near Puffendorf.[41]

---

### Attacking the Mine Problem

Mines were a serious problem for tanks everywhere along the front. In November, the Army gave a hard look at special mine-exploding tanks, which had been used (apparently only in a few armored divisions) on a limited scale since Normandy. The British Crab, or Scorpion, flail tank (which detonated mines with chains attached to a spinning drum mounted on the front of the vehicle) was found to be far superior to the roller-style detonators T1E1 and T1E3 in American production. Beginning that month, the Army placed orders with British authorities for growing numbers of the Crabs. The 738th and 739th MX Tank battalions each had a company of mine-clearing Shermans, initially including both flail and roller style. The roller style units were abandoned for good, at least in the 739th, in February 1945.[42]

---

XIX Corps finally reached the Roer River on 28 November. Back in the VII Corps' zone in the Hürtgen Forest, the 83d Infantry Division, with the 744th Tank Battalion attached, moved into the line to press the attack to the final objective at Düren beginning 10 December. In fighting around the town of Strass, one company of the 744th was largely destroyed.

The tankers nonetheless advanced behind a mine-clearing flail tank borrowed from the 5th Armored Division. Mop-up operations continued despite the German offensive in the Ardennes, and by Christmas day the west bank of the Roer was cleared.[43]

On 13 December, V Corps launched a third attack in the direction of Schmidt, this time with the express goal of capturing the Roer River dams. The 78th Infantry Division, supported by the 709th Tank Battalion, attacked on the left toward Kesternich, where initially light resistance toughened quickly. Fighting in the town was confused and marred by weak coordination between tanks and infantry; the battalion lost five tanks around Kesternich during 14–16 December.

The 2d Infantry Division, with the 741st Tank Battalion attached, attacked on the right while supported by an advance by one regiment of the neighboring 99th Infantry Division. But the V Corps' operation was hardly off the ground when the German Ardennes offensive ran right into it.[44]

## Listening In

The following is a slightly edited extract from the radio logs of the 743d Tank Battalion during the fighting in November 1944 on the Roer Plain. In this small selection of the radio chatter, the reader will discern a remarkable range of illustrations for issues that have been discussed previously: the challenges that faced tankers in coordinating with the infantry, the frustration tankers felt when ordered to stay in the line at night, and the healthy respect tankers held for both the German foe and their own air forces. Here are the voices of nineteen-year-olds as they calmly discuss someone's attempts to kill them.

17 November

Company A: GEORGE [G]
Company B: VICTOR [V]
Company C: SUGAR [S]
HQ Company: QUEEN [Q]

| TIME | FROM | TO | MESSAGE |
|------|------|-----|---------|
| 0710 | V15 | | Prepare to move in five minutes. |
| 0715 | V15 | | Turn them over. Prepare to follow me. |
| | V10 | | Ten vehicles moving out of town. |
| | V10 | V | We are moving out now. |
| | V | | All stations 10: Get the [air recognition?] panels out. . . . Here come the German boys. |
| 0725 | G | G15 | Are you moving out? |
| | G15 | G | Roger. Out. |
| 0817 | G | G10 | We are moving on down to help Company C. They are at Phase Line Orange. |
| 0820 | G14 | G | There is a mistake in their location. They are half-way between Green and Orange. There is another unit at Orange. |
| 0835 | G14 | G | They need support immediately at Orange phase line. |
| | G | G14 | We will not get up there until they sweep this road, so we can't get there no matter if they do need us. |
| | G14 | G | That unit you requested is coming up to take care of that sweeping. |
| 0852 | G10 | G | Engineer officer wants to know where you are located. |
| | G | G10 | Crossroads straight ahead. Go slightly left of that. |

| | | | |
|---|---|---|---|
| 0856 | G9 | G14 | What was that coming in here? |
| | G14 | G9 | Sounded like AP. |
| | G9 | G14 | Thought it was 20mm. |
| | G14 | G9 | We will pull over to the left if we have to. |
| | G10 | G | That unit went to the left instead of straight ahead. |
| | G | G10 | Send somebody to get ahold of them and get 'em on the right road. |
| 0900 | G22 | G | George 13 has already left on his way back, is that correct? |
| | G | G22 | That is correct. Has bad engine or something. Don't know where he is, but he should be back, in that former area where 15 was. |
| | G10 | G | Can you make out what that is? |
| | G | G10 | No, but I don't think it's going to bother us. |
| | G14 | G | They're throwing artillery here. |
| | G10 | G | It's coming from the right flank. |
| | G11 | G | The doughs are pinned down by an MG. Want us to do something? |
| 0903 | G14 | G | They are throwing some AP in here. |
| | G | G14 | Take cover by these buildings. |
| 0910 | G | G11 | How far up is the MG? |
| | G11 | G | Two hundred yards. |
| | G | G11 | Can you pull up and see what's up that street? |
| | G11 | G | Roger. |
| 0912 | G14 | G | Should we start on our way with this road in this shape? |
| | G | G10 | See if you can pull your section around that corner. It will be better than sitting here. |

|      | G11 | G   | Can't see a thing. No doughs or nothing. |
|------|-----|-----|------------------------------------------|
|      | G   | G11 | The doughs should be up ahead. |
| 0915 | G   | G14 | If you move cautiously, maybe they will help us. |
| 0916 | G10 | G11 | Cover me as I move out. |
| 0917 | G14 | G   | The doughs would like us to fire in haystacks just beyond Phase Line 3. There are vehicle tracks there. |
| 0918 | G11 | G10 | There are friendly doughs in there up ahead. Let me pull up with you to help them. |
| 0919 | G10 | G11 | Don't go sticking your head out for trouble. Be careful! |
| 0920 | G11 | G10 | I can see that machine gun that is firing at us, and if our doughs will get down, I can dispose of it. |
|      | G   | G11 | Be careful of our doughs! |
|      | G14 | G   | The doughs are 300 yards beyond Phase Line Green. |
|      | G   | G14 | Give us coordinates, and we will give 'em help. |
|      | G11 | G   | We put AP and HE in there. Soon as we move, I will let you know. I think we did some good because there is no more firing coming out of there. |
| 0922 | G14 | G   | One of our boys is laying some in there now. |
| 0924 | G11 | G   | The doughs want us to lay a few big ones in there because they believe it to be a pillbox. |
| 0935 | G   | G14 | I know Company C wants help to take the objective, but I will not take any more chances on roads not swept. We are with Company B now. |

| 0937 | G11 | G10 | Better put out panels, hadn't we? Plenty of air support up there. |
| 0938 | G11 | G10 | Roger. What is that red smoke? |
| | G10 | G11 | Something about friendly units. |
| 1003 | G | G10 | Two enemy tanks reported moving toward you parallel to Orange. Queen 7 [probably battalion S-3] wants to know if you can bring fire on them. |
| 1005 | G14 | G | The [tank destroyer] unit supporting us there is self-propelled. |
| 1010 | Q7 | G | Do you know whether G15 sent two of his tanks over to Easy unit or not? |
| 1015 | Q15 | G22 | Send your T2 back and pick up the Able Company dozer. He is in a ditch about halfway up. |
| 1017 | G11 | G10 | Did you pick a spot for me? You wait until we get past. Then you will have your move. |
| 1019 | G | G5 | If we get these doughs started, we are going down to Orange. |
| 1025 | G5 | G | Did you say those vehicles on our left were friendly? |
| 1028 | G10 | G11 | You can move up to my position and fire support. |
| 1030 | G10 | G11 | Keep your eyes open and don't get any of our own doughs, but if you see any Jerries, you know what to do. |
| 1032 | G15 | G18 | How are you coming? Have you met the unit you are supposed to work with? |
| 1035 | G | G10 | All set. Ready to move out when we get a little room. |
| 1039 | G11 | G10 | Is that pillbox to my right taken? |
| 1040 | G | G11 | There are friendly doughs two hundred yards to our right. |

| 1043 | G | G10 | We can't move up until the doughs get up, but keep them covered and keep spraying these red-and-white buildings. |
| 1046 | G9 | G | Can't move up. They have a good place to move to. |
| 1048 | G | G9 | There is not a very good field of fire down there. |
| 1053 | Q15 | G22 | Has your T2 left yet to get that dozer? |
| | G22 | Q15 | We are almost there now. |
| 1055 | G11 | G | We are down here where we can let them have it. How about an HE? |
| 1057 | G | G11 | Be sure there are no doughs near there, then let the son of a bitch have it. |
| 1058 | G15 | G18 | There is a doughboy coming down to where you are. He is going to point out a machine-gun nest to you, so be on the lookout for him. |
| 1104 | G | G10 | Watch that white house. That is ours. |
| 1107 | G11 | G15 | Do you know who is on our left? |
| 1109 | G15 | G11 | I believe it is 15. |
| 1125 | G11 | G | The doughs are in that house now. |
| | G | G11 | That's fine. Move on up now. |
| 1127 | G | Q | We are on Orange now. |
| ? | G15 | G17 | Cover road to your left front. I want you to fire on that building when I tell you. |
| | G12 | G | Potato mashers [German grenades] are being thrown over wall. |
| | G | G12 | Fire on the wall and see what that will bring out. |
| | G14 | G | Butch [probably infantry HQ] would like us to lay down fire on everything that looks suspicious before we jump off. |
| | G | G14 | We will tell Butch when we are set. |
| 1130 | G10 | G | What was that? |

| | | | |
|---|---|---|---|
| | G | G10 | That was 12 firing on the wall. |
| | G | Q7 | There is some fire on Phase Line Orange from right to left. |
| | Q7 | G | Are you continuing to advance? |
| 1131 | G | Q7 | We just got here, so it will take a little time to get set to move on. |
| | G12 | G | The doughs say there is fire coming from that big building on our right. |
| | G | G12 | Do you mean that red one? |
| 1135 | G12 | G | Yes, that's the one. |
| | G | G12 | Be sure you know who is in there. I saw some of our doughs near there. |
| 1136 | G12 | G | The doughs said they had fire coming from there. |
| 1137 | G | G12 | Okay. Just make sure you get the right target. |
| 1142 | G | G10 | Move on up and take a position now. |
| | G12 | G | Can you see the left wing of that house? My shots seem to do no good. They have the windows sandbagged. They seem to have made a strongpoint out of it. |
| 1145 | G | G12 | Yes, I see it. I will see what I can do about it. I am in a position to get it. |
| | G | G12 | We are going to put a shot in there now. On the way. |
| | G12 | G | Raise it just a little. |
| 1150 | G | G12 | That shot went in. Wait 'til the smoke clears. They should be pretty well toasted in there. [This may indicate the tank fired "Willy Peter"—white phosphorous—into the building.] |
| 1155 | Q7 | G | Custer is on Baker, on the western edge of Charlie. They have not gone into |

| | | | |
|---|---|---|---|
| | | | Xray. [These are references to coded map locations.] |
| 1204 | Q7 | G | The CO wants to know location of G15 and if you are with the doughs. |
| 1206 | G15 | G | I am on Phase Line Orange and waiting for unit to come up. |
| 1210 | G | Q7 | I believe it is G18, G19 that encountered that antitank gun. They are laying in smoke on something. |
| 1215 | G18 | G | I can lay some into that house if they need it. |
| 1217 | G | G18 | We haven't got it to waste, so hold it. |
| 1230 | G | G11 | Edge over so I can get up there by you, so we can deliver and help them out. |
| 1231 | G18 | G | I believe an 88 is the cause of some of this around here. |
| 1232 | G | G18 | It is hazy, but we can nail a few with a little observing. |
| | G15 | G | They got a gun dug in and are firing through the hedge. |
| | G | G10 | Okay. We are going to move up to it. |
| 1238 | G11 | G | There are Jerries back of that hedgerow, and that is where the shooting is coming from. |
| 1243 | G | G11 | Don't fire, 19! There are doughs all around that building. |
| 1250 | G | G12 | 19, move on up here now. |
| | G9 | | I am right behind you. 12 is alongside you. |
| | G15 | G18 | Are you at the objective yet? |
| | G18 | G15 | No, not yet. |
| | G15 | G18 | Are you still near where you were this morning? |
| | G18 | G15 | Yes, we are. |

| 1255 | G15 | G18 | We have been going to beat Hell this morning. We are way down from you. |
| 1316 | Q7 | G | Enemy tanks are at [map coordinates] 903499. |
| 1320 | G14 | G | If you come directly up this road in this section, there are mines. |
| | G12 | G9 | Do you see that object up there? It looks like a self-propelled. |
| 1322 | G9 | G12 | I don't see it. |
| 1323 | G9 | G | The doughs tell me that firing is coming from behind that house. Do you see it? |
| 1324 | | | No, I can't see a damn thing. |
| | G16 | | Move on up the street. The doughs are with you. |
| 1355 | G18 | | Don't move on up too far. Don't get yourself out in the open. |
| 1420 | | G16 | Pull ahead of that building there. Cover that road to the right. |
| | G15 | G16 | That looks like a pillbox. Try AP on that. |
| 1425 | G15 | G16 | Stop firing, cut your motor. We will be here for a while 'til they see what it is. |
| 1430 | G14 | G | They are getting ready to shove off. I think that is a bazooka that come in here just now. |
| 1450 | G11 | G16 | They want you to spray those houses over there. Give them hell. |
| | | | |
| 1921 | G | Q7 | [Company A commander to probable battalion S-3.] Is it right that we are to move 10 up tonight? |
| 1925 | Q7 | | Yes, that is correct. |
| | G | Q7 | I would like to talk to the CO and find out what is up. What made it change all |

|  |  |  | at once? I know we are outranked, but we always get the last end of the deal. But if it is a direct order, we will go up. |
|---|---|---|---|
| 1933 | Q7 | G | I called up and did all I could, and they said you could stay there, but then they called and said you should go up. What is your story on it? |
|  | G | Q7 | Well, there just isn't any sense to it. If there was any armor reported in that location, it would be different, and just our three vehicles can't do any good alone. I know that there are some pillboxes in there that aren't cleared yet, and we may get bazookas, because moving up in the dark is bad business. It was just about dark when we started to service and it was dark before we got finished. |
|  | Q7 | G | I'll call again and see what I can do, but if you have to go up, I'll tell them to send some boys back to go up with you. |
| 1937 | G | Q7 | Roger. Out. |
|  | Q7 | G | You will have to go ahead and go up. You should call and get some infantry to go with you. |
|  | G | Q7 | Okay. We will go, but if I have some AWOLs, don't blame me. Roger. Out. |
|  | G | G11 | Did you hear that? |
|  | G11 | G | Yes, I heard it all. So we will go. There is one man here now to guide us up. |
| 1950 | G | G11 | You tell him to get about fifteen more and then go up. I suppose I'll have a court martial on my hands one of these days with the temper I have. |

| 1952 | G11 |     | Roger. Out. |
|------|-----|-----|-------------|
|      | G17 | G   | Send a medic up here right away. 19 has a man hurt bad. |
|      | G   | G11 | I will do that right away. |
| 2020 | Q7  | G   | The CO would like to know who that man was that got hurt and how. |
|      | G   | Q7  | William Klusterman, on guard duty, and artillery. |
|      | Q7  |     | Roger. Out. |
|      | G   | G15 | I want someone from 19 to go out and meet the medic. They are going past here now. |
| 2105 | G   | G15 | If you can't get 19, one of you better go out and show him the way. |
|      | G15 |     | Roger. Out. |
|      | G   | G19 | Has the medic got there yet? |
|      | G19 |     | Yes. |
|      | G22 | Q15 | Sergeant Morton should bring one replacement along when he brings up supply in the morning—a bow gunner—and make certain to come up early. |

## MUD AND FORTS

Being forced to hunker down did not sit well with Patton, so he ordered part of the Third Army back onto the offensive in late September. XX Corps—including the 5th, 83d, and 90th Infantry divisions, with the 735th, 774th, and the 712th Tank battalions, respectively—jumped off first on the north flank. The 83d Infantry Division pushed northeast on the road to Trier. The 90th Infantry Division passed easily through the Maginot Line, where the 712th tankers used the fortifications to practice for the imminent attack on the West Wall.[45]

The most dramatic action, and most egregious display of

how *not* to use infantry-support tanks, was the 5th Infantry Division's attack on the first of the Metz fortifications, Fort Driant, beginning 27 September. The main works stood on a hill 360 meters tall and consisted of four casemates with reinforced concrete walls seven feet thick and a central fort shaped like a pentagon. All the elements were connected by tunnels. Each casemate mounted a three-gun battery of either 100mm or 150mm, and the southern side received additional cover from a detached fort mounting three 100mm gun turrets. The central fort was surrounded by a dry moat running up to thirty feet deep. Barbed wire surrounded the entire fortification and wove among its individual elements. The gun turrets, as it turned out, could shrug off repeated hits by American 8-inch guns.[46]

The first battalion-sized attack received artillery, air, and tank destroyer support, all of which proved ineffective against the fortifications. The infantry became pinned down by small-arms, machine-gun, and mortar fire, and the effort was called off after about four hours.[47]

After the failure of the first operation, the 735th Tank Battalion (which would develop a specialty in attacking forts) was brought into the fight as part of a carefully constructed assault plan. For the special operation, on 30 September the battalion assembled a composite company consisting of its eleven tanks with 76mm guns, four 105mm assault guns, and a single 75mm Sherman for an artillery observer. They trained in the use of the explosive "snake," designed to blow a path through barbed wire much like the bangalore torpedo, and the use of concrete-piercing ammunition. (This would be the only tactical use of the snake on record in the ETO.)[48] The battalion's AAR describes the action against Driant beginning on 3 October:

The special company of tanks attacked with the 2d Battalion, 11th Infantry, Fort Driant at 1100. This attack was delayed waiting for the air support to bomb and soften up the fort. Two tanks from Company A moved out to the LD approximately eight hundred yards from the fort and approached the barb-wire enclosure at the north end of the fort. Their mission was to destroy any machine-gun and rifle fire which might hold up the infantry who were to follow thirty minutes later. Lieutenant Jones, who commanded the A platoon, moved out with two tanks and one 105mm assault gun from HQ Company and the supporting Company E infantry. They were to secure and protect the left flank from any enemy counterattacks and fire on targets of opportunity. After this flank had been secured, Lieutenant Jones moved his tank out about one hundred yards in front of his platoon. He was trying to reduce sniper fire when an enemy bazooka hit the turret of his tank forcing the crew to abandon their tank. Lieutenant Jones, the loader, and the gunner were wounded and evacuated.

In the meantime, Lieutenant Galbreath had moved up with Lieutenant Town's Company C platoon. Lieutenant Galbreath had observed the bazooka team that fired on and hit Lieutenant Jones's tank. He directed fire on this team and destroyed them with his .30-cal "co-ax."

One Company C tank was dragging a snake. A tank was following which was to push this snake into position. This snake was to be detonated by an electric wire running through the bow gun porthole. Upon arrival at the barb wire, a steep incline was encountered which made it impossible to push the snake into the wire. At this particular point, the diagram of the fort showed the wire outside of the ditch when it was actually inside. From this position, Lieutenant Town and his platoon fired harassing missions. Two tank dozers were attached to Lieutenant Town's platoon to make a crossing of the ditch in front of the fort. The two dozers had mechanical troubles and were not of much value to this operation. Lieutenant Town's platoon now reverted to a holding mission at this point.

Lieutenant Bauer, Company B, and his platoon moved up on the right flank to breach the wire at the south end of the fort. One tank of his platoon was pulling a snake. This snake broke when the tank made a right turn. The snake was abandoned and the platoon continued on its mission toward the barb wire. With his platoon, he laid a ladder of HE fire into the wire and was thereby permitted to breach the wire. His tank passed through this gap followed by his platoon. The mission of his platoon was to secure [map location] B-4; after B-4 was secured, his platoon attacked B-1, supported by Company B infantry. Lieutenant Bauer moved his tank approximately fifty yards out in front of his platoon when his tank was hit in the turret and he was blown from the tank. Lieutenant Bauer, the gunner, and the loader were killed. At this time, the supporting infantry became pinned down by heavy machine-gun and rifle fire, which could not be observed due to the thick brush and undergrowth. . . .

Along about midnight, the enemy counterattacked and infiltrated into our position. The Company B infantry, after suffering heavy losses, withdrew without notifying the tanks. This action resulted in the capture by the enemy of one tank of Company B and six enlisted men. The remaining three tanks (one B medium, and two HQ Company 105s) from the Company B platoon were hit by enemy bazookas at point-blank ranges. The entire Company B platoon was knocked out of action. Lieutenant Town's Company C platoon and one squad of infantry beat off this counterattack and our ground gained was saved. . . .

The concrete-piercing ammunition was not effective and it was reported by tank commanders later that AP and HE ammunition was more effective.

[4–5 October 1944:] All ground taken from the enemy was consolidated. The 1st Battalion of the 10th Infantry relieved the 2d Battalion of the 11th Infantry. Tanks were not permitted to be relieved. . . . The tanks had no field of fire and their mobility was restricted due to the unfavorable terrain.

Early in the morning of 6 October 1944, an enemy tank approached our right flank. . . . This enemy tank passed around our right flank and fired on Staff Sergeant Olson's tank of Company C. His tank was destroyed.

The next action by tanks [on 7 October] was when the infantry moved out to attack B-4. Lieutenant Town's platoon of three tanks were to move along the bottom of the ditch which was the only route of approach. The infantry was to secure the top of the ditch while the tanks advanced. After moving less than one hundred yards, Lieutenant Town's tank was hit by direct fire coming from some point farther up the ditch. The hit was in the suspension system, causing his tank to block the ditch and not permitting any further advance by the tanks. . . . This was the last action by the tanks, and on 8 October 1944, the tanks were permitted to withdraw to a position approximately 1,200 yards southwest of the fort and placed in mobile reserve.

On 9 October, American commanders decided that the attack—which thus far had cost 21 officers and 485 men killed, wounded, or missing in action—was too costly to continue. This decision ushered in a period of relative quiet in most of the Third Army zone.[49] In some areas, however, October saw limited-objective advances against heavy German resistance marked by counterattacks so frequent that at times it was debatable who was on the offensive.[50] The 90th Infantry Division spent nearly an entire month taking the town of Maizières-les-Metz; the Army's official history records that tanks of the 712th Tank Battalion played little role in the battle, but battalion veterans remember tough street fighting.[51] During one sixteen-day "break" in offensive operations, moreover, tanks of the 737th Tank Battalion fired approximately fourteen thousand rounds of 75mm in indirect-fire missions from static positions. By the end of the month, Patton's troops had breached the Moselle River line to a depth of a dozen miles.[52]

Almost stymied since September, Patton—with Bradley's blessing—resolved to launch a major offensive by 6 November that he hoped would quickly cross the Saar River, breach the West Wall, and reach the Rhine. Patton's plan was to capture the Saar-Moselle triangle and Trier, the major stronghold. Success would turn the flank of the Siegfried Line in the Third Army sector and open the route to the Rhine at Koblenz, fifty miles distant.[53] Incessant rain during the days before the attack, however, forced delays and turned the entire front into a quagmire. Every bridge on the Moselle save one was knocked out by floodwaters, and movement across fields for even tracked vehicles became virtually impossible. Patton would not be dissuaded and ordered his troops ahead on 8 November.

The German defenders, judging that no one in his right mind would attack under such conditions, were initially caught by surprise. They quickly recovered, fell back on prepared positions, and turned the conditions to their advantage on the defense. The Third Army advanced only fifteen miles in eight days. XXII Corps battered its way across the Saar and finally came close to the Siegfried Line in early December when it captured Sarreguemines. XX Corps took on Metz and its ring of thirty-five forts; Metz had not been taken by assault since A.D. 451.[54]

In the XII Corps' zone, tanks of the 737th (attached to the 35th Division) fought through prepared enemy defenses, extensive minefields, unfavorable weather, mud-soaked terrain, and moderate-to-heavy resistance. The battalion lost eighteen tanks—including two of the new Jumbos—in the first half of the month.[55] On a typical day, Company A commander reported that his men had "moved from Laneuville to Fonteny starting with fifteen tanks—two stuck in mud, then two were hit by AT guns and burned, one broke down in Fonteny, and one was hit by AT fire, breaking the sprocket. Enemy tanks in Fonteny held north portion of town and Able rallied at 1800, remaining all night under artillery with no doughs—only three tanks remain in shape to move. . . . The infantry knocked out a German tank with a bazooka. Now I have seen everything."[56] Tanks of the 737th were the first in the corps to enter Germany in early December.[57]

The 26th Infantry Division attacked with support from the newly committed 761st "Black Panthers" Tank Battalion, the first African-American armored unit to see combat. The battalion also recorded rough going through rain, mud, cold, and driving sleet. Upon the battalion's arrival in France in October, Patton had told the outfit, "Men, you're the first Negro tankers to ever fight in the American Army. I would never have asked for you if you weren't good. I have nothing but the best in my Army. I don't care what color you are as long as you go up there and kill those kraut sons of bitches. Everyone has their eyes on you and is expecting great things from you. Most of all, your race is looking forward to you. Don't let them down and damn you, don't let me down!"[58]

\* \* \*

The XX Corps' attack on Metz, meanwhile, involved four parts: a wide envelopment to the north by the 90th Infantry and 10th Armored divisions, a close-in envelopment from the south by the 5th Infantry Division, a containing action west of the Moselle by the 95th Infantry Division, and a final assault on both sides of the river.[59]

Despite grave difficulties getting tanks across the flooded Moselle River (the first Shermans of the 712th Tank Battalion followed the infantry across after a two-day delay), the 90th Infantry Division advanced steadily through the muck and fortifications. The only stiff challenge came in the form of an infantry-armor counterattack at Distroff on 15 November. American troops had to call friendly artillery down on their own positions, because German infantry penetrated so deeply. Losses were heavy on both sides.[60]

The untested 95th Infantry Division, supported by the in-experienced 778th Tank Battalion, tangled with floodwaters and a series of stubborn forts against which the tanks appear to have been unable to render much assistance. Beginning on 15 November, however, the division made steady progress against folding resistance.[61]

The 5th Infantry Division slugged its way through strong-point after strongpoint, and tankers of the 735th and doughs of the 11th Infantry Regiment spent two days clearing the airfield at Frescaty. Patrols reached the city limits of Metz on 17 November.[62]

Hostilities formally ceased in Metz on 22 November, although several forts continued to hold out. The official U.S. Army history asserts that, because XX Corps CG Maj. Gen. Walton Walker had forbidden direct assaults on the forts and because artillery shells had to be conserved to support a projected drive on the Saar River, the isolated forts were left to "wither on the vine."[63] In fact, tanks of the 735th were employed in a new approach to fort-busting.

On 24 November, the battalion received an initial allocation of six hundred rounds of French-made 75mm white phosphorous (WP) shells to fire at the fortifications. On 25 November, tank crews that lobbed two hundred shells into Fort Privot reported no appreciable results. Forts Jeanne d'Arc and Driant received similar treatment over the following days; the battalion poured hundreds of rounds daily into the German garrisons. Initial skepticism among the tankers gradually gave way as the results of sustained WP bombardment became apparent. Fort Privot surrendered on 29 November, with more than 10 percent of the troops suffering from burns. Artillery observers reported on 30 November that they could hear German troops inside Fort Driant screaming.[64] Fort Jeanne d'Arc was the last to capitulate, doing so on 13 December.

---

### Well, It Sounded Good!

In early December, ordnance began to equip some tanks in select battalions—including the 702d, 712th, 743d, 753d, and 781st—with turret-mounted multiple rocket launchers intended to provide high-volume area-saturation fire.[65] The fairly common T34 Calliope model consisted of a 60-tube 4.5-inch rocket launcher mounted on a frame above the turret. Typically, about one company per battalion was outfitted with the launchers. The crew controlled elevation by using the main gun, which was connected to the launcher above by an extension. Much to the annoyance of the crews, initial models prevented firing of the main gun unless the aiming arm was removed.[66] Captured German soldiers reported that they found the rocket fire worse than artillery and extremely demoralizing.[67] But more than one tank battalion objected to the loss of tanks in their

primary role, the vulnerability of the launchers to damage, and the
additional supply and maintenance headaches. Several battalions,
with the backing of infantry commanders, dumped the launchers after only weeks of use.[68]

---

Alarmed by the threat the Third Army posed to the
planned Ardennes offensive, the Germans moved several divisions in to reinforce the front. Moreover, German forces fell
back into one of the most extensively fortified parts of the
West Wall. Patton's planned dash ground to a halt. The 90th
Infantry Division, for example, had barely crossed the Saar
and succeeded in clearing the steel town of Dillingen after
bloody house-to-house fighting when the Third Army had to
turn north to deal with the Bulge.

The 95th Infantry Division spent the entire month of December trying to capture the city of Saarlautern on the east
side of the Saar River.[69] The attached 778th Tank Battalion had
hardly reached the front, and the men were now embroiled in
street fighting for which they had received no training. The
battalion AAR suggests that they made it up as they went.

On 17 December, the 735th relieved elements of the 778th
Tank Battalion in Saarlautern. The battalion history of the
735th for December describes the nature of the fighting faced
by men of both battalions:

There was tedious street fighting in this area with Jerry
battling for every house. Tanks were not of much value.

The buildings in Saarlautern were incorporated in the
Siegfried Line. Inasmuch as most basements were pillboxes, tanks were able to run right through buildings
without caving the floors. Tanks would blow a hole, move
in, blow another hole, fire through it, and then move in
again, repeating the process over and over. There were

many dummy or fake constructions. A gas station complete with pumps was actually a pillbox, a theater ticket window was actually a small pillbox. Snipers were to be found everywhere and were hard to locate and rout out.

## First to the Rhine

The 6th Army Group (which had been activated on 15 September under Gen. Jacob Devers to exercise control over the U.S. Seventh and French First armies) at the extreme south of the front made the most significant Allied gains in November. On 13 November, Lt. Gen. Alexander Patch's U.S. Seventh Army launched an offensive through the Vosges Mountains toward Strasbourg. Spearheaded by the French 2d Armored Division (which advanced on the city in virtual defiance of orders in a repeat of its behavior under U.S. First Army command at Paris),[70] Seventh Army forces liberated Strasbourg on 23 November and pushed on to the Rhine.

To the south, the First French Army struck on 14 November and rolled through the Belfort Gap to the Upper Rhine. By mid-December, the Army Group occupied positions from south of Bitche through Wissembourg to the Rhine, and thence south along the river to the Swiss border. The Germans retained only one sector west of the Rhine, which became known as the Colmar Pocket.[71] Hitler insisted that the pocket be held and gave Heinrich Himmler personal command.[72]

## Battle of the Bulge: The Big Picture

While the Allies bludgeoned their way into the border marches of the Reich, Hitler carefully husbanded Germany's last reserves of tanks and infantry for a desperate attempt to reverse the situation in the west. On 16 December powerful German forces struck the lightly held sector of the First Army front south of Monschau in the Ardennes. German armored spearheads drove toward the Meuse River, aiming at Antwerp. Aided by bad weather, a variety of deceptive measures, and the failure of Allied intelligence correctly to interpret the signs of an impending attack, German forces achieved complete surprise. Elements of five U.S. divisions plus support troops fell back in confusion. Two regiments of the 106th Infantry Division, cut off and surrounded atop the mountainous Schnee Eifel, surrendered after only brief fighting—the largest battlefield surrender of U.S. troops in World War II. . . .

Scattered American units, fighting desperate rearguard actions, disrupted the German timetable, obstructing or holding key choke points—road junctions, narrow defiles, and single-lane bridges across unfordable streams—to buy time. Defenders at the town of St. Vith held out for six days; V Corps troops at Elsenborn Ridge repelled furious attacks, jamming the northern shoulder of the enemy advance. To the south armored and airborne troops, although completely surrounded and under heavy German attack, held Bastogne for the duration of the battle. German efforts to widen the southern shoulder of the bulge along the Sauer River came to nothing.

Short of fuel, denied critical road networks, hammered by air attacks, and confronted by American armor, the German spearheads recoiled short of the Meuse. Meanwhile, Patton had altered the Third Army's axis of advance and attacked northward, relieving Bastogne on 26 December. On 3 January First and Ninth army troops and British forces launched attacks against the northern shoulder of the bulge. Meanwhile, a secondary German offensive, Operation

Nordwind, failed in the south. . . . By the end of January the Allies had retaken all the ground lost in both German offensives. The Battle of the Bulge was over.

*A Brief History of the U.S. Army in World War II,* Center of Military History, United States Army, Washington, D.C., 1992

# 7
# HITLER'S LAST GAMBLE

It is now certain that attrition is steadily sapping the strength of German forces on the western front and the crust of defense is thinner, more brittle, and more vulnerable than it appears on our G-2 maps or to the troops in the line.

> U.S. 12th Army Group intelligence
> summary, 12 December 1944.
> Quoted by Colonel Robert Allen in
> *Patton's Third Army, Lucky*
> *Forward*

The enemy is at present fighting a defensive campaign on all fronts; his situation is such that he cannot stage major offensive operations. Furthermore, at all costs he has to prevent the war from entering a mobile phase; he has not the transport or the petrol that would be necessary for mobile operations, nor could his tanks compete with ours in the mobile battle.

> British 21st Army Group
> appreciation, 15 December 1944.
> Quoted by Colonel Robert Allen in
> *Patton's Third Army, Lucky*
> *Forward*

By early December, Hitler had assembled twenty-eight divisions for his Ardennes offensive, Operation Wacht Am Rhein (Watch on the Rhine), and another six for a planned supporting offensive, Operation Nordwind (Northwind), in Alsace. This

was the largest reserve Germany had been able to accumulate
in two years, albeit much weaker than the strike force available when German troops had rolled through the same area
in 1940. Factories and repair shops, working furiously, had
supplied 1,349 tanks and assault guns in November, and another 950 were delivered in December.[1] Troops below the
level of officers and NCOs, however, often were new to battle.

Hitler's plan, delivered to Feldmarschall Gerd von Rundstedt complete to the last detail with "NOT TO BE ALTERED"
scrawled across it in the Führer's own handwriting, called for
a three-pronged offensive along a seventy-five-mile front between Monschau and Echternach.[2] In the north, the SS-heavy
Sixth Panzer Army was to strike to and then across the Meuse
River before heading northwest for Antwerp. In the center, the
Fifth Panzer Army was to attack through Namur and Dinant
toward Brussels. The German Seventh Army was to reel out a
line of infantry divisions to protect the southern flank of the
operation. A "Trojan Horse" unit under special operations veteran SS Hauptsturmführer (Lieutenant Colonel) Otto Skorzeny, using captured American vehicles and uniforms, was to
ease the way to the Meuse once the initial breakthrough was
achieved.

Despite elaborate German safeguards, Allied intelligence
picked up many signs of the build-up but, by and large, dis-
missed the possibility of a German offensive because of a false
preconception: Such an attack would be doomed to defeat and
therefore irrational to undertake. Hitler was rolling the dice in
a bigger game. He hoped that he could drive a wedge deep
enough in the Allied camp to induce his enemies to come to
terms rather than insist on unconditional surrender.

At its greatest penetration, the Bulge extended sixty miles
deep and forty miles wide. By the end of the six-week battle,
600,000 American troops and perhaps 50,000 British soldiers

had fought 550,000 Germans. For the most part, the fighting did not turn on the well-planned movements of large formations. Instead, much of it unfolded at the level of small units and individuals—what generals and commentators at the time described as "fluid."[3] In a sense, it was the war with which infantry tankers were well familiar.

## ABSORBING THE BLOW:
## THE STORY OF THREE TANK BATTALIONS

Three separate tank battalions, two of them D day veterans, were in the thinly held Ardennes sector when Wacht Am Rhein blasted out of the fog on 16 December. By the end of the month, another dozen would arrive as the Allies scrambled to block the expansion of the Bulge and lay the groundwork for its annihilation. Most of these battalions were by now experienced outfits with battle-hardened men. The tankers had learned their lessons and paid their tuition in blood. Now they were ready to teach the Germans a thing or two.

The 741st Tank Battalion was split on the northern shoulder of the German attack zone, facing the Sixth SS Panzer Army. The battalion itself was attached to the 2d Infantry Division, but one platoon (expanded to companies C and D on 16 December) was attached to the neighboring 99th Infantry Division. In the center and directly in the path of the Fifth Panzer Army, the 707th Tank Battalion and 28th Infantry Division were recovering from the trauma of the failed operation at Schmidt the previous month. On the southern shoulder facing the German Seventh Army, the 70th Tank Battalion and 4th Infantry Division were also recuperating from the battering they had suffered in the Hürtgen Forest. The one other infantry division in the line, the untested 106th, was supported by CCB of the 9th Armored Division.

## Locked and Loaded

The 741st Tank Battalion was supporting offensive operations toward the Roer River dams by the 2d Infantry Division near Rocherath, Belgium, when the Sixth SS Panzer Army struck, so the battalion was well prepared for battle.[4] On 15 December, one platoon of Company C was attached to the 395th Infantry Regiment of the 99th Infantry Division, which was positioned just to the south of the 2d Infantry Division. The 2d and 99th Infantry divisions (the latter subordinated to the control of the former after having several units overrun in the first days of the battle) ultimately would serve as a firm wall along the northern shoulder of the German penetration, forming a defensive line along the Elsenborn Ridge.

The day of 16 December was spent responding to initial reports of the German offensive. At 1520 hours, the 2d Infantry Division requested that the battalion deploy two platoons of Company A to critical points defended by the 2d Battalion, 38th Infantry Regiment. At 1724, Division instructed that all of Company C was to operate with the 99th Infantry Division under formal attachment to the 2d Infantry Division's 23d Infantry Regiment. At 2030, Company D was ordered to proceed to Camp Elsenborn to join Company B of the 612th Tank Destroyer Battalion. At 2249, Company B, 741st, and the remaining platoon of Company A were alerted for quick movement and designated as the division reserve.

On 17 December, the 741st Tank Battalion met the full force of the 12th SS Panzer Division attack in the fiercest armor battle experienced by a separate tank battalion during the war. The fight proved that battle-savvy American tankers—all still operating the 75mm Sherman or M5 light tank—could take on and beat concentrated German armor, particularly when they enjoyed the advantages of being on the defense.

About 1100 hours, 741st tanks knocked out three Mark IVs

near Wirtzfeld. At midday the S-3 recorded that the situation was developing favorably as battalion troops recaptured Bullingen and took the high ground near Krinkelt. By midafternoon, however, reports were pouring into the battalion CP of heavier German tanks supported by infantry approaching from several directions. At Rocherath, Sgt. Ray Wilson, a gunner in a Company B Sherman, fired on a panzer that had appeared a mere seventy-five yards away. The shell bounced off. These were Tigers! Nearby, Sergeant Dickson and his crew—who thought they had a cushy assignment in reserve—sweated and laid very low as nine German tanks appeared in front of them.[5]

As the battalion's records dryly state, there was "much shifting of tanks" in order to meet enemy attacks. In Rocherath, every available man was thrown into hasty defenses erected around the battalion CP. The infantry was preparing the bridges for demolition, which was definitely not a good sign.

Lieutenant Joseph Dew and his platoon sat in defensive positions on the perimeter of Rocherath. The weather was cold and bleak, and eighteen inches of snow blanketed the ground. As frantic messages inundated the radio net, Dew knew that another replacement platoon leader in Company C (Lt. Victor Miller was his name) was engaging Tiger tanks east of town. Miller had called for help against three approaching panzers but was told that he was on his own. Soon, two Shermans and the lieutenant's life had been lost, but they had exacted a steep price from the Germans; two of the hulking panzers were burning, too.

Panthers also were on the prowl, and four of them penetrated to within 150 yards of the battalion CP that night, destroying three Shermans. The infantry hit three of the panzers with bazookas to no effect, but they finally disabled one Mark V, and the Germans retreated.[6]

At 0920 hours on 18 December, the radio net again crackled

with furious traffic. Tiger tanks were crawling into Rocherath down a street approximately 150 yards from the battalion CP. Fog and smoke from burning buildings reduced visibility to almost zero.[7] Two deadlined Company B tanks placed in a lane just east of the CP for antitank defense opened fire on the Tigers' flanks with devastating effect. When the smoke cleared, these two "disabled" tanks had destroyed five Tigers. One surviving Mark VI continued through town on the road to Bullingen, but sergeants Angelletti and Padgett of Company B carefully maneuvered behind the panzer and destroyed it.

At almost the same moment as the drama near the CP, Lieutenant Dew spotted seven enemy tanks advancing toward his position. He ordered his gunner to open fire. Soon, one German tank was disabled and four others had been hit, and the enemy withdrew. Dew's crew counted their remaining ammo. They had only four rounds of AP left. With visions of six German tanks reappearing, Dew thumbed the radio and reported his plight. Within minutes, crews from other Company C tanks rushed some of their rounds to his position, and Battalion placed a hasty request to Division for three truck-loads of ammo—70 percent AP. Early that afternoon, Jerry came on again, and Dew's crew accounted for two more tanks. But the company was losing Shermans, too—three that day, and in the confusion nobody knew how many men from those crews had survived.

At dusk, the tankers were told that they would begin servicing and refueling a few vehicles at a time. Dew knew that soon his crew would be called out. The work might even seem a welcome break after sitting in a freezing tank all day. Shooting and shouts from the forward infantry positions snapped him back to watchfulness; it sounded like a tank moving in his direction, and Dew made sure that the gunner had AP loaded. A dark bulk gradually separated itself from the gloom, and

Dew brought his gun to bear and fired. Another burning wreck joined his day's tally.

Over in Company B's area, the tankers were surprised by searchlights stabbing out of the dark and seeking their positions. A spotlight fell on a Sherman, and an 88mm round followed. The lights were mounted on Tigers! The Shermans fired up their engines, slammed into gear, and moved to less-exposed venues. By now, several buildings nearby were burning, making the task of staying hidden more difficult.

On 19 December, the German attack resumed. No new assault came down the road Dew was defending. The lieutenant pumped six rounds into a German tank he was not certain had been knocked out, however, and made sure he saw flames before he stopped. Nearby, Sergeant Dickson played ring-around-the-rosy with some Tigers, as he later recalled:

> We found a kraut tank on the opposite side of the building that we were behind. It had two tanks supporting its flanks. To attract the kraut's attention, [Sergeant] Case fired on the left flank from a covered position, while we moved up on the right flank between two buildings, about forty-five yards from the enemy. Corporal Kroeger fired four rounds of AP, which ricocheted off the kraut armor like pebbles falling on a tin roof. Then one of the enemy's supporting tanks fired on us but missed us and hit the building. A piece of shrapnel knocked a hole about the size of a half-dollar in my steel helmet. We immediately backed up and took cover behind a building, and the krauts started an encircling movement on us. We soon found out we were under observation and direct fire from any direction in which we tried to move. We started sweating blood. We called for artillery and additional support, but we thought we'd never get it in time. . . .

The building on our right was in flames, which was to our advantage, as we were hoping for a smoke screen. It finally got fairly thick, and I decided to make a break for it. We took off like a bat out of hell under the cover of smoke. Luckily we reached cover without drawing fire. As we reached cover, the enemy [tank] on our right completed his encirclement by breaking through a stone wall, which put him in direct [line of] fire from Sergeant Mazzio's tank. Mazzio's gunner, Corporal Snike, immediately knocked the tank out, and the situation was relieved entirely. During the excitement, our artillery dropped a round on the turret of a Tiger tank, knocking it out. With the additional support of a Company A tank, the three remaining kraut tanks were knocked out. . . .[8]

At 1440 hours, Division ordered 741st battalion commander Lt. Col. Robert N. Skaggs to withdraw behind Wirtzfeld. Division put Company C of the 644th Tank Destroyer Battalion under his command and ordered the armor to act as rear guard to screen the infantry's withdrawal. Skaggs was to destroy all equipment left behind.

Skaggs instructed companies A, B, and C to ensure protection of the critical Krinkelt-Wirtzfeld road junction. The tankers fended off German attacks throughout the afternoon and reported the destruction of several more enemy tanks. As if the battalion did not have problems enough, German planes bombed its rear positions at 1600 hours.

At 1810, Dew helped a TD locate and destroy yet one more Tiger tank. About two hours later, the rear guard began to extricate itself from Rocherath. At 2030 hours, Company B reported that the last tanks had cleared the town and that the engineers who laid antitank mines behind them were riding the Shermans to safety. The tankers did not withdraw far, and the line held with little flexing in this area.

The 741st AAR recorded:

> In the fierce three-day action at Rocherath, tankers of the 741st Tank Battalion proved themselves adept at the art of way-laying and killing Tigers. From well-camouflaged positions, by expert maneuvering and stalking, tank after tank of the enemy forces was destroyed by flank and tail shots of the battalion's gunners. Recapitulation at the end of the encounter showed the battalion as having knocked out twenty-seven enemy tanks (mostly Mark VIs), one SP gun, two armored cars, two halftracks, and two trucks.
>
> In contrast to the number of enemy vehicles destroyed, our tank losses were comparatively small. A total of eight tanks were lost to enemy action.

Amazingly, only eight battalion men died and six were wounded during the furious December fighting.[9] The 741st received a Presidential Unit Citation for its actions around Rocherath.

## Shattered

Almost everything had gone right for the 741st—a full swing in the fortunes of war from the battalion's washout on D day. But fortune had no such plans for the 707th, now completely rebuilt after its misadventure at Kommerscheidt.[10]

On 16 December, the 707th was in 28th Infantry Division reserve. Assembly areas for direct support of the doughs had been reconnoitered, and the battalion was ready to deploy as needed. Division alerted the 707th at 0600 hours and reported that the enemy had infiltrated the MLR (main line of resistance) and at dawn attacked several sectors. Companies A and B were attached to the 110th Infantry Regiment, Company C to the 109th, and Company D to the 112th. The Assault

Gun Platoon was tied in with division artillery and was prepared to fire indirect missions.

Company B made first contact with the enemy in the vicinity
of Buchholz, and companies A and C also committed to action
during the day. Action on the first day was entirely against infantry formations, and all 28th Infantry Division strongpoints
remained intact when night fell. Only one 707th tank was temporarily knocked out of action.

Unfortunately, most of the tanks and assault guns in the
German Seventh Army and two panzer corps from the Fifth
Panzer Army hit the 28th Infantry Division sector.[11] On 17 December, the battalion recorded "[h]eavy fighting throughout
the sector against overwhelming odds." At 0100 hours, German tanks and infantry struck the 1st Platoon of Company A,
which was deployed in the Clerf-Marnach-Hosingen-Drauffel
area in support of the infantry. Companies A and B battled armor and infantry the entire day, during which the Germans
overran Urspelt, Clerf, Drauffel, Hosingen, and Hoscheid. Company D advanced toward Marnach down route N16 but ran into
direct 88mm fire that knocked out eight light tanks on the spot.
At 2200 hours, heavy enemy pressure forced the battalion headquarters to withdraw from Wilwerwiltz. The 707th claimed a
total of six Mark IV and V tanks and four self-propelled guns
knocked out that day. But by evening the battalion had lost all
of its light tanks, sixteen Shermans, and one T2. Wounded enlisted men totaled 14, but 5 officers and 111 enlisted men were
listed as missing. Company C was the only line unit that had
not been badly mauled.

The remnants of companies A and B, Battalion HQ, and the
Assault Gun Platoon were withdrawn to Wiltz—on the road to
Bastogne—and combined into a composite unit on 19 December under the CO of Company B. Together with the remnants
of the 110th Infantry and 28th Division headquarters person-

nel, the tankers fought off continual heavy attacks throughout the day. Company C and the 109th Infantry withdrew slightly to Diekirch, also under heavy pressure. The battalion reported having knocked out one Tiger tank and a halftrack, but it had lost another seven Shermans, with four enlisted men wounded and two officers and twenty enlisted men MIA.

On 19 December, the survivors of the composite company in Wiltz found themselves surrounded. At 2400 hours, the battalion commander mounted an unsuccessful effort to break out, after which he ordered all vehicles destroyed and organized personnel into groups under officers with orders to exfiltrate to Boulaide. Company C was ordered to cover the withdrawal of the 109th Infantry to Ettelbruck, which mission it accomplished at 2330 hours. The 707th lost 14 Shermans, 6 assault guns, 11 halftracks, 2 enlisted men wounded, and 15 officers and 131 enlisted men MIA that day.

The battalion's few remaining tanks supported the defense of Vichten, and then Neufchateau, over the next few days, but the 707th had ceased to exist as a fighting force, as had the 28th Infantry Division. Their sacrifice had not been in vain, however, because their tenacious defense had disrupted the German timetable for the capture of the key road junction at Bastogne.[12] On 31 December, Lt. Col. H. S. Streeter assumed command of the remnants of the 707th.

## Playing a Tricky Hand

On the Bulge's southern shoulder, the German offensive caught the 70th Tank Battalion with its pants down, but the battalion had the good fortune to face virtually no enemy armor, and its combat experience enabled the tankers to recover quickly.[13]

The battalion had just arrived in the country of Luxembourg after the rugged fighting in the Hürtgen Forest, and

many of its tanks were stripped down for complete maintenance and parts replacement. Spares, however, were difficult
to come by, which precluded some needed repairs.

All companies of the 70th were alerted at 1100 on 16 December. Service Company men at once speeded up work on
the disabled tanks, and the few that were ready to roll immediately deployed to support the 12th Infantry Regiment, which
was under attack by the 212th Volksgrenadier Division. The
4th Infantry Division line already was beginning to sag under
German pressure. Company D was in the best shape, so it
moved two platoons forward. Company A contributed a platoon. Company B could field only three Shermans. The tankers
found that several companies of the 12th Infantry had been
cut off at separate points, and the first day was spent trying
to reopen communications lines with mixed success. Company D's M5s proved useful for hauling doughs and fighting
off German infantry that had no armor support.

The battalion reported on 17 December in its AAR, "Today
was a gray foggy day, and the situation was extremely vague."
Tankers had difficulty spotting enemy activity through the
dense fog. All communication had been lost with the 3d Battalion, 12th Infantry, in Osweiler and Dickweiler. Three tanks
from Company B were out of radio contact, their fate unknown.

The battalion continued efforts to reach the surrounded
doughs, each tank carrying five infantrymen—all who were
available. The tanks fought their way into Bergdorf, where the
doughs of Company F were isolated. Spotting a large hotel
that had been the company CP, the lead tank pumped several
76mm rounds into the building before noticing an American
flag being unfurled on the roof. The sixty grinning GIs still
holding the hotel met the tankers at the door.

A relief attack on Echternach failed because of a lack of infantry support. At Consdorf, one Sherman manned by two crewmen, assisted by seven cooks, MPs, and stragglers, formed the

defense as a German regiment approached; a Company B Sherman and two light tanks, accompanied by a handful of infantry, arrived just in time to help beat back the first German probe.

On 18 December, task forces from the 9th and 10th Armored divisions (the latter advancing from the Third Army zone) arrived to assist the 4th Infantry Division. The 70th Tank Battalion remained committed, and much of the time the tank radios provided the only means of communication between infantry companies and their battalion CPs. The 70th deployed halftracks to strategic locations to act as relay stations, which enabled the battalion to maintain contact with all its tanks.

By 19 December, many 70th tankers found themselves making tactical advances. The greatest setback was a bazooka ambush that knocked out two and damaged one tank from 3d Platoon of Company A. Artillery and mortar fire were intense. Two Company B tanks in Osweiler rocked as buildings collapsed around them. One bathroom, less bathtub, was blown away, and the commode and sink came to rest on one tank's rear deck. The crew immediately complained about the lack of bathing facilities.

On 21 December, 70th Battalion was transferred from First Army control to Patton's Third Army. Company C's three remaining tanks moved to the top of a hill north of Consdorf, where they would remain for the next four days; they were so badly in need of maintenance that they could no longer move.

The 70th continued to fight until 24 December, when it was relieved. The battalion's losses during the Bulge were comparatively light: five Shermans, one M5, one halftrack, one officer and five enlisted men KIA, and three officers and twenty-one enlisted men WIA. Colonel R. H. Chance, CO of the 12th Infantry, praised the battalion for providing "the most outstanding tank support that this infantry regiment has ever witnessed."

## HELP ARRIVES

Almost immediately after the German offensive struck, additional tank battalions moved to the threatened sector. Most arrived with their partner infantry divisions, but others were reattached to divisions already in the area.

### Northwind, American Style

One of Patton's most famous gestures took place on 18 December when he boldly promised Eisenhower that he would have three divisions moving north to the Ardennes within forty-eight hours (he made good). But the first units to redeploy in response to the crisis came from the north: well-seasoned outfits all, if lacking Patton's fame. The 30th Infantry Division and 743d Tank Battalion arrived on 16 December, and the 1st and 9th Infantry divisions (745th and 746th Tank battalions attached, respectively) followed the next day. The newly arrived 740th Tank Battalion also entered the fray on 19 December.

The 743d was engaged in rocket-launcher training near Hongen, Germany, on 16 December, when it was alerted to move to the Ardennes.[14] Through a cold rain, the battalion conducted an all-night road march south the night of 17 December to take up immediate fighting positions in the vicinity of Malmedy, Belgium. During the march, the column was on the alert for German paratroopers. Enemy aerial activity was intense, and antiaircraft fire speared upward on all sides. As they arrived in Malmedy, companies were divided among the battalions of the 117th Infantry Regiment, which were moving into defensive positions around Malmedy, Masta, and Stavelot. Lieutenant Colonel William Duncan, battalion CO, set up his HQ in a large hotel room. Asked the situation by one of his officers, he replied, "I don't know what the situation is beyond

this: The Germans are on the loose and can be expected anywhere anytime. It's our job to find out where they are and then
stabilize a line to stop them and hold them."[15] The men knew
no more, and rumors spread like wildfire.

When they arrived in Stavelot, Company B, with three
assault guns attached, found the Germans already there and
in control of the northern half of the town. Lieutenant Jean
Hansen's 3d Platoon moved in and spent the night on one side
of the main square with the infantry; the Germans were only
about eighty yards away on the other side. Hansen told a battalion officer that he knew nothing about what was going on
around him except that the Germans were mighty damn close
because they kept shooting at him.[16] The boys of the 1st SS
Panzer Division appeared to be suffering some confusion of
their own. During the first several hours, three vehicles loaded
with German infantry drove into the square; the Americans
easily dispatched all these "attacks."

In Masta, the 743d's tanks were strafed by friendly P-47s.

At 1900, the battalion CO was ordered to send a company
to Stoumont in support of the 119th Infantry—a task he assigned to Company C.

The company B and C tankers in Stavelot and Stoumont bore
the brunt of the fighting on 19 December as the 30th Infantry
Division extended the wall sealing off the northern edge of the
German salient westward. Not that Company A was having an
easy time; as its Shermans maneuvered toward La Gleize,
they encountered Panther and Tiger tanks. One M4 was lost to
88mm fire, but tankers helped a friendly AT gun knock out a
Mark V.

In Stavelot, Hansen's tanks moved up a street to support
the doughs, who were trying to eject the SS from the northern

part of town. A Tiger tank rounded the corner a mere fifty
yards ahead. A friendly TD fired one ineffective round and
scuttled to safety. The lead Sherman fired four rounds of AP
at the panzer, but none penetrated even at this close range.
The American crew fired a smoke shell and backed around a
corner.

Hansen deployed his Shermans to flank the Tiger and gain
a side or rear shot, but this German commander knew his
business, too. The Mark VI maneuvered constantly to counter
the Shermans. Stalemate ensued. The American tanks established an ambush roadblock in case the German decided to
come out and fight, but the next day the two sides were still
locked in a Mexican standoff.[17]

Unfortunately, the American line was still falling back
when Company C arrived in Stoumont. The tankers ran into
advancing SS troops of Kampfgruppe Peiper almost immediately, as recorded in the AAR:

> The 3d Platoon, Company C, was attached to the 2d Battal-
> ion, 119th Infantry, and made an early morning move to
> Chevron. At about 0615 hours the 1st and 2d platoons with
> the company commander moved to join the 3d Battalion,
> 119th Infantry, at Stoumont, Belgium. The tanks reached
> Stoumont at 0700 hours and went into immediate defen-
> sive positions. The 1st Platoon deployed into a position on
> the high ground at the eastern edge of the town where
> they joined Company I, 119th Infantry. The 2d Platoon
> moved into a position at about (VK633026) and supported
> Company L, Infantry.
>
> Within the quarter-hour, the enemy counterattacked
> from the south and east with about forty tanks plus a battal-
> ion of infantry with halftracks. Heavy enemy fire consisting
> of direct, mortar, small-arms, and automatic-weapons fire
> became intense during the three-hour fight that followed.

Infantry companies I and L began withdrawing toward the north and west. The 2d Platoon, 743d Tank Battalion, knocked out three enemy tanks, two halftracks, and many enemy doughs as the enemy tried to advance from the east. The 1st Platoon, meanwhile, accounted for two enemy tanks, one halftrack, and many enemy infantry who were advancing from the south.

As the 3d Battalion, Infantry, withdrew, the tanks laid down intense fire on the enemy; then the 1st Platoon pulled back by sections with some of the infantry riding on the rear decks of the vehicles. The 2d Platoon supported with fire during the withdrawal of the 1st Platoon, and then it, too, withdrew by sections. As the tanks moved to the rear, they exchanged direct fire with the enemy.

The 743d tanks withdrew to a makeshift defensive line to the west of Stoumont. At this point, the histories of one of the Army's most experienced tank battalions crossed with that of an untested outfit, the 740th, which was engaged in making its own incredible story.

## Can Anybody Spare a Tank?

Back in the States, the 740th Tank Battalion had been organized as a special battalion to be issued top secret CDL spotlight tanks.[18] The battalion never actually received its CDL equipment despite a considerable amount of special training. So Lt. Col. George K. Rubel, a veteran of North Africa and the battalion CO, stressed standard tank battalion instruction—especially accurate gunnery—a decision that probably saved the lives of many of his men in December 1944.[19] The 740th arrived in Belgium in November having no tanks but with an order to convert to a standard tank battalion. The battalion did sport a bold new code name: Daredevil. Rubel borrowed nine

Shermans, three M5s, and two assault guns from the tank-short First Army to begin retraining. None of the men had ever used the M5 or fired a 105mm howitzer.

The 740th, which expected its first combat to take place in January, had tentative orders to join the 99th Infantry Division in the Ardennes. When the German attack struck on 16 December, however, several things occurred. First, the 740th was ordered to turn over all its Shermans to the 745th Tank Battalion. Second, on 17 December, Rubel was informed that the battalion might have to enter battle with its three M5s and two assault guns, and with the remainder of the personnel fighting as infantry. Third, on 18 December, the battalion was ordered to the front but was told to salvage what vehicles it could from an ordnance repair depot in Sprimont, Belgium. Upon arrival at the depot, the battalion was shocked to find that only three Sherman tanks were on the "ready for issue" line, and that they were short essential equipment. Of the twenty-five tanks in the park, only fifteen could be made operable, and even these were missing generators, starters, breech parts, radios, tools, rammer-staffs, and other items. None had a basic ammo load. Battalion personnel worked all night and until noon the next day cannibalizing tanks to put the fifteen selected into running condition. Nonetheless, one tank crew headed to battle from Sprimont without a breech block, ammunition, or .30-caliber machine guns.

Rubel put crews into anything that could fight: M4s, M5s, M8s (M5s with short-barrel 75mm howitzers), two M24s, M7 self-propelled 105mm howitzers, and M36 and M10 tank destroyers. Few vehicles had radios, and the commanders had to use arm signals.

Staff Sergeant Charlie W. Loopey was one tank commander. Loopey had the reputation of being a bit of a playboy back in the States, but he would prove a fearless and steady man in combat.[20] He and his crew picked out one of the M36s.

Although they had not trained on the equipment, the M36 was a tank-like self-propelled gun mounted on a Sherman chassis. It had a 90mm converted antiaircraft cannon, which was the best antitank weapon in the American arsenal. On the downside, the vehicle had an open-topped turret that would leave Loopey and his gun crew exposed to the elements, shrapnel, and small-arms fire from higher elevations such as second-story windows. The hull and turret armor, moreover, was even thinner than that on the Sherman, offering protection against little more than bullets and shrapnel. The M36 also lacked the coaxial and hull-mounted machine guns that were so important to the Sherman's punch. The only machine gun provided was mounted facing the rear for antiaircraft defense. If German infantry got too close, the crewmen had only tommy guns and grenades for defense.

Lieutenant Charles B. Powers, Loopey's boss and leader of the 2d Platoon, Company C, picked a 75mm Sherman for himself. Powers was a quiet, likeable gentleman who nevertheless was always ready to stand up for his men.[21] Powers's platoon moved out for Remouchamps in the late hours of 19 December, following company commander Captain Berry in his peep. They soon encountered the S-2 of the 119th Infantry, 30th Infantry Division, who was on his way to regimental CP. He related that one battalion of the regiment had been overrun and that the other two were under 50-percent strength and slowly losing ground. He requested assistance, and did so again when Lieutenant Colonel Rubel arrived. Rubel noted that he had orders to stay where he was, so at 1400 hours Maj. Gen. Leland Hobbs, division CG, appeared with authority from First Army to attach the 740th. The tankers moved out immediately.

As it arrived at the 119th Infantry's positions, the 740th encountered the withdrawing tanks of the 743d (which were low on fuel and ammo), whose crews reported that five Panthers were advancing up the Ambleve River road about one thousand yards distant. After consulting with regimental commander Col. Edward Sutherland—who had so angered tankers of the 743d during the St. Lô breakout with his orders for unsupported tank probes—it was agreed that the lead platoon of the 740th would attack thirty minutes later at 1600 hours. The infantry would advance as the tanks came abreast. Sutherland had learned a few things about how to use tanks.

Powers and the 2d Platoon spearheaded the attack in thick fog. After advancing 800 yards, Powers spotted a Panther 150 yards ahead at a curve in the road. His first round hit the shot trap under the gun mantlet, ricocheted downward, killed the driver and bow gunner, and set the Mark V on fire. Another hundred yards on, Powers spotted a second Panther. His first shot glanced off the front plate, and his second round jammed in his gun. Sergeant Loopey pulled forward in his M36 tank destroyer and set the second Panther alight with his 90mm while Powers cleared his jam. The platoon pressed on and encountered a third Panther. Powers's first shot blew the muzzle brake off the Mark V, and his next two shots set it on fire. (Other accounts claim that these Panthers were already disabled.)[22] Both Powers and Loopey were awarded the Silver Star for their actions.

After this brisk thirty-minute firefight, the tide turned. The doughs, supported by the 740th armor spraying German infantry on the hillsides with machine guns, advanced a thousand yards. Peiper's spearhead would not use this road.

Rubel engaged in another bit of unorthodox equipment requisition and employment several days later during fighting near La Gleize. On 23 December, he dug up a 155mm SP gun, augmented the crew with his cooks, radio operators, and peep driver, and sited the weapon on high ground where it could fire into the German defenses over open sights. He ordered his 105mm assault guns to keep the Germans' heads down. As he stood on a wall and directed fire, the gun pumped 192 rounds into La Gleize. Prisoners later said they had never experienced anything so terrible.[23]

## The Northern Jaw Gains More Teeth

Between 16 and 18 December, the 1st Infantry Division moved into defensive positions between the 2d, 99th, and 30th Infantry divisions. This added one more well-fired brick to the wall along the northern edge of the Bulge.

The 745th Tank Battalion moved into the line with the Big Red One, as usual, and encountered the strongest armor attacks it had yet faced. During the period of 20–22 December—when twelve German divisions, seven of them armored, threw a ferocious fresh attack against the northern shoulder defenses along the Malmedy-Bütgenbach-Monschau line—Company C alone destroyed thirteen tanks and one SP gun near Bütgenbach.[24]

The 750th Tank Battalion left the 104th Infantry Division behind in defensive positions along the Roer and rolled into the Ardennes on 22 December after an all-night road march. Now attached to the untried 75th Infantry Division, the 750th spent most of its time until mid-January providing a mobile reserve to the infantry regiments. At no time during this period was even an entire company committed to action.[25]

Lieutenant Colonel Rubel, meanwhile, was learning that tank and infantry communities did not always become the tightly knit family portrayed in the official history. On 28 December, he reported to the headquarters of the 82d Airborne Division, to which the 740th had been attached for an assault southward toward Lierneux, and met with a universally chilly reception. The paratroop officers told him that tanks had usually been more of a hindrance than a help to them because tankers refused to keep up with their men. Rubel, who evoked memories of Patton among some of his men, replied that his boys had come to fight.[26] At Rubel's urging, the paratroopers and tankers ran exercises together before attacking on 3 January. Within a few days, the tankers and doughs knew each other's first names, and after their first engagement together, the paratroopers told Rubel that his was the first outfit that *they* couldn't keep up with.[27]

## The Southern Jaw Clamps Tight

Beginning 18 December, Patton turned the weight of Third Army more than 90 degrees and tore into the southern flank of the Bulge. His men moved 125 miles through a blizzard to accomplish this feat, and through 23 December, 133,178 motor vehicles traversed a total of 1,654,042 miles. III Corps, including the 4th Armored and 80th and 26th Infantry divisions, attacked on 22 December to relieve the surrounded "Battling Bastards of Bastogne," primarily paratroopers from the 101st Airborne Division. German commanders who calculated that Patton would never be able to react so quickly were wrong.[28] On the other hand, German intelligence easily detected the Third Army shift, and by the time Patton's spearhead arrived, the Germans had deployed strong blocking forces on all approach routes.[29]

The 735th Tank Battalion took part in Patton's remarkable redeployment.[30] On 20 December, companies A and C were on the east bank of the Saar supporting doughs of the 2d Infantry Regiment, 5th Infantry Division, fighting in Saarlautern. At 1230 hours, the battalion received warning orders to move to the vicinity of Stuckange, where the CO was to report to XX Corps Headquarters. The 735th was told to move as a unit, which was impossible to do because its elements were engaged with the enemy and spread out across one hundred square miles. The companies were given their routes by special couriers and told to join up as quickly as they could. Sometime after 1500 hours, the battalion halted briefly at a bridge near Bouzanville, which was the first opportunity to discover if all companies had formed up. They had.

The 735th's march orders were for Luxembourg, where a liaison officer from the 26th Infantry Division informed the battalion of its attachment to that unit and sent the tankers on to Arlon, Belgium. In about twelve hours, the 735th had arrived in its new sector after a sixty-mile, overnight, blacked-out road march that passed through parts of Germany, France, Luxembourg, and Belgium. The tankers reached their partner units on 21 December and engaged the enemy the next day, initially meeting light resistance. By 24 December, the infantry and tanks had run into fierce resistance. In a single action on 27 December, German assault guns claimed three of the 735th's M4A3E2 Jumbos.

Redeployment of tank battalions to unfamiliar infantry divisions reintroduced some of the old problems experienced in Normandy when fighting beside new partners. Despite a concerted effort by 735th Tank Battalion CO Lt. Col. Abe Bock to work out the terms for tank-infantry cooperation with Headquarters, 26th Infantry Division, problems due to unfamiliarity arose almost immediately. On 23 December, Company B supported a drive by the 104th Infantry Regiment toward Dellev. The 735th's AAR described the problem and the tankers' reaction to being forced to risk their lives with strangers:

> Very little resistance was met, and the tanks did little firing. The town of Dellev was taken by the tanks as the infantry would not go into it ahead of them. This attitude seemed to be prevalent among the infantry units here. Apparently they do not realize the ease with which tanks can be knocked out in restricted areas such as towns and that they could easily be left without any tank support whatsoever by running them into a trap such as that. . . .

Transfer of the 735th Tank Battalion and its attachment

to a new division led inevitably to a feeling of doubt and in some cases to downright confusion on the battlefield. This doubt and confusion is directly traceable to the fact that the two units have different histories and have been confronted by different problems for which they have arrived at different solutions. Infantry-tank cooperation has suffered greatly by the change in attachment—which can only be regained by long association.[31]

---

### Tankers' Christmas in the 735th Battalion

The 25th was the same as any other day though everyone knew it was Christmas.

One platoon of Company D was added to [Task Force Hamilton]. This TF continued to assault Eschdorf. Due to tank losses and mechanical difficulties, there were only three tanks able to fight out of the two platoons of Company A that were with the TF. One tank commanded by Sergeant Maloney was hit by a 75mm gun on a German Mark V at about 0615, and the tank exploded, presumably killing all the crew. The tank commanded by Sergeant Leet, which had approached Eschdorf the night before, was hit by an 88mm round at about 1000, killing two men and wounding three. This crew had attempted to move earlier, but the engine failed them, and they had a choice of leaving or fighting from the tank. Choosing the latter, they fought for several hours until hit. The cold weather and excessive amount of movement without a chance for maintenance was taking its toll of vehicles at a time that was critical. Due to this shortage of tanks, the platoon of Company D was attached at 1100 and moved from Niederpallen at 1130 to join the TF located at 704434. After bitter fighting all that day, the enemy finally was almost cleared from the town. Company A accounted for the Mark V that had hit one of their tanks. Lieutenant (Cowboy) Harris caught the

Jerry behind a building in such a position that he couldn't move without exposing himself. Thereupon he lined up all the tanks he had in position to hit him as he moved, then waited until he pulled out and gave him one round from his own gun and finished the tank. This was at extremely short range. There were no prisoners from the tank.

*AAR, 735th Tank Battalion*

---

The 737th Tank Battalion also participated in the Third Army counteroffensive.[32] Attached to the 35th Infantry Division near Sarreguemines, the battalion was ordered north on 21 December. The 737th assembled in the vicinity of Detrange, Luxembourg, at 0300 hours on 23 December following a grueling 120-mile road march. The equipment was not in its best shape, and tankers worked frantically to perform what maintenance they could in the bitter cold and snow. By noon, the tanks were committed in support of 5th Infantry Division doughs. The 737th had an unusually positive experience in terms of the rapid integration of tanks and infantry even though the battalion had never fought before with the "Red Diamond" Division. Staff Sergeant Clint O'Davaney, a platoon sergeant, Company B, exclaimed, "These guys from the 5th are fighting bastards. Ain't it the truth!"

By Christmas, Wacht Am Rhein was spent as an offensive operation. That day, the 2d Armored Division stopped the 2d Panzer Division at Celles, four miles from the Meuse River. The same day, the 3d Armored Division blocked the 2d SS Panzer Division drive on Namur. Bastogne still held, and on 26 December the lead elements of a relief force from the 4th

Armored Division punched through. The American lines along the shoulders of the Bulge held firm.[33] Hitler had coal in his stocking.

Interestingly enough, the tank battalions that had not borne the brunt of the initial German assault suffered low losses during the December fighting, probably because they for once held the advantages of the defender. The 743d, for example, saw plenty of tough fighting—it knocked out at least six Panthers and Tigers—but lost only five men KIA (and their Sherman) and four men WIA during late December.[34]

## NORTHWIND, GERMAN STYLE

The night of 31 December 1944, eight German divisions—including the 21st Panzer and 17th SS Panzergrenadier divisions—attacked Seventh Army positions in a would-be pincer movement from the Saar River and Colmar Pocket: Operation Nordwind. Ultra had revealed that the attack was coming. Inasmuch as Patton was moving north to attack the Bulge, Eisenhower ordered Devers's 6th Army Group in the south to take responsibility for some of the Third Army front and to hold the line at any price. Eisenhower had no more reserves between the Ardennes and Switzerland.

Eisenhower's preference was for a broad withdrawal to shorten the lines—all the way to the Vosges Mountains, if necessary. This was a bit of good military thinking that, unfortunately, would entail abandoning the French city of Strasbourg. De Gaulle ordered the First French Army to defend Strasbourg regardless of American orders. After exchanges of threats, including de Gaulle's to cut all American supply routes through France, Eisenhower agreed to shift the line between the U.S. Seventh and First French armies and permit the latter to protect the city.[35]

Standing in the way of the main German thrust were the

44th and 100th Infantry divisions (with the 749th Tank Battalion initially attached to the former and then split between the two), the 45th and 103d Infantry divisions (most of the 191st Tank Battalion and Company B of the 756th attached, respectively), the 36th Infantry Division, and the untried 70th Infantry Division (with parts of the 753d, 191st, and 781st Tank battalions attached during the first few days). The 79th Infantry Division (which lost the 781st to the 70th Infantry Division on 3 January) soon joined the fray after pulling back to a new MLR parallel to the Maginot Line. Company C, 781st Tank Battalion, was the last unit to pull out during this move. The unit history records that as the tankers withdrew, "the people stood in groups on street corners and looked scared. French flags weren't hanging from the windows any more and no little kids waved. Moving back was a new and unwelcome experience."[36]

For the tankers, the period was one of support for the infantry in generally defensive operations. Deep snow and icy roads rendered movement difficult. On the other hand, in some areas the frozen ground permitted cross-country maneuver, a luxury long lacking during the rain-soaked fall. At times, ice-covered roads on hilly terrain close to the Vosges Mountains left tanks with no option but to cut cross-country the long way around.[37]

The 781st was in the thick of the fighting. Its informal history recorded one wintry debacle:

[On 9 January] at 0600, Company A's tanks were warmed up in the cold Alsatian dawn. There was a foot of snow on the ground and the air was misty. A carefully coordinated tank-infantry attack had been worked out at 0200 that morning. At a few minutes before 0700, tanks and infantry arrived together at the edge of Sessenheim as planned. It was still dark but, in spite of the mist and darkness, they could see the town. Several buildings in it had been set afire by the artillery.

A few minutes after 0700, they were a bare four hundred yards from a group of buildings on the outskirts of the town. At that moment every tank radio carried Sergeant Sexton's voice saying in tense amazement, "My God, it's as big as a house!" "It" was one of four Mark VI German Tiger tanks, dug in and painted white, that had been brought into town secretly during the night. A moment after the sergeant spoke, 75mm shells from our tanks found their way to the Nazi tanks, but as Sergeant Johnson put it, "They bounced off like tennis balls." It wasn't long before shells from 88s, antitank, and self-propelled guns were everywhere. Technician Grade 5 Huya saw one shell hit to the right of Johnson's tank, then the left, then one left a trail of sparks as it scraped harmlessly along the belly of the tank. Eight tanks out of eight were hit in as many minutes. The attack on Sessenheim ended with eleven men killed or MIA, fifteen seriously wounded, and with six of our tanks left burning in the snow at the edge of town.[38]

Nordwind's last gasp occurred on the night of 24 January, when five divisions tried unsuccessfully to break the American line at the Moder River. That same week, on 20 January, Eisenhower sent one American and five French divisions, and then XXI Corps, to clear out the Colmar Pocket once and for all. The 709th Tank Battalion, attached to the 75th Infantry Division, reported, "Although the operations in Colmar first started in extremely low temperatures and through snow, the resultant thaw afforded an excellent opportunity to view the help given by duckbills on the tank tracks. . . . The Colmar area afforded this battalion the best tank terrain for operation and maneuver it has yet encountered."[39]

Vigorous antitank defenses and frequent counterattacks marked the fierce fighting around Colmar. The 756th Tank Battalion, for example, lost twenty medium tanks there in late January. Since landing in France, the battalion had lost seven of its nine platoon leaders and many of its enlisted tank commanders, and had received inferior replacements. Tough fighting, with line company strength reduced by half, and the superiority of German tank guns hurt morale. The battalion CO concluded by late January that his unit's cohesion was at risk.[40]

By 9 February, however, the Colmar Pocket had been eliminated. The Americans and French had closed the line of the Rhine.[41]

## DENOUEMENT

On 3 January 1945, Hitler admitted that his Ardennes offensive no longer offered promise of success. He had shot his last bolt. On 8 January, he authorized a withdrawal to the Ourthe River. Although Operation Nordwind was still unfolding in Alsace, it would burn out within two weeks. The Allies could now turn to the task of overrunning the heart of Germany.[42]

Field Marshal Montgomery had carefully hoarded the First Army's VII Corps to spearhead the inevitable counterstroke against the German line from the north, an operation that he ordered to commence on 3 January in the general direction of Houffalize—about the mid-point of the Bulge. The corps commander, Maj. Gen. J. Lawton Collins, planned to strike with two armored divisions, the 2d and 3d, and follow through with the 84th and 83d Infantry divisions, which would mop up bypassed resistance. Attached to those divisions were, respectively, the 774th and 771st Tank battalions. The 75th Infantry Division (750th Tank Battalion attached) would act

as the corps reserve. The II SS Panzer Corps, made up of the
2d SS Panzer Division and two volksgrenadier divisions, barred
the way.[43]

Other American divisions already in the line pressed forward, too. The 82d Airborne Division, for example, was attacking near Arbrefontaine when Sgt. Nello J. Fasoli of the
2d platoon, Company A, 740th Tank Battalion, had a rare and
unwelcome encounter with a pair of Royal Tigers: 70-ton,
thickly armored behemoths armed with the powerful 88mm
gun. Lieutenant Colonel Rubel recorded:

[On 7 January at about 0830 hours, w]ord came down that
a [Royal Tiger] was shooting hell out of things not very far
down the road. Staff Sergeant Hendrix and Sergeant Fasoli
advanced to take it out. While Staff Sergeant Hendrix covered the tank, Sergeant Fasoli fired five rounds, which
were all direct hits. They apparently jammed the turret,
but the tank could not be destroyed. Seeing this, Lieutenant Tribby called up two tank destroyers, which carried
90mm guns. The Tiger swung his gun on them, knocked
them both out, and they both burned. Lieutenant Tribby
then called up another TD and a 57mm AT gun. Lieutenant Tribby and Sergeant Fasoli led these guns into position on foot. The TD fired fifteen rounds into the side of
the Tiger at a range of a little over 150 yards, but no rounds
penetrated. However, the Tiger finally did catch fire, and
the crew bailed out. With this tank out of the way the attack was resumed, with Sergeant Fasoli spearheading and
Sergeant Hendrix and Lieutenant Tribby following.

Sergeant Fasoli entered the town [probably Goronne]
where he encountered the second Mark VI [also a Royal
Tiger]. He fired twice at this tank at about fifty yards'
range—then backed up into cover of a building and fired
three more rounds. They just glanced off. The Mark VI

fired three rounds at him and missed with all three. A bazooka team armed with captured German Panzerfausts was called up to engage the Tiger, but while it was coming up, the tank withdrew. Sergeant Fasoli then knocked out three machine-gun nests to the right of his tank.

Confronting snow or rain, snowdrifts up to four feet deep, bad roads, rough terrain, and German resistance, the armored divisions failed to break through, and the infantry divisions became deeply embroiled in the same frustrating fighting.

Meanwhile, Patton was pressing northward with his III and VIII corps against similar physical conditions and fierce resistance. In addition to the 6th Armored Division, III Corps had two veteran infantry divisions—the 26th and 35th, elements of both supported by the 735th Tank Battalion.

The veteran 90th Infantry Division and 712th Tank Battalion soon joined them after being withdrawn from the Saar region. The tankers moved into the Ardennes on 7 January 1945, arriving at Rippweiler, Luxembourg, after a forty-nine-mile road march over snow-covered roads. The battalion was committed again on 9 January near Berle, Luxembourg. Once again, now battle-honed American tankers proved they could beat German armor. On 12 January, for example, camouflaged Shermans of the 2d Platoon, Company B, knocked out six tanks and six self-propelled guns, netting 150 prisoners. The next day, the same platoon knocked out three Panthers and three assault guns. Only three days later, two platoons from Company A, firing from defensive positions on good ground, destroyed eight Panthers and crippled a Tiger.[44]

By January, VIII Corps had available the 17th Airborne Division, 11th Armored Division, and the newly arrived 87th Infantry Division, to which the 761st Tank Battalion was attached.[45]

On 15 January, First and Third army troops finally met
at Houffalize. On 17 January, the First Army was returned to
Bradley's 12th Army Group; it could now turn eastward to erase
the remnant of the Bulge, adding V Corps' 30th Infantry Division and 743d Tank Battalion to the effort.


Physical conditions remained atrocious for the men, many of
whom had been in the line for nearly a month. The 743d's AAR
for 17 January noted that the battalion "had a number of NBC
[nonbattle casualty] illnesses not requiring hospitalization,
most of these a result of the extreme cold and difficult operating conditions in the tanks which one man, with grim humor,
referred to as 'Armored Frigidaires.' " Advancing in deep
woods, the 750th tankers found that the snow from the trees fell
into the open turrets of the tanks in such quantities that crewmen were unable to extract ammunition from the floor racks.
Commanders had to keep the hatches open because periscopes
were frosted over.[46] The crews of the 740th, attacking to retake
St. Vith on 20 January, encountered snow so deep that the paratroopers working with them had to walk in trenches dug by
the tank tracks or ride the vehicles in order to make any head-
way at all. The snow also created unexpected hazards. Tanks
would tip without warning into snow-filled bomb craters up to
twenty feet deep, sometimes rolling completely and usually
bending the gun barrel and stripping the elevation and traverse mechanisms. Tanks also risked crashing through the
crust into streambeds, where they could sink into the mud up
to their turrets.[47]

The challenge of moving tanks across icy roads gave birth
to some creative ideas. In the 750th, for example, companies A
and B discovered that by turning some of the track guides over
and cutting the prongs down some with a torch, they could give
their tanks very effective cleats. Company C welded metal lugs

onto the tracks.[48] The 737th Tank Battalion also welded lugs onto steel chevron blocks, which tankers then used to replace every sixth section on each track. The 740th found by experimentation that using only six standard grousers per tread worked on ice, and Lieutenant Colonel Rubel sent his men out to find knocked-out tank destroyers, whose crews usually kept a dozen or more grousers attached to their turrets (to counterbalance the heavy gun).[49] One idea that did not fully pan out was to use the amazing tank dozer as a snowplow. Deep snow piled up in front of the blade, at times stopping the tank within forty yards.[50] Nevertheless, the dozer was often the only way to open a road.

The crews did the best they could to adapt to these miserable conditions. Lieutenant Colonel Rubel offered a description of the combined affects of carrying infantry and gradually accruing minimal creature comforts:

In [the] attack a tank was a strange looking object. There were usually from ten to twenty men riding on top of it. It was usually towing a trailer loaded down with rations, machine guns, tripods, and the usual miscellany of gear that a combat soldier takes along with him. In addition, the tankers had placed sand bags on the front slope plate of the tank, the sides, and sometimes around the turrets for protection against Panzerfausts. Add to this conglomeration the tankers' housekeeping tools, which usually included a liberated heating stove, three or four joints of stovepipe, two or three frying pans, and two or three ordinary black pots. The pots were multipurpose articles. They were used for converting snow into drinking water, washing clothes, cooking food, and pouring gasoline. They were also used as carriers for other smaller articles while enroute. The load on the back of the tank usually included, in addition to all the other items mentioned, several extra boxes of .30- and .50-cal ammunition and occasionally the carcass of a deer or cow that had been killed while attacking the tank. The tank thus laden turned out to be an excellent camouflage job. At a distance of fifty yards it was impossible to tell what kind of a vehicle it was—even if you determined that it actually was a vehicle.[51]

American tankers also adapted to the wintry landscape once the U.S. Army finally began to provide the necessary whitewash. Generally, supplies came very late. The 741st was notified on 10 January that calcimine had become available.[52] The 743d Tank Battalion, which had seen some of the toughest fighting in the Bulge, was first able to apply coats of lime to its tanks of the line on 11 January 1945.[53] The 749th was not able to apply winter camouflage until 19 January.[54] The 753d Tank Battalion noted one problem with the improving use of white camouflage by American forces: In fighting on 8 January near Mackwiller in the Seventh Army zone, tankers experienced difficulty distinguishing between the infantry of the two armies.[55]

Despite—or perhaps because of—the terrible weather, January generally proved to be a time of relatively low battle casualty rates for the tank battalions in the Ardennes sector. The 743d, for example, lost seven men KIA and three officers and sixteen men WIA, as well as four M4s and four M5s, despite being on the attack and encountering German armor with some frequency (the battalion destroyed nine and captured four Mark IVs and knocked out two Mark Vs).[56] The 750th also attacked during the period and lost only two Shermans and two M5s, all to mines.[57] The 741st lost two enlisted men killed and one officer and two enlisted men wounded— and lost no vehicles—during its push south near the Elsenborn Ridge.[58] And the 737th recorded in its AAR, "Our tanks destroyed one Royal Tiger, two Panthers, eight Mk IV tanks, ten SP vehicles, eight halftracks, four 75mm AT guns, one 75mm howitzer . . . [a]s against a total of eight casualties and five tanks being disabled by enemy action. . . . All of our tanks had covered thousands of miles and all were equipped with the 75mm gun."

The 740th, however, lost thirteen Shermans and one M5 and was down to an average of seven operational tanks per company at month's end. It also suffered proportionate losses in men (seven KIA and twenty-eight WIA).[59] The tendency of inexperienced battalions to suffer high losses early in their deployments may account for these figures in part, but the battalion's destruction of four Tigers, one Royal Tiger, and five other tanks and assault guns underscores the tough fighting the men endured. The 712th also suffered heavy losses during its deployment into the area, including that of battalion commander Lt. Col. George B. Randolph, who was killed by shellfire.


740th platoon leader Lieutenant Powers and tank commander Loopey at about this time were having another run-in with the Germans. On 27 January, the platoon attacked toward the town of Heeresbach with the 504th Parachute Infantry Regiment against light resistance. About two thousand yards short of the objective, Powers received word that a counterattack was heading his way, with the German infantry advancing in parallel columns up the road. Powers loaded paratroopers onto his four Shermans and raced to meet the head of the columns. The tanks opened fire on the surprised enemy with all weapons, and in two minutes they had killed 65 enemy troops and induced 201 to surrender. Shortly thereafter, the tanks destroyed an SP howitzer. The tankers and paratroopers took Heeresbach, but they did not sleep easily that night. Two more counterattacks struck before dawn.[60]

Powers and his men needed the sleep. The 82d Airborne

Division had been attacking day and night in order to prevent the Germans from retreating in a leapfrog fashion and preparing new defensive positions each time. The problem for the tank crews was that the parachute regiments attacked in rotation, but the 740th had to support each and every assault. The only tankers who got a full night's sleep were those lucky enough to live through having their tank knocked out.[61]

Patton, meanwhile, launched an attack he had been pressing Bradley to approve on the base of the Bulge with XII Corps. He pushed the 4th, 5th, and 80th Infantry divisions (supported by the 70th, 737th, and 702d Tank battalions, respectively) across the Sauer River on 18 January.[62] Commanders had to lead their tanks forward on foot over the icy roads in some cases.[63]

Because towns offered protection and shelter from the elements, they became the centerpieces of the fighting. The official U.S. Army history credits tanks and tank destroyers during this period with playing an invaluable role for the infantry by blasting German defenders from the sturdy structures. Minefields again became a constant menace, particularly when hidden by a new layer of snow.[64]

Although Hitler had finally recognized that his offensive in the Ardennes had failed, he authorized a withdrawal only as far as the West Wall (except for SS units he transferred to the crumbling Eastern Front) despite the pleas of Rundstedt and Army Group B commander Feldmarschall Walter Model that they be permitted to retreat to the east bank of the Rhine. This stubborn decision set the stage for the annihilation of much of the remaining German resources in the West.[65] The separate tank battalions would again play their part.

## The Reich Overrun: The Big Picture

Eisenhower had earlier decided that his armies should advance to the Rhine all along its length before crossing. . . .

[T]he Canadian First Army cleared the area between the Maas and Rhine rivers. At the same time, the [U.S.] First Army advanced and finally seized the Roer River dams but found that the Germans had destroyed the controls. The resultant flooding delayed the Ninth Army's advance by two weeks. That attack finally began in late February and linked up with the Canadians, cutting off German forces facing the British. Meanwhile, the First Army's drive to the Rhine culminated in the capture of Cologne and on 7 March the seizure of an intact bridge at the town of Remagen.

As American divisions poured into the bridgehead, the Third and Seventh armies launched coordinated attacks to the south. On the 22d and the 25th, Third Army troops made assault crossings of the Rhine. On 23 March the British Second Army and the U.S. Ninth Army staged massive crossings in the Rees-Wesel-Dinslaken area, supported by the largest airborne landings of the war, while the Seventh Army crossed on the 26th near Worms. Now Allied columns fanned out across Germany, overrunning isolated pockets of resistance. While Montgomery's forces drove northward toward the great German ports of Bremen, Hamburg, and Luebeck, the Ninth Army advanced along the axis Muenster-Magdeburg. Ninth and First Army troops met on 1 April, encircling the industrial region of the Ruhr and capturing 325,000 prisoners. The First Army continued eastward toward Kassel and Leipzig while the Third Army rolled through Frankfurt, Eisenach, and Erfurt toward Dresden, then southward toward Czechoslovakia and Austria. The 6th Army Group advanced into Bavaria toward Munich and Salzburg. . . .

British, American, and Soviet forces neared previously negotiated stop lines along the Elbe and Mulde Rivers. The First Army made contact with Soviet troops on 25 April. . . . On 7 May the

German High Command surrendered all its forces unconditionally, and 8 May was officially proclaimed V-E Day.

*A Brief History of the U.S. Army in World War II,* Center of Military History, United States Army, Washington, D.C., 1992

# 8

# THE REICH OVERRUN

We spent February licking our wounds. There were new men to be trained, battle lessons to be passed on, and new tanks to be processed. We all knew what we were getting ready for. The Germans had thrown their Sunday punch, now we were going to throw ours.

*Up From Marseille,*
*781st Tank Battalion*

Late January found American commanders once again contemplating plans to breach the West Wall and capture the Roer River dams. This time, however, Lt. Gen. Omar Bradley decided to work around the Hürtgen Forest. The advance during late January and early February was limited far more by deep snow, icy or collapsing roads, and freezing temperatures than it was by patchwork—albeit sometimes spirited—German resistance.

*Patchwork* belies the fury on the ground if you just happened to be at one of those spots showing spirited defense. On 1 February with four hours' notice, the 740th Tank Battalion assaulted the Siegfried Line in the vicinity of Neuhof in support of the 82d Airborne Division paratroopers. Lieutenant Powers's 3d Platoon was ordered to spearhead the attack by Company C and the 325th Glider Infantry on Udenbreth. The platoon was already short one Sherman. Proving again that the Daredevil Tankers were an outfit that could outrun the airborne, Powers's tanks pulled a good half-hour ahead of the infantry and entered Udenbreth alone, shooting up everything

in sight. Sergeant Loopey suddenly became aware of the menacing, blocky shape of a Mark IV tank, which he engaged and
destroyed. It was not alone; in the ensuing firefight, Loopey
knocked out two more Mark IVs and an antitank gun. While
the battle played out, however, the Germans maneuvered one
of the big cats, a Tiger, into position, and at noon an 88mm
shell smashed into Powers's tank, killing his gunner and wounding the lieutenant. Loopey quickly took command of the platoon, but minutes later another Sherman went up in flames.
Loopey had no choice. The two surviving Shermans pulled
back to join the rest of the company in defensive positions
short of the objective. Powers was evacuated, but he would return to duty fairly quickly.[1]

Paratroopers who had jumped in North Africa, Italy, Normandy, and the Netherlands said the fighting in this area was
the worst they had witnessed. The 740th, when relieved on
5 February by the 750th, was down to eighteen operational
tanks, some of them manned by emergency crews drawn from
the Headquarters and Service companies. There would be little rest, however. On 6 February, the battalion was ordered
north to join the 8th Infantry Division in VII Corps.[2]

Eisenhower on 1 February ordered Bradley to throttle back
the effort, because he wanted to shift the emphasis northward
to the Ninth Army in support of Montgomery. Bradley and Patton interpreted those orders liberally, as usual. The First Army
nevertheless had to surrender several divisions to the Ninth.
One division, however, was transferred in the other direction;
the 78th Infantry Division attacked through the Monschau
Corridor and by 9 February finally captured the Roer dams.

The official U.S. Army history credits CCA of the 5th Armored Division with providing the armored support in this operation, but the 774th "Blackcat" Tank Battalion was attached

to the 78th on 3 February and participated in the attack. By 5 February, all combat units of the battalion had passed through the Siegfried Line defenses into positions with the 309th and 310th Infantry regiments. The ultimate objective was the Schwammenauel Dam, a huge earthen construction holding back a large artificial lake, which if entirely released by the enemy would result in flooding a great length of the Roer River valley and block any further advances into enemy territory for a long time. By now, the Americans knew that the Germans would defend the approaches vigorously. The challenge was to punch through before enemy engineers could blow the dam.

From 6 February to 10 February, the Blackcats, in support of the infantry, fought a fiercely contested battle for this ground. The tankers and doughs applied now well-tuned bunker-busting tactics to fortifications and pounded strongpoints on the high hills east of Schmidt with indirect fire. The tankers lost so many Shermans and crewmen to mines that when the fighting ended, the battalion welded extra armor plate onto the bottom of all its tanks. Nonetheless, the Americans captured the dams. Friendly engineers reached the control towers and reported no demolitions, although the Germans had jammed some valves in an open position, releasing a part of the great body of water through a sluice gate. Even this was sufficient to partially flood the river and increase its speed beyond the point where it could be bridged under combat conditions.[3]

## DRIVE TO THE RHINE

Downstream from the Roer dams, the 743d Tank Battalion had moved back to the Aachen area in great secrecy and radio silence along with the 30th Infantry Division; their mission was to breach the Roer River defensive line. Arnhem Mary, who broadcast German propaganda in English as did Axis Sally, observed,

"Okay, 30th Division—you can put back on those shoulder patches. We know you're at Aachen. . . ."[4] The Ninth Army, under Monty's overall command, would be part of a British-Canadian-American assault along almost the entire river.

On 8 February, the battalion moved into assault positions near Rohe, Germany. That same day, the Germans partially sabotaged the Roer River dams; the river began to rise, and the attack was delayed for twenty-four hours to 9 February. Battalion officers made last-minute plans and poured over aerial photos of enemy positions. But the river was now flowing at ten miles per hour; crossings that had been fifty feet were now three hundred. D day was postponed indefinitely. There was one positive development: The battalion received its first Easy 8 Shermans with improved suspension and 76mm gun sporting a muzzle brake.[5]

The floodwaters began to recede on 19 February. Supported by an intensive artillery barrage, infantry units forced the Roer at 0300 hours on 23 February. With the bridgehead secure, engineers began building bridges, and at 2300 hours Company A assumed the point on a night march that took the 743d across the river and forward to support the doughs. Overhead in an L4 observation plane, the battalion executive officer helped spot friendly and enemy forces while maintaining constant radio contact with the tanks and division artillery. Tank commanders, in turn, could request artillery support against targets as small as individual German tanks and anti-tank guns.[6] This practice, which provided constant real-time intelligence to tank crews in action, became widespread among the separate tank battalions.

The tank-infantry team once again found itself fighting a strongpoint-by-strongpoint battle, beginning with the town of Steinstrasse. The team lost a few more tanks each day. Tragedy struck during night operations on 26 February, when Com-

pany B opened fire on tank movement where there was supposed to be none and accidentally destroyed four British flail
tanks moving up in support. In general, however, the night
attacks—made under bright moonlight—were popular with
the tankers, who were fighting on terrain that was flat and de-
void of natural cover.[7]

The 30th Infantry Division's attack was part of Operation
Grenade, in which the Ninth Army deployed ten divisions
along the Roer River, with the 35th Infantry Division in reserve. First Army's VII Corps had four more divisions available
to support the Ninth Army attack. Each corps included an armored division, and each infantry division had an attached
tank battalion, for a total of 1,394 tanks—more than two-thirds
of which were still 75mm Shermans. The assault force also
could draw on the dedicated support of the XXIX TAC and
robust fire support: one artillery piece per ten yards of front.[8]

Specialized tank battalions also pitched in. The 739th supplied twenty-seven tank drivers to operate LVTs (landing vehicles, tracked), also known as (Water) Buffaloes, which ferried
personnel and equipment across the Roer River during the
assault crossing. The Buffalo was a fully tracked amphibious
vehicle of lightweight construction that was capable of negotiating five to six feet of surf. Track rotation provided propul-
sion and steering, and maximum speed in water was about six
miles per hour. There were several different models of the
LVT, including a cargo vehicle and armored amphibious tanks
mounting either a 37mm cannon or 75mm howitzer in a turret. The swift current forced the 739th to discontinue use of
the LVTs.

\* \* \*

As in Normandy, Monty's forces pinned the German reserves, and American forces penetrated the line and raced cross-country.[9] By 2 March, Ninth Army's right wing had reached the Rhine River south of Düsseldorf. On 3 March, the left wing—including the 784th Tank Battalion, the second of two comprising black enlisted men and mostly white officers—linked with Canadian forces driving southward out of the Nijmegan bridgehead at Venlo.

In VII Corps' zone, the 8th and 104th Infantry divisions (740th and 750th Tank battalions attached, respectively) faced the somewhat more difficult task of attacking across the Roer into an urban area, Düren, and the woods of Hambach Forest.[10] An artillery bombardment including the assault guns of the 740th commenced at 0215 hours on 23 February. Lieutenant Colonel George Rubel, watching the bombardment, observed, "The buildings still standing in Düren appeared to be literally melting down, and fields for miles around appeared to be boiling."[11] The infantry of the 8th Infantry Division nonetheless faced withering machine-gun fire during the assault. Bridging efforts were shot up as quickly as the engineers could begin them, and it was not until 24 February that tanks could cross to support the doughs. A tough fight followed from strongpoint to strongpoint. Huge coal pits further complicated progress; they effectively created a series of narrow bridges that advancing units had to cross—sometimes against mutually supporting 88mm guns and sometimes against tanks and SP guns.

Lieutenant Powers, back in charge of his 3d Platoon, Company C, was wounded for a second time on 25 February near Gibelsrath. The company—after having its request for smoke and artillery fire rejected—had to advance over several thousand yards of open terrain under fire from 88mm antitank guns. One can only speculate why the local infantry commanders did not use night attacks similar to those in neighboring sectors. The 1st and 2d platoons each left three Shermans burning when the company broke off the attack, and 2d Platoon alone lost its commander, two others killed, and eight men wounded. Sergeant Loopey once more took charge of 3d Platoon. This time, Powers had his "million-dollar wound." The war was over for him.[12]

Rubel recorded, "From this point to Cologne our entire action was a nightmarish routine of attachment and detachment from one regiment to another." Tankers of the 740th initially experienced some unpleasant incidents when trying to work with the 8th Infantry Division, to which it was now attached. Several regimental and battalion commanders were relieved during the first few days of fighting, and under pressure from Division, the new commanders began consulting Rubel regarding the use of his tanks.[13] Finally, on 7 March, the 740th fought its way to within sight of the Rhine River just south of Cologne. By now the tankers and doughs worked together extremely effectively. The infantry kept abreast of the tanks and shot at snipers and bazooka men, and the tanks hosed down buildings and streets with machine-gun fire and pasted basements and upper stories with AP and HE rounds.[14]

On 9 March the battalion entered Knapsack, about six thousand yards from Cologne. Rubel informed the bürgermeister that all weapons must be surrendered and that quick reprisals would meet any shooting. Some shooting developed that night, so Rubel ordered that one house be torched. There were no more problems. On 12 March, the battalion was notified that it was being transferred south to the Seventh Army (where it would stay for only two weeks!).[15]

Tanks of the 750th also were first able to cross the Roer on 24 February. The battalion had the good fortune to support infantry commanders who resorted to night attacks to negate the German advantage in open terrain. Wet turf was as big a challenge as the German defense. On 26 February, the 3d Armored Division passed through the 104th Infantry Division, and from that point the tankers of the 750th had the relative luck to be engaged in mop-up operations. On 5 March, the battalion supported the doughs in the capture of Cologne, where it faced only scattered light resistance in street fighting.[16]


By 1 March, when the 774th Tank Battalion crossed the Roer to support the 78th Infantry Division's drive to the Rhine, German resistance was collapsing. On these rolling plains, the tanks were in their element; in eight days in a fast-moving operation, the 774th received credit for helping the infantry take twenty-three towns, capture several hundred prisoners, and destroy a large number of guns and vehicles. The battalion CP advanced almost daily, everyone was on the move, and on 9 March the first units reached the Rhine.[17] The experience may have reminded the tankers of the race across France, but this time there were no welcoming crowds—only the sullen stares of German civilians.

Lieutenant Dew in the 741st, meanwhile, had seen everything. He was now running a taxi service, and the "drive" to the Rhine had taken on a whole new meaning. On 6 March, Company C had loaded infantry on the tanks near Mechernich and charged ahead—standard operating procedure. This time, however, somebody up the chain of command thought that the idea had more potential and sent the tankers back to the line of departure to pick up more doughs. The shuttle service continued and was employed again between the next two points in the advance.[18]

Once resistance broke down, the race to the Rhine was another welcome period of low casualties for most separate tank battalions in the north. The 741st, for example, lost seven men killed and eighteen wounded during all of March. The 743d suffered only seventeen casualties of all types for the month.[19]

## PATTON PUSHES

Third Army spent February clearing the Vianden Bulge and capturing Bitburg, a limited-objective operation that left Patton's forces poised as far east as the Kyll River for the drive to the Rhine. XII Corps would assume the main burden, supported by harassing attacks from III Corps farther north aimed at preventing the Germans from shifting troops to strengthen the defenses west of Bitburg. Unfortunately, the spring thaw set in, the mud was back, and rivers—including the Sauer directly in front of the planned advance—were again flowing at troublesome levels.

The veteran 5th Infantry Division, with the 737th Tank Battalion, made the main effort on the right. The 80th Infantry Division, with the 702d Tank Battalion and armored infantry from the 4th Armored Division attached, attacked on the left.

Bridging the raging Sauer beginning 6 February turned out to be the hardest part of the operation, because the Germans fought knowing that they had little available to stem the advance once the doughs were finally across. After the bridgehead was secure, the 702d and 737th Tank battalions made heavy use of the T34 rocket launchers mounted on their Shermans. The 737th entered Germany for the second time on Lincoln's Birthday. Beginning 18 February, the 90th Infantry Division, supported as usual by the 712th Tank Battalion, launched a supporting attack southward out of the VIII Corps sector. The German defenses gradually caved in across the zone of advance, and on 28 February the 5th Infantry Division occupied Bitburg. The 737th boasted in its history: "On the drive through the Siegfried Line to Bitburg, despite fixed fortifications of the Siegfried Line, mined roads, rough terrain, and heavy antitank fire, none of our tanks were destroyed by enemy fire and only three were disabled by mines. The daily result of operations may best be characterized by the statement of Captain Zurman, 'Many krauts suspended operations against the Allies today.' "[20]

Farther south in the Saar-Moselle triangle, the 94th Infantry Division, XX Corps, on 14 January had begun operations against the "Siegfried Switch" (an extension of the West Wall) that would open the door to the capture of the triangle and the city of Trier. The division initially had no tank battalion attached, which left the doughs in a world of trouble when the 11th Panzer Division launched a counterattack in their sector. On 16 February, however, the 778th Tank Battalion was attached, and within days battalion tanks had helped the doughs punch through the last of the fortifications. The 10th Armored Division roared through the gap torn by the slogging doughs and their supporting tanks. The 94th Infantry Division again opened a way for the armor across the Saar River. Fighting off pressure to return the 10th Armored Division to SHAEF reserve, Patton threw its tanks toward Trier while turning the 76th Infantry Division toward the same objective from its supporting position in the attack on Bitburg. The armored division grabbed Trier the night of 1 March, along with an intact Roman-era bridge across the Moselle River.[21]

The attack continued across the Kyll River in early March. The 712th Tank Battalion soon had a graphic reminder that, despite Captain Zurman's boasts to the contrary, the enemy could still become unexpectedly dangerous, as recorded in the AAR:

On 9 March a task force of the 2d Combat Team consisting of the 2d Battalion, 2d Infantry; Company D and the Assault Gun Platoon of this battalion; the Cannon Company, 2d Infantry; one platoon of the 7th Engineers; and the 5th Reconnaissance Troop, less one platoon, known as Task Force Graham, jumped off at 0700 and advanced against light opposition. . . . As the task force approached Manderscheid, a platoon of Company D, commanded by 1st Lt. Harvey E. Winoski, was in the lead. Suddenly a Jag Panther [Jagdpanther] opened up on the column. A fierce firefight ensued. Three of our light tanks were hit and the platoon leader mortally wounded. Staff Sergeant Donald S. Simons, the platoon sergeant, immediately assumed command and maneuvered the remaining tanks into a position to outflank the enemy gun. Although the 37mm shells of the light tanks failed to penetrate the armor of the German tank, the enemy was sufficiently engaged so that 1st Lt. William H. Van Loon was able to move his assault guns into a position to fire on the enemy vehicle. The 105mm howitzers opened up and disabled the Jag Panther. . . .[22]

After the 5th Infantry Division established a bridgehead, the 4th Armored Division passed through, and the doughs and tankers mopped up behind the armored columns. The 5th Infantry Division then turned toward the Moselle River, and on 14 March the 737th jumped off at 0200 as part of the Third Army's envelopment that would trap hundreds of thousands of German troops west of the Rhine. Once again, the 4th Armored Division passed through the door the doughs and tankers had kicked open and raced southward.[23] By 24 March, the Allies held the west bank of the Rhine for its entire length.[24]

## CROSSING THE RHINE: A THREE-TURRET-RING CIRCUS

The Rhine River was supposed to pose a major defensive obstacle to the Allies, but four separate operations easily forced the river during March. Eisenhower had agreed that Monty would make the big push across the Rhine in the north. Things did not work out that way.

On 7 March, the First Army's 9th Armored Division captured

the Ludendorff railroad bridge at Remagen intact and—while engineers disabled most of the demolitions—boldly threw five battalions of infantry and tanks across the Rhine. Not only had the 9th Armored Division breached the Rhine, but it had cut off the escape route for the remnants of eleven German divisions trapped between the advancing First and Third armies.[25]

The 746th Tank Battalion crossed the Remagen bridge on 8 March—the first separate tank battalion to cross the river. The 774th began crossing the next day, and the unit history recorded the scene:

[O]n 9 March the first units of the battalion crossed the historic Rhine on the partially demolished Ludendorff railroad bridge at Remagen. On 10 March the rear elements of the battalion were ferried across, being unable to use the bridge because of almost incessant air bombing attacks and an intense concentration of enemy artillery trying desperately to destroy our tiny hold on the east bank of the river. One Service Company truck, loaded with ammunition, had received a direct hit as it was leaving the bridge and went up in flames. By 1400 the entire battalion was on the east bank, under heavy artillery fire to be sure, but there—ready for action. . . .

In the momentous days from 11 March to 21 March the 774th's tanks and the 78th Infantry Division together fought desperately to hold and enlarge the Remagen bridgehead. Immediately after crossing, the [tank] platoons fanned out with their respective infantry units, reaching as far south as Honnef and west of Kalenborn by that first night. At Kalenborn the enemy was prepared with tank-mounted 88s dug into strategic positions commanding all approaches to the town and their famous autobahn. The infantry were driven back time after time by the withering fire, and with terrible losses. The tanks went on alone, but the high-velocity 88mm shells ripped into them as soon as they left the protection of the wooded areas outside the town. It took four days of continuous and fierce attack to drive the Tigers from their lairs. Tankers who thought they did not have a chance of coming through alive stayed right in there fighting, with all the skill and guts that four months of combat had brought. One entire platoon of tanks [was] nothing but twisted and charred heaps of metal, another had four tanks disabled, but many of the men crawled to safety, to take their places in new tanks which were hurriedly brought up—and Kalenborn fell. From here the battalion drove on to take town after town along the Rhine River bank, some thirty-four in all. The 774th captured more than a thousand Germans and killed seven hundred enemy. By 21 March the bridgehead, extending some twenty miles along the east bank of the Rhine to a depth of six to twelve miles, was firmly secured, and there was now room for the big armored outfits to come in and make their weight felt."[26]

On 21 March in the predawn gray, Corporal Ocasio and his fellow crewmen in a 746th Jumbo advanced cautiously toward Windhagen, supporting the doughs along with a few TDs. The armor pulled up near a spiderweb of roads that joined the autobahn near the town. As infantry patrols disappeared among the buildings, the tankers waited and watched before pulling up near some woods to establish a roadblock. Riflemen soon came pounding back down the road out of Windhagen, a clear sign that something was amiss. Soon, the wedge shapes of Jagdpanthers appeared on the edge of town. Both sides opened fire as the Shermans attempted to maneuver to the flank. Two 88mm rounds struck Ocasio's bulked-up Sherman, and the crew bailed out. Perhaps a tribute to its thicker armor, the Jumbo did not burn.

The crew dove for cover as the German counterattack swept by them. Ocasio eyed his tank and suggested a crazy idea to crewmate Technician 5th Grade Coy. The two men sprinted back to the Jumbo, vaulted to the deck, and squirmed quickly into the turret. Ocasio spun the gun toward one of the nearby Jagdpanthers, which now presented its thinner flank armor. The two men pumped six AP rounds into the German vehicle. As the enemy crew took its turn to bail out, the Americans switched to HE and killed them all. The rest of Ocasio's platoon and the TDs were still blazing away, too. The Germans soon retreated, leaving two smoking hulks in their wake. The attack on Windhagen resumed.[27]

On 22 March, Patton beat Monty to the punch and slipped across the Rhine at Oppenheim, a small barge harbor halfway between Mainz and Worms. The 5th Infantry Division made the assault crossing at the cost of only eight killed and twenty wounded, and the 737th Tank Battalion joined the doughs on 23 March. Within thirty-six hours, the bridgehead was five miles deep and seven miles wide. The 90th Infantry and 4th Armored divisions now crossed the river unmolested and headed east. By 28 March, tanks of Company C, 737th Tank Battalion, had crossed the Main River and entered Frankfurt.[28]

When news of Patton's stroke reached Hitler, he called for immediate countermeasures, but German commanders had nothing with which to respond. The only "reserve" was an assortment of five panzers under repair at a tank depot one hundred miles away. The bottom of the barrel had been scraped.[29]

On 23 March, Montgomery finally launched his operatic assault, complete with massive air strikes, airborne assaults by two divisions, and well-organized media coverage. He had slowly amassed twenty-five divisions and a quarter-million tons of ammunition and other supplies on the west bank of the

Rhine. Opposing him in the thirty-five-mile stretch of river that he planned to cross were only five exhausted German divisions. The Ninth Army, which furnished half the assaulting infantry, lost only forty men killed during the crossing. Still, nervous about the Germans despite the near total absence of serious resistance, Monty would authorize no general advance eastward until he had moved 20 divisions and 1,500 tanks into the bridgehead.[30]

But first the bridgehead had to be enlarged. The 743d Tank Battalion had crossed the Rhine with the 30th Infantry Division as part of the assault wave, and it ran into a last-gasp German effort to staunch the wound as the 116th Panzer Division shifted into the tankers' path from the Canadian front. Several days of renewed limited-objective fighting against stiff resistance ensued. But the German effort was futile, because two American armored divisions were crossing the river behind the infantry. On 29 November, having again opened the door, the doughs and tankers settled down as the big armor passed through the lines and swept over the defenders.[31]

On 26 March, Seventh Army forced the Rhine near Worms. One assault division, the 3d Infantry, had a tough time, but the second, the 45th Infantry, faced only modest resistance. The lead elements of the 756th Tank Battalion crossed the river at 1615 hours, mostly on pontoon rafts, to support the 3d Infantry Division doughs. Within three days, four more divisions, including two armored, had poured across—and more would follow.[32]


The Rhine crossing featured an almost circus-like use of the good and not-so-good special capabilities that had been foisted on some of the separate tank battalions—almost as if higher command decided it needed to use the whole panoply to justify the cost.

DD tanks had proven themselves already, and Monty had a veritable naval task force of them ready: sixty-six British and seventeen American. The use of the 70th, 741st, and 743d Tank battalions, which had used DD tanks in the Normandy landings, was considered. The losses among the tank crews had been so high since Normandy, however, that those outfits would have required as much training as those that had never used the equipment. Company C of the 736th Tank Battalion was instead trained and fitted out with DD tanks and attached to the 743d for the actual crossing, during which the tankers faced virtually no resistance. Prior to the Seventh Army crossing, Company C of the 756th Tank Battalion—the only medium tank company in the battalion that had *not* used DD tanks in Operation Dragoon—had received hurried training on DD Shermans. The DD tanks participated in the crossing in support of the 3d Infantry Division. Launching at daylight, three successfully made the crossing in the 7th Infantry Regiment sector, but three sank, and one was destroyed by artillery; in the 30th Infantry Regiment sector, six made it, and one sank.[33] Technically, Patton in late March also used DD tanks that were supplied to the 748th Tank Battalion. Eight of the fifty-one DD Shermans actually entered the Rhine, but one sank. Most of the rest were so badly damaged by road march that they could no longer maintain buoyancy. The river crossing was not an assault crossing, however; the 748th was merely moving up to support the 65th and 89th Infantry divisions.[34]

The 747th Tank Battalion was issued LVTs, and between 24 and 26 March made 1,112 roundtrips across the Rhine in support of the Ninth Army. The Buffaloes carried elements of the 30th and 79th Infantry divisions, including infantry, artillery, AT guns, and ammunition. Two LVTs were damaged by artillery fire.[35] For Homer Wilkes and the rest of the battalion (except, briefly, for Company B and the assault guns), the Rhine crossing was the last action under fire of the war.

The Ninth Army reequipped Company B of the 739th MX Tank Battalion with CDL tanks to illuminate bridging sites beginning 23 March. First Army had been using a handful of CDL tanks from the 738th MX Tank Battalion for the same purpose at the Remagen bridgehead since 9 March and deployed additional CDL tanks on 21 and 23 March. Third Army also used three platoons of CDL tanks from the 748th at St. Goar, Bad Salsig, and Mainz.[36]

## POCKETING THE RUHR

The envelopment and capture of the Ruhr industrial basin was the last large-scale battle facing American troops in Europe. The Ninth Army—still under Monty's command until 4 April, when it was returned to Bradley—raced around the north, while the First Army, in concert with the Third, looped around the south. The encirclement was mainly a story of the 2d Armored Division, spearheading the northern sweep, and the 3d Armored Division to the south. The infantry divisions and attached tank battalions played only a supporting role.

On 1 April, American forces linked at Lippstadt. The defenders in the Ruhr Pocket held out for eighteen days, but when the fighting was over, 325,000 Germans had surrendered. Feldmarschall Walter Model chose to kill himself rather than give up.[37]

Mopping up the Ruhr Pocket was no cakewalk, although some areas fell almost without a shot.[38] The 8th Infantry Division, in a typical example, was ordered to cut the pocket in half by driving north through Olpe to Wuppertal, but without tank support. Pushing out of Siegen in the last days of March, the doughs were thrown back with heavy losses. On 8 April, the 740th Tank Battalion was sent to support the frustrated doughs. The tanks spearheaded the renewed attack, with infantrymen mounted on the rear decks. Their orders were to

race ahead, with the doughs dismounting only to clear roadblocks; these usually comprised a log barricade defended by
two or three bazooka teams, one or two machine guns, and two
or more antitank guns. Unfortunately, if the Germans chose to
fight, the first indication that a roadblock lay ahead was usually the destruction of the lead 740th tank. In a growing number of cases, however, the dispirited defenders surrendered
when the tanks rolled up.[39]

The 3d Platoon, Company C, of the 740th was under
new management. Staff Sergeant Charlie Loopey had received
a battlefield commission to second lieutenant and taken
over the platoon for good. On 9 April, Loopey and his men
supported the 2d Battalion, 121st Infantry Regiment, in its
advance through Rahrbach. Just as Loopey approached the
village of Welschen Ennestt, two enormous seventy-ton Jagdtiger tank-killers mounting 128mm guns came out of the forest ahead. Either could have obliterated Loopey's Sherman
with a single round, and he stood no chance of penetrating the
thick frontal armor of the German vehicles at any range. For-
tunately, the Jagdtigers were evidently trying to escape because they turned the other direction and headed north. No
one will ever know why the escape hatches on both were open.
The escape hatch was a circular hole in the back of the super-
structure normally covered by an armored door and was about
two feet in diameter. Loopey's gunner put a couple of rounds of
HE through these holes on both vehicles and knocked them
out, killing their crews.[40]

The doughs pushed forward relentlessly; the American infantry regiments were able to leapfrog one another, but once
more the tankers went into the line every day. The 740th again
experienced considerable friction with infantry commanders
in an unfamiliar partner division who were tasting their first
battle.[41] Nevertheless, American forces were in Olpe by 11 April.

On 12 April, only four days before the 740th would experience hostile fire for the last time, Lieutenant Loopey's platoon jumped off at 0800 hours from Hombert. In Oberbrugge, the tankers spotted a roadblock but also noticed a bypass that appeared to lead around the obstruction. Easing forward, Loopey realized that the Germans had set a bazooka ambush on the bypass, and he opened fire. The ambushers dispersed, and the tanks pressed ahead and swung back to take the roadblock from the rear. They found a target-rich environment and destroyed one self-propelled flak gun, one halftrack, and many wheeled vehicles. Loopey, per standard practice, had his head protruding out of his hatch. A shell struck the turret, showering Loopey's face and neck with fragments. He was evacuated at about 1130 hours. The war was over for him, too. But the military machine clanked on: Staff Sergeant Fleming assumed command of 3d Platoon.

On 14 April, the 8th Infantry Division linked with the 79th Infantry Division, which had pushed southward from the Ninth Army at Wetter in the Roer heartland. Lieutenant Colonel Rubel recorded: "The battle of the Roer Pocket was over. In many ways it had been a steeplechase, and from the infantry's standpoint it was an easy operation. From the tanker's standpoint, it was a hundred miles of spearheading, and a grueling, exhausting battle. We had lost as many tanks here as we had lost in the Battle of the Ardennes. We hoped that the war would soon be over."[42]

On 18 April, Rubel received orders putting the 740th on occupation duty in Düsseldorf. Rubel himself took on the duties of lord mayor of the city. The colonel delivering the orders chuckled and added, "The last Lord Mayor of Düsseldorf was killed a few days ago, you know. Don't let it become a habit."[43]

## RACE TO THE FINISH LINE

The tankers of the separate battalions were now among the most savvy graduates of the school of war. They knew how to storm cities and deal with small groups of defenders in villages or at crossroads. They could slog through fortifications and run like the cavalry of old. By and large, they had worked out effective teamwork strategies with the infantry, TDs, and artillery, even if still a bit ambivalent about their friends in the fighter-bombers above them. They had learned to beat better tanks and worked out a series of pragmatic technical solutions to problems ranging from communication to moving on ice.

They had to do it only a little while longer before they could return to their lives and families.

Cornelius Ryan captured the essence of the final push: "The race was on. Never in the history of warfare had so many men moved so fast. The speed of the Anglo-American offensive was contagious, and all along the front the drive was taking on the proportions of a giant contest."[44] So fast, indeed; between 24 and 30 April, the 737th Tank Battalion moved 520 miles.[45] A detailed accounting of the actions of each battalion during this period would be a dull recitation of long lists of towns passed through, sometimes involving a firefight but often not.

The Ninth Army pounded in the direction of Berlin all the way to the Elbe River. Just to the south, First Army advanced to the Mulde River. Patton's Third Army drove toward Czechoslovakia, and Seventh Army pushed through Bavaria toward the rumored Nazi National Redoubt in the Bavarian Alps and Austria.[46]

The tankers rolled past columns of German POWs heading for the rear, often with no supervision. Increasingly, displaced persons and released Allied POWs also appeared.

## Spearheads

There were not enough armored divisions to sweep every-where, and some infantry divisions with their attached tank battalions joined the operation to overrun the Reich at the pointy end of the spear. Doughs piled onto the tanks. In some cases, artillery observers rode with the forward elements. Tank battalions attached to the infantry divisions following the spearheads spent their days scooping up wandering German soldiers and clearing out the scattered towns and villages where German forces refused to give up.

The 736th Tank Battalion (attached to the 83d Infantry Division) was one of the units leading the charge. Their column became engaged in an intense rivalry with the neighboring 2d Armored Division to see who could move farthest fastest. The doughs requisitioned every vehicle they came across (and one German ME-109 fighter plane, to boot, painting "83d Inf. Div." across the underside) and soon became known as the "Rag-Tag Circus." The two divisions reluctantly conceded a tie at the Weser River. Then, on they pelted. The 2d Armored reached the Elbe River late on 11 April and slipped armored infantry across; doughs of the 83d Division reached the east bank of the river on 13 April. The 736th's tanks crossed the Elbe on 20 April, but Eisenhower had already decided that his troops would press no closer to Berlin.[47] This would be the farthest penetration for a separate tank battalion in Germany.

The 702d Tank Battalion, dashing through central Germany with the 80th Infantry Division, described in its AAR the conditions tankers of most units encountered much of the time:

Throughout the month of April, enemy attempts at resistance were marked by their continued feebleness. At only two periods was there any show of strength, and by late in the month our assault had lost its character, and the only proper description for operations engaged in by the battalion was "road march."

The cities of Kassel and Erfurt were the focal points of resistance, and in the defense of the former, tanks were used in limited numbers. Flak units were the manpower basis for this defense. But these fanatical sacrifice operations served to no value, for the miscellaneous grab-bag units crumbled before our organized assaults after only a token-plus resistance. . . .

The attitude of the German soldier was one of complete abandonment to his fate. He found his fate lay only in two directions, death or the PW camp, and with a little physical persuasion, generally chose the latter. PW figures grew astronomically, and interrogation degenerated into a simple counting of those who passed through the tills of the PW cage. The German people were completely confused and confusing. Many of them went out of their way to be hospitable to the conquering American, and overt acts by the civilians against our military forces were rare.[48]

Not all German forces had abandoned the fight. Advancing columns frequently encountered small units that fought briefly, claiming a few more American lives, before giving up, running, or dying. The SS were a particular problem. American troops had a simple rule: If a town showed white flags and no resistance, they rolled through. If American troops came under fire, they smashed the community. Indeed, any sympathy for the civilian populace declined as advancing forces began liberating the concentration camps. The 70th Tank Battalion's informal history recorded that "The tanks swept across open fields from village to village, blasting relentlessly at every sign of resistance. Any town or city that tried to delay the advance soon became a raging inferno. The German landscape was dotted with burning villages. More white flags began to appear."[49]

Lieutenant Dew in the 741st was fighting a series of these small but deadly engagements as his battalion advanced with the 2d Infantry Division through central Germany. After crossing the Weser, on 8 April his tankers had to destroy 20mm antiaircraft guns firing on the column near Kleine Lengdon. They suppressed small-arms fire in a few small villages during the next several days. On 13 April, the column again encountered antiaircraft fire at Dorstewitz. Dew decided to rush the town and outflank the gun positions, and he ordered his platoon forward. As the Shermans swung into the village, an unseen enemy soldier fired a bazooka. The round easily punctured Dew's tank, wounding the lieutenant and killing his driver. The battalion would experience its final hostile fire only five days later. It seemed so senseless to lose a man at this stage. Dew would return to duty on 5 May after the 741st had fired its last shot.

Now and again, the fights were big and dismaying. For example, after crossing the Rhine, the 100th Infantry Division and the 781st Tank Battalion advanced rapidly until reaching the west bank of the Neckar River in the vicinity of Heilbronn on 3 April. The doughs crossed the river in assault boats the next day to find themselves battling a remarkably effective defense made up of Wehrmacht, Volksturm, Hitler Youth, and SS—so effective that the Germans counterattacked and almost threw the doughs back into the Neckar. Accurate artillery fire disrupted every American attempt to erect a bridge and get the tanks across. Higher headquarters frantically arranged for the delivery of ten DD Shermans, and crews were given a day of training. The tanks entered the water but were unable to climb the other side, and three sank. Finally, on 8 April, two platoons made the trip across a temporary bridge that was immediately knocked out by enemy artillery. On 12 April, American doughs and tanks pushed the German artillery out of range of the bridging sites, and on the next day Heilbronn fell.[50]

And, on 17 April, tankers of the 756th rolled into the Nazi citadel of Nürnberg, and with the doughs of the 3d Infantry Division for three days fought street to street against determined resistance in the form of antitank, bazooka, and small-arms fire. The 191st Tank Battalion and 45th Infantry Division pushed in from the south. SS and mountain troops, backed by thirty-five tanks brought from the Grafenwoehr Proving Grounds, defended the city. German snipers with Panzerfausts picked off tanks from the rooftops, and it became standard practice for the tanks to blast any building that even looked as if it might hide such a sniper. On 22 April, with victory finally at hand, the 756th patrolled the streets of the city in a show of strength.[51]

Control and maintenance problems cropped up as they had during the long road marches across France. The 735th Tank Battalion, for example, in April noted in its AAR, "It was once again demonstrated in the rapid movement across Germany . . . that in a rapidly moving situation it is impossible to keep contact with the tank COs with the present means of communication by FM radio. . . . At this time, the entire battalion is badly in need of maintenance after having traveled several hundred miles in the past few days. New tracks are especially needed at this time." The 746th reported in April, "All companies experienced difficulty in maintaining the full-tracked vehicles enroute."[52]

Even this late in the game, airstrikes by friendly fighter-bombers continued to be a problem. On 20 April, a rare incident took place: Elements of the 772d Tank Battalion fired back on eight P-47s that were attacking the column, downing four. The battalion's AAR claimed that the P-47s were obviously "enemy owned and operated."

## Resting Arms

The war had effectively ended for a growing number of the tank battalions. As early as 8 April, the 747th Tank Battalion started military government duties around Wulfen. After two days of street combat in Magdeburg, the fighting was over for the D day veterans of the 743d Tank Battalion on 19 April. The 735th halted at the advance limiting line by 20 April and saw no further action. Another D day outfit, the 745th, wrapped up fighting in the Harz Mountains on 22 April.

On 16 April, the strategic bombing campaign was suspended for want of targets in Germany. On 25 April, First Army linked with Soviet troops at Torgau.[53] On 30 April, Hitler shot himself in the Führerbunker in Berlin. When word reached German troops in the field, resistance virtually ceased.[54]

Nevertheless, other battalions continued to push forward through Germany and into Austria and Czechoslovakia. On 4 May, tankers of the 781st and doughs of the 103d Infantry Division traversed Brenner Pass and linked up with the U.S. Fifth Army eight miles inside Italy.[55]

German formations continued to surrender en masse, and it was clear that the end was near. The AAR of the 774th Tank Battalion recorded the following entry for 5 May:

Incoming message: GERMAN ARMY GROUP G, ON FRONT OF XXI CORPS AND 101 ABN DIV HAS SURRENDERED. HALT ALL TROOPS IN PLACE. NO FURTHER ADVANCE EXCEPT ON ORDERS THIS HEADQUARTERS.

FURTHER DETAILS AND ORDERS WILL FOLLOW. NEC-
ESSARY SECURITY MEASURES WILL BE TAKEN. HOW-
EVER, TROOPS WILL FIRE ONLY IF FIRED UPON.

> TAYLOR
> Maj Gen
> Cmdg

German representatives signed documents of capitulation in the early hours of 7 May. To the world, General of the Army Dwight Eisenhower declared simply, "The mission of this Allied Force was fulfilled at 0241, local time, May 7, 1945." At midnight on 8 May, the war in Europe was over for everyone. The 717th Tank Battalion Record offered the following vignette in its history: "V-E Day was not what anyone had thought it would be. No one celebrated; the work went right on. In the old SS barracks at Bottrop, chow was being served for the noon meal when Lieutenant Howard walked into the officers' mess. Very quickly, he read the TWX [telegram] announcing the end of the European war. Then he went outside to the main mess hall and read the same wire to Headquarters Company. There were a few cheers, and a few 'Thank God's'. The end was really too big to believe."

On 9 May, the 774th recorded simply in its AAR, "The entire battalion gathered for memorial services, paying tribute to the memory of our departed comrades."

# Appendix A

# BATTALION PROFILES

### 70TH TANK BATTALION

First GHQ medium tank battalion in U.S. Army. Formed from 67th Infantry (medium tanks) at Fort Meade, Maryland, on 15 June 1940 under Lt. Col. Stephen G. Henry. Redesignated 70th Light Tank Battalion 7 October 1941. Company C detached 15 February 1942, sent to Iceland; new Company C formed 19 May. Company A landed at Algiers 8 November 1942 as part of 39th ICT (infantry combat team, regimental), 1st Infantry Division. Landed in Sicily July 1943. Arrived England in November 1943, reequipped as standard tank battalion; former Company C reattached as Company D. Landed D day on Utah Beach supporting 4th Infantry Division. Companies A and B used amphibious DD Shermans. Joined drive on Cherbourg and breakout at St. Lô. Fought at St. Pois, Villedieu, and Mortain, and entered Paris. Spearheaded 4th Infantry Division's drive into Belgium, entered Germany on 13 September 1944. Moved to Hürtgen Forest in November, where the battalion experienced some of the worst fighting of the war. Moved to Ardennes with the 4th Infantry Division in December, fighting in Battle of the Bulge. Crossed Rhine near Worms 29 March 1945, pursued retreating German forces. With TF Rodwell stormed SS stronghold in Aalen on 21 April. Crossed Danube 25 April at Langen. Ended war near Austrian border at Gmund, Miesbach, and Holz.[1]

### 191ST TANK BATTALION

Organized 1 September 1940 out of four National Guard tank companies from New York, Massachusetts, Virginia, and Connecticut. Assembled at Fort Meade, Maryland, in February 1941 under Maj. Littleton A. Roberts. Reorganized as medium tank battalion June 1942. Landed in North Africa but saw first combat in Italy, landing at Salerno in September 1943. Landed at Anzio January 1944 and joined attack on Rome, during which battalion suffered high losses. Landed in southern France

15 August 1944. Usually attached to 45th Infantry Division, battalion joined drive to the Vosges Mountains. Fought in Lorraine and Alsace in November 1944. Slashed through Homburg and Kaiserslautern to Rhine with TF Dolvin March 1945. Company B DD tanks led river crossing on 25 March. Battalion entered Bamberg, Nürnberg, and Munich, where it ended war.[2]

## 701ST TANK BATTALION

Activated 1 March 1943 at Camp Cambell, Kentucky, under Lt. Col. F. J. Simpson. Originally organized as special battalion equipped with CDL spotlight tanks. Landed in Liverpool on 1 May 1944 and shipped to France in August, where battalion stayed until reorganized as standard tank battalion after 23 October. Moved to front on 19 December 1944 in Ubach, Germany, attached to 102d Infantry Division. Joined the assault across Roer River on 23 February 1945. Attacked northward, reaching Rhine at Krefeld. Crossed Rhine beginning 26 March attached to the 75th Infantry Division. Reattached to 102d Infantry Division for drive through Muenster and across Weser River. Ended the war in Gardelegen.[3]

## 702D TANK BATTALION

Activated 1 March 1943 at Camp Cambell, Kentucky, under Maj. Ralph Talbott III. Transited England, debarked at Utah Beach 6 August 1944; confusingly, a 702d Tank Destroyer Battalion already deployed in same area. Attached to the 80th Infantry Division on 8 August, operated in Argentan-Bordeaux area during closure of Falaise Gap. Fought along Moselle River September and October 1944. Supported 80th Infantry Division offensive in vicinity of Metz November. Moved to Luxembourg City upon outbreak of Battle of the Bulge. Joined 80th Infantry Division attack across Ourthe and Sauer rivers into Siegfried Line in February 1945. Briefly attached to 76th Infantry Division in late February and advanced toward Trier. Advance to Rhine in March with TF Onaway, then shifted to Luxembourg to rejoin 80th Infantry Division. Crossed Rhine near Mainz on 28 March. Advanced rapidly through Germany, including Kassel, Gotha, Erfurt, Jena, Weimar, Gera, Bamberg, Nürnberg, and Regensburg.[4]

## 707TH TANK BATTALION

Activated 20 September 1943 out of 3d Battalion, 81st Armored Regiment, 5th Armored Division at Pine Camp, New York, under Lt. Col. Richard W. Ripple. Landed in France 1 September 1944. Committed to battle near Krinkelt, Germany, 10 October 1944 attached to 28th Infantry Division. Participated in 28th Infantry Division's disastrous attack on Schmidt in November, during which Company A was destroyed. Withdrew to Luxembourg 20 November for intensive rehabilitation. On 16 December, battalion found itself in path of the German Ardennes offensive and shattered. Company C put into defensive positions on Meuse River on 1 January 1945 attached to 17th Airborne Division, battalion then moved to Belgium. Battalion deployed to Germany in April near Seebachin attached to the 89th Infantry Division. Last action at Neu Wursohnitz on 6 May.[5]

## 709TH TANK BATTALION

Activated on 20 September 1943 from 3d Battalion, 40th Armored Regiment, 7th Armored Division under command of Lt. Col. Odis L. Harmon. Landed at Liverpool, England, 11 March 1944. Debarked at Utah Beach 10 July 1944. Attached to 8th Infantry Division, fought in Normandy during breakout and into Brittany. Much of battalion joined 83d Infantry Division in fighting at St. Malo, Dinard, and Brest. Performed "occupation" duty in Luxembourg in October and November 1944. Entered Hürtgen Forest on 19 November. On 12 December, 709th was attached to 78th Infantry Division for attack near the Kesternich-Simmarath Ridge. Participated in fighting in Colmar Pocket in February 1945. Joined race to Rhine in March. Crossed river on 3 April and fought in Ruhr industrial region. Entered military government status in late April 1945.[6]

## 712TH TANK BATTALION

Activated on 20 September 1943 at Camp Gordon, Georgia, out of 3d Battalion, 11th Armored Regiment, 10th Armored Division, Maj. William E. Eckles commanding. Landed in France 29 and 30 June 1944. Battalion less Company A committed 2 July near St. Jore attached to 90th Infantry Division; Company A attached to 82d Airborne Division.

After breakout, battalion crossed Seine near Mayenne. Joined drive on Le Mans and closing of Falaise Pocket in August 1944. On 8 September near Landres, France, battalion had rare encounter with large German armored force (thirty-five tanks) and destroyed about half. Advanced to the Moselle near Metz in mid-September. Participated in fight for Maizières-les-Metz in October and in Metz offensive in November. Deployed to Rippweiler, Luxembourg, on 7 January 1945 to join fighting around the Bulge. Battalion CO Lt. Col. George B. Randolph KIA 9 January. Reentered Germany in February in 90th Infantry Division and SHAEF reserve. Engaged in elimination of German forces west of Rhine in March, crossing Moselle River yet again. Advanced through series of small German towns in April, ending up at border with Czechoslovakia. Entered the Sudetenland in May 1945.[7]

## 717TH TANK BATTALION

Activated 10 September 1943 at Camp Chaffee, Arkansas, out of 16th Armored Division under Lt. Col. Raymond W. Odor. Assigned to Armored Board, Fort Knox, Kentucky, testing new equipment, including M26 Pershing. Sailed for Europe 26 December 1944 and landed in France February 1945. Fired first shot 24 March at Rhine River, attached to 79th Infantry Division. After crossing Rhine, participated in operations in Ruhr Valley during April, including assault on Essen in support of 17th Airborne Division. Ended the war in Bottrop, Germany.[8]

## 735TH TANK BATTALION

Activated on 10 January 1943 at Fort Lewis, Washington, under Lt. Col. Ralph Alexander, commanding. Committed on 15 July 1944 in Normandy near Sallen. After breakout, fought at Angers, Chartres, and Reims. Crossed the Moselle in early September and became embroiled in fighting around Metz. Joined fruitless assault on Fort Driant in October 1944. In November, supported 5th Infantry Division's drive into Metz and reduction of forts still holding out. Relieved elements of 778th Tank Battalion in Saarlautern east of Saar River on 17 December. Deployed northward to join fighting in Ardennes beginning 21 December. Remained in Luxembourg until February 1945, during which month the battalion conducted limited offensive operations against Siegfried Line with the 87th Infantry Division. Reached Rhine near Koblenz 13 March and crossed 25 March on rafts as part of the 87th Infantry Division assault. Dashed across Germany, reaching Saale River on 13 April. Crossed the Weisse Elster near Brockav on 16 April and went onto defensive.[9]

## 736TH TANK BATTALION

Activated 1 February 1943 at Camp Rucker, Alabama, Maj. William H. Dodge, commanding. Organized as special battalion equipped with top secret CDL spotlight tanks. Arrived in the United Kingdom on 1 April 1944 and Utah Beach in August. Reorganized as standard tank battalion in November and attached to 94th Infantry Division in St. Nazaire-Lorient sector. Again selected for special equipment—DD tanks to be used for crossing of the Rhine—to which one company was devoted. Moved to front on 26 January 1945 and joined attack on Kesternich. Reached Rhine in March with 83d Infantry Division. Company C DD tanks supported Rhine crossing. Reached Elbe River at Barby on 13 April. Contacted Russian forces 4 May 1945.[10]

## 737TH TANK BATTALION

Activated 1 February 1943 at Fort Lewis, Washington, with Col. S. L. Buracker, commanding. Arrived in England 12 February 1944. Debarked at Omaha Beach 12 July and attached to 35th Infantry Division. While with that division, fought at St. Lô, Mortain, and Le Mans. First tank battalion of Third Army to cross Moselle and Meurthe rivers. Entered Germany east of Sarreguemines on 15 December 1944. On 22 December, redeployed to the Ardennes and joined 5th Infantry Division. Supported division's crossing of Sauer River January 1945 and drive through Siegfried Line to Bitburg in February. Drove along Moselle to the Rhine and then south as part of envelopment of German forces in March. Crossed Rhine 25 March near Russelheim, raced to Frankfurt am Main. Turned north toward Ruhr Pocket in April, then conducted 520-mile road march to return to the Third Army, reaching Bavaria on 1 May. Entered Czechoslovakia south of Winterberg on 3 May 1945.[11]

## 738TH TANK BATTALION

Activated on 16 February 1943 at Fort Benning, Georgia, under command of Lt. Col. Raymond W. Odor. Reorganized on 19 November 1943 as special battalion equipped with top secret CDL spotlight tanks. Arrived in England April 1944. In September, mission changed to operation of special equipment for breaching and clearing minefields. On 12 October 1944, redesignated 738th Medium Tank Battalion, Special (Mine Exploder). Debarked at Le Havre, France, on 11 November 1944 and moved to Aachen, Germany. On 7 December 1944, Company A attached to 3d Armored Division, cleared roads during capture of Obergeich. Performed almost daily missions attached to diverse units thereafter.[12]

## 739TH TANK BATTALION

Activated on 1 March 1943 at Fort Lewis, Washington, under command of Maj. Bethuel M. Kitchen. Reorganized in December 1944 as special battalion equipped with CDL spotlight tanks. Arrived in England August 1944. On 12 October, mission changed to operation of special equipment for breaching and clearing minefields; battalion redesignated 739th Medium Tank Battalion, Special (Mine Exploder). One company obtained flamethrower tanks—probably British Crocodiles supplied for evaluation. Departed for Netherlands on 28 November 1944. On 18 December, one platoon of Company C detonated mines near Suggerath. Beginning in January 1945, mine-clearing elements performed almost daily missions attached to diverse units. Flamethrower platoon first used in Jülich, Germany, on 7 February. In late February, battalion supplied tank drivers to operate LVTs used to ferry personnel and equipment across Roer River during assault. In March, one company detached for training in use of DD tanks. Company B deployed CDLs on 23 March during Rhine crossing. CDL tanks used again twice in April, once in failed effort to capture bridges near Henrichenburg and again to illuminate bridge construction across Dortmund-Ems Canal and Lippe River.[13]

## 740TH TANK BATTALION

Activated on 1 March 1943 at Fort Knox, Kentucky, under command of Maj. Harry C. Anderson. Reorganized 10 September 1943 as special battalion to be issued CDL spotlight tanks, but never received equipment despite considerable special training. Arrived in Belgium November 1944 with no tanks but with order to convert to standard tank battalion. Clashed with Peiper's spearhead in December 1944 in first action. Attached to 82d Airborne Division in January 1945, attacked north side of the Bulge. Assaulted Siegfried Line in February. Crossed the Roer with 8th Infantry Division on 24 March and joined drive on Cologne. After reaching the Rhine, transferred 350 miles south and attached to 63d Infantry Division for another attack through Siegfried Line toward Saarbrucken. Returned to 8th Infantry Division to hammer at Ruhr Pocket in April 1945, after which took on occupation duties in Düsseldorf.[14]

## 741ST TANK BATTALION

Activated on 15 March 1942 at Fort Meade, Maryland, under command of Lt. Col. Jacob R. Moon. Two companies equipped with DD tanks, and battalion formed part of assault wave at Omaha Beach on 6 June 1944 attached to 1st Infantry Division. Reattached to 2d Infantry Division in Normandy and participated in breakthrough at Vire River in July and August. Reached Paris 27 August. Advanced through France and Belgium, reaching Siegfried Line on 13 September. Attacked toward Roer River with 2d Infantry Division on 13 December 1944, turned south at outbreak of German Ardennes offensive. Supported 2d Infantry Division push to eliminate Bulge and drive into Germany in January and February 1945. Crossed Rhine at Remagen in March, reached Weser River on 5 April. Entered Leipzig 19 April and Czechoslovakia 5 May near Pilsen.[15]

## 743D TANK BATTALION

Activated as a light tank battalion on 16 May 1942 at Fort Lewis, Washington, under command of Maj. John Upham. Redesignated as medium tank battalion on 19 August 1942. Arrived in England November 1943. Two companies equipped with DD tanks, and battalion formed part of the assault wave at Omaha Beach on 6 June 1944 attached to 29th Infantry Division. On 14 June, attached to 30th Infantry Division, with which battalion fought for rest of war. Participated in St. Lô breakout in July and Battle of Mortain in August 1944. Entered Belgium on 3 September 1944. Company A supported capture of Fort Eben Emael on 10 September. Supported operations against Siegfried Line in October and attack to Roer River beginning 16 November 1944. Shifted to Ardennes on 17 December, fighting in Malmedy, Stavelot, and Stoumont. Took part in attack on Bulge from the north in January 1945. Shifted back to Aachen area in February and supported Roer River crossing. On 24 March, with one DD-equipped company of 736th Tank Battalion attached, crossed the Rhine near Spellen. Raced across Germany, entering Magdeburg (the last major city on autobahn to Berlin) on 16 April 1945. Ended war there.[16]

## 744TH LIGHT TANK BATTALION

Activated on 27 April 1942 at Camp Bowie, Texas, under command of Maj. Richard J. Hunt. Arrived in England 9 January 1944. Debarked at Utah Beach on 29 June 1944. First combat on 26 July near St. Germain in support of 2d Infantry Division. After breakout, attached to 28th Infantry Division for drive to the Seine. On 19 September 1944, moved to Netherlands where it supported 113th Cavalry Group and Belgian Brigade for two months. Moved to Frelenberg, Germany, in November 1944 and joined attacks on fortifications near Suggerath, after which entered Corps reserve. Crossed the Roer with 30th Infantry Division on 24 February 1945, fighting through Hambach Forest. Crossed Rhine on 23 March and fought in Ruhr area with 75th Infantry Division. Took up occupation in Olpe.[17]

## 745TH TANK BATTALION

Activated on 15 August 1942 at Camp Bowie, Texas, under command of Maj. Thomas B. Burns. Formed part of the assault echelon at Omaha Beach on D day, landing its first company on 6 June 1944 in support of 29th Infantry Division. Fought in St. Lô breakout and envelopment of Falaise Pocket. Raced east in wake of 3d Armored Division. Supported 1st Infantry Division near and in Aachen in September 1944 and attack toward Roer River beginning 16 November. Ordered south with 1st Infantry Division on 16 December to help stop Ardennes offensive, continued to support division against Bulge and Siegfried Line through February 1945. Participated in assault across Ruhr River on 25 February. Reached Rhine at Bonn on 11 March. Crossed Rhine into Remagen bridgehead. Took part in Ruhr Pocket envelopment in April. Crossed Weser River and advanced into Harz Mountains and then to the Czechoslovakian border, where further movement eastward was halted on 7 May 1945.[18]

## 746TH TANK BATTALION

Activated on 20 August 1942 at Camp Rucker, Alabama, under command of Maj. Loveaire A. Hedges. Shipped to England January 1944. Formed part of the assault echelon at Utah Beach on D day, landing on 6 June 1944 in support of 82d Airborne Division and 4th Infantry Division. Participated in capture of Cherbourg and the defense of Carentan. Supported 9th Infantry Division breakthrough near Villedieu les Poeles in August 1944 and race across France to the Belgian border. Fought in Hürtgen Forest September and October. Transferred to Belgium and supported attack toward Roer River in November. Attacked again toward Roer River in January 1945. Advanced to Rhine in March, crossing Remagen bridge (first separate tank battalion to cross the river). Advanced to Ruhr Pocket in April 1945. Shifted east to Harz Mountains, ending war along Mulde River.[19]

## 747TH TANK BATTALION

Activated on 10 November 1942 at Camp Bowie, Texas, under command of Maj. Sidney G. Brown Jr. Shipped to England February 1944. Landed at Omaha Beach on 7 June 1944 and joined 29th Infantry Division. Aided in closing Falaise Pocket in August. Attacked toward Brussels and then Bastogne in September, entering Germany near Sevenig. Supported 29th Infantry Division's attack toward Roer River in November. Mopped up, fired across river December 1944 and January 1945. Supported assault across the Roer on 23 February. In March, trained to operate LVTs. On 24 March, battalion LVTs attached to 30th Infantry Division participated in Rhine assault crossing. One company conducted brief operations against Ruhr Pocket in April, after which battalion took on military government duties, ending war in Schnega.[20]

## 748TH TANK BATTALION

Activated on 20 August 1942 at Camp Rucker, Alabama. On 20 April 1943, reorganized as a special battalion equipped with CDL spotlight tanks. Shipped to Wales April 1944 and disembarked at Utah Beach on 24 August. Reorganized as standard tank battalion after 23 October. Moved to front on 20 January 1945 near Buschdorf, Germany, attached to 94th Infantry Division. Fought through West Wall defenses in February. Trained with DD and CDL tanks 1–15 March. Moved to Saarlautern area to support 65th Infantry Division operations against Siegfried Line defenses. Withdrawn again on 20 March to draw DD tanks, attached to 5th Infantry Division near Bad Kreuznach, Germany. Long road marches damaged many DDs, but a few crossed the Rhine on 23 March 1945. CDL tanks deployed to support bridging operations. Turned in all special tanks by mid-April 1945. Advanced with 65th Infantry Division to Danube at Gundelhausen. Entered Regensburg on 27 April. In early May, took Passau and entered Austria, ending war near Linz.[21]

## 749TH TANK BATTALION

Activated on 2 December 1942 at Camp Bowie, Texas, under command of Maj. Donald Donaldson. Debarked at Utah Beach from England on 29 June 1944 and joined 79th Infantry Division. In August, raced across France, passing through Laval to Le Mans; 79th Infantry Division was first American division to cross the Seine. Entered Belgium on 2 September, fighting near Neufchateau and vicinity of the Foret de Parroy. Months of fighting against prepared defenses followed in drive to Saar River near Sarreguemines. Battled German Nordwind offensive in January 1945. On 13 March, attached to 71st Infantry Division for Seventh Army offensive through Siegfried Line to the Rhine. Crossed Rhine on 30 March at Mainz. Crossed the Weisse River on 13 April near Zeitz and went into defensive posture near Limbach until V-E Day.[22]

## 750TH TANK BATTALION

Activated on 1 January 1943 at Fort Knox, Kentucky. Served as tank test unit. On 8 July, newly arrived CO Lt. Col. Sidney T. Telfords unofficially christened battalion the "Seven-five-zero," a name that stuck. Sailed to

England and then to Omaha Beach in September 1944. Attached to the 104th Infantry Division near Aachen, Germany, in October 1944. First real combat on 16 November in operations against Siegfried Line; spent next month pushing toward Roer River. Participated in counterattack against Bulge December 1944 and January 1945. Supported crossing of Roer River on 23 February. Reached Cologne on Rhine River on 5 March. Crossed into Remagen bridgehead and swung north toward Ruhr Pocket in the wake of 3d Armored Division. Crossed Weser River and reached Halle in April. Encountered Russian forces on Mulde River after 21 April 1945.[23]

## 753D TANK BATTALION

Constituted on 16 December 1940, activated on 1 June 1941 at Fort Benning, Georgia, under command of Lt. Col. Robert B. Ennis. Landed in North Africa on 26 May 1943, Sicily on 10 July 1943, Italy on 9 September 1943, and southern France on 15 August 1944. Participated in drive toward Germany. In December, supported both the 3d and 36th Infantry divisions in fierce fighting in the Selestat-Ribeauville-Kaysersberg area, then moved with the 36th into the Strasbourg area. Fought against German Nordwind offensive in January 1945. On 15 March, jumped off in support of 36th's attack through Siegfried Line toward Rhine River. Crossed Rhine under Corps control in April, attached to 63d Infantry Division for limited pursuit of enemy and cleaning up bypassed strongpoints, including Heilbronn. Located in Kufstein, Austria, when cease-fire orders received on 7 May 1945.[24]

## 756TH TANK BATTALION

Activated (originally as light tank battalion) on 1 June 1941 at Fort Lewis, Washington. Landed in North Africa on 24 January 1943, Italy on 17 September 1943, and southern France on 15 August 1944. Companies A and B equipped with DD tanks for landing near St. Tropez. Drove to Belfort Gap with 3d Infantry Division. Fought in Vosges Mountains, entered Strasbourg on 26 November 1944. Fought in Colmar Pocket January and February 1945. Supported 3d Infantry Division in late March through Siegfried Line and across Rhine near Worms, crossing on 26 March. Company C supported crossing with DD tanks. Participated in assault on Nürnberg 17–20 April. Attacked south through Augsburg and Munich, formed part of the spearhead that seized Berchtesgaden and Salzburg in early May 1945.[25]

## 759TH LIGHT TANK BATTALION

Activated on 1 June 1941 at Fort Knox, Kentucky, under command of Lt. Col. Kenneth C. Althaus. Stationed in Iceland for eleven months and finally shipped to the United Kingdom in August 1943. Landed in Normandy on 16 June 1944 and was committed attached to 2d Infantry Division. From 21 August 1944 until end of the war, attached to 4th Cavalry Group. Passed through Chartres and crossed the Seine on 26 August 1944; crossed the Meuse River at Dinant and liberated Celles, Rauersim, Stavelot, and Malmedy. Entered Germany on 13 September. Ordered into the Ardennes in December. Spent early 1945 in defensive positions or out of the line. Reached Rhine River on 5 March at Zons. Captured series of obscure German towns in April, ending month in Aschersleben, where occupation duty began.[26]

## 761ST TANK BATTALION

Activated on 1 April 1942 at Camp Claiborne, Louisiana, as a light tank battalion manned by black enlisted personnel. Major Edward E. Cruise assumed command. First black officers joined in July 1942. Converted to medium tank battalion in September 1943. Arrived in England in September 1944 and France on 10 October. Saw first action on 8 November with Third Army. Entered Germany on 14 December. Participated in American counteroffensive after the Battle of the Bulge from 31 December 1944 to 2 February 1945. In March served as spearhead of 103d Infantry Division in penetrating Siegfried Line. Among first American units to link with Soviet forces, doing so on 5 May 1945 in Steyr, Austria.[27]

## 771ST TANK BATTALION

Activated on 10 September 1943 at Camp Bowie, Texas, as part of reorganization of 4th Armored Division. Lieutenant Colonel Jack C. Childers assumed command. Probably landed in France in October 1944. Saw first combat attached to 102d Infantry Division on 21 November. Fought along Roer River until 21 December, when sent to Ardennes with 84th Infantry Division. Joined breakthrough from Metzerath, Germany, in February 1945. Reached Rhine at Homburg on 4 March. On 19 March, attached to 17th Airborne Division, with which battalion was to link after paratroopers landed as part of Rhine River assault. Crossed river night of 25 March, linked up, attacked eastward. Reached Hanover on 10 April. Reached vicinity of Elbe River by mid-month. Took up occupation duties in the vicinity of Salzwedel, Germany, on 4 May 1945.[28]

## 772D TANK BATTALION

Activated on 20 September 1943 at Pine Camp, New York, under temporary command of Maj. L. L. Willard. Disembarked at Le Havre, France, on 8 February 1945. Crossed Rhine on 27 March and saw first real combat at Mannheim. Marched along Main River to Werbachhausen and across the Danube to Ulm in April. Operating in area of Imst, Austria, when hostilities in sector ended on 5 May 1945.[29]

## 774TH TANK BATTALION

"Blackcat" battalion activated on 20 September 1943 at Fort Benning, Georgia, from 1st Battalion, 31st Armored Regiment, 7th Armored Division, under command of Lt. Col. N. K. Markle Jr. Arrived in Scotland on 12 July 1944; disembarked at Utah Beach on 24 August. Helped 83d Infantry Division protect Patton's right in September. Entered Luxembourg in October, then participated in operations along Moselle River. Moved to Hürtgen Forest in December 1944 to support the 83d Infantry Division's drive toward Roer River. Supported 83d Infantry Division operations against north flank of the Bulge in January 1945 and the 78th Infantry Division capture of the Roer River dams. Crossed Rhine via the Remagen bridge in March, then attacked Ruhr Pocket in April. Raced 280 miles southeastward to join 101st Airborne Division in drive toward mythical Nazi National Redoubt in Alps near Berchtesgaden. Ended war near Kempfenhausen, Germany.[30]

## 777TH TANK BATTALION

Activated on 20 September 1943 at Fort Gordon, Georgia, from 1st Battalion, 3d Armored Regiment, 10th Armored Division. Arrived in England on 27 December 1944; disembarked at Le Havre, France, on 6 February 1945. Took part in Operation Damnation in April attached to 69th Infantry Division, in turn attached to 9th Armored Division. Crossed Weser River, and Company C entered Colditz on 15 April, liberating five hundred French officers and Stalin's son. Other tanks entered Leipzig on the 18 April. Moved to Thrana in early May 1945.[31]

## 778TH TANK BATTALION

Activated on 20 September 1943 at Camp Barkeley, Texas, under command of Lt. Col. Frank J. Spettel. Shipped to France in September 1944. Joined battle around Metz attached to 95th Infantry Division on 15 November, including fighting in Maizières-les-Metz. Supported 95th Infantry Division's attack across Saar River in December and helped clear Saarlautern; held defensive positions in this area into February 1945. Beginning 6 February, most of battalion attached to 94th Infantry Division to support its operations against the Siegfried Switch line of fortifications. Crossed Rhine with 26th Infantry Division on 25 March. Supported the division's advance across Germany behind 11th Armored Division in April in direction of Linz, Austria. Advanced toward Prague until 7 May 1945.[32]

## 781ST TANK BATTALION

Activated (originally as light tank battalion) on 2 January 1943 at Fort Knox, Kentucky, under command of Lt. Col. Harry L. Kinne Jr. Arrived at Marseille in October 1944. Entered combat in Alsace on 7 December attached to 100th Infantry Division, which was attacking toward Maginot Line stronghold of Bitche. From December 1944 to January 1945, battalion supported five different infantry divisions, entering Germany attached to 79th. Battled Nordwind offensive in January. Supported 100th Infantry Division attack that finally captured Bitche in March, then drove to Rhine near Mannheim. Crossed the river on 31 March and seized Heilbronn in April. Crossed Neckar River and swung toward Munich. Most of battalion entered Austria near Innsbruck in May, while Company C entered Brenner Pass with 103d Infantry Division.[33]

## 782D TANK BATTALION

Activated (originally as light tank battalion) on 1 February 1943 at Camp Cambell, Kentucky. Converted to standard tank battalion on 16 October. Shipped to France in January 1945, arriving at Le Havre. Moved into Germany at Aachen on 8 April. Attached to 97th Infantry Division on 23 April and saw first real action on 30 April at Wittichsthal. Entered Czechoslovakia on 4 May 1945 and ceased operations in vicinity of Sluzetin on 7 May.[34]

## 784TH TANK BATTALION

Activated (originally as light tank battalion) on 1 April 1943 at Camp Claiborne, Louisiana, under command of Maj. George C. Dalia. One of three separate tank battalions with black enlisted personnel and mostly white officers. Reorganized as regular tank battalion on 15 September. Shipped to England in November 1944 and landed on Continent 25 December. Committed on 30 December attached to 104th Infantry Division near Eschweiler, Germany. Reattached to 35th Infantry Division on 4 February 1945 and crossed Roer River on 26 February. Formed part of Task Force Byrnes, which linked up with Canadian forces in Venlo, Netherlands, in early March. Crossed Rhine on 26 March and fought in Ruhr Pocket. By 15 April, was helping to clear woods west of Elbe River. Took on occupation duties in vicinity of Immensen on 27 April.[35]

## 786TH TANK BATTALION

Activated on 20 September 1943 at Camp Chaffee, Arkansas, out of 1st Battalion, 47th Armored Regiment, 14th Armored Division. Major Charles F. Ryan assumed command. Shipped to United Kingdom, arriving December 1944, and landed at Le Havre, France, on 22 January 1945. Attached to 99th Infantry Division in February and moved to front near Weisweiler, Germany. Supported division's attack to Rhine near Düsseldorf in early March. Crossed Rhine at Remagen on 10 March. Advanced to Weid River, then conducted fast-moving operations along the Frankfurt-Düsseldorf autobahn. Conducted mop-up operations in Ruhr Pocket in April. On 17 April, transferred with 99th Infantry Division to Third Army and advanced to Bamberg. Ceased combat operations on 1 May 1945 near Landshut.[36]

## 787TH TANK BATTALION

Activated on 10 September 1943 at Camp Chaffee, Arkansas, out of 3d Battalion, 16th Armored Regiment, 16th Armored Division. Major David L. Hollingsworth assumed command. Shipped to France, arriving in March 1945. Due to collision off Bermuda, ship carrying the battalion's equipment did not arrive until April 1945, by which time battalion had moved to Wurzburg, Germany. Between 3 and 6 May, conducted road march to join 86th Infantry Division near Erding. Entered Austria on 6 May 1945. Experienced no contact with the enemy.[37]

# Appendix B

# INDEPENDENT TANK BATTALION/ ARMORED GROUP ATTACHMENTS TO INFANTRY AND AIRBORNE DIVISIONS, ETO

## 1ST INFANTRY DIVISION

745th Tank Battalion, 6 June 44 to 8 May 45
747th Tank Battalion, 7–13 June 44
741st Tank Battalion, 7–15 June 44
743d Tank Battalion, 11–13 June 44
3d Armored Group (–747th Tank Battalion), 1–15 June 44

## 2D INFANTRY DIVISION

Company B, 747th Tank Battalion, 8–15 June 44
Company D, 747th Tank Battalion, 11–15 June 44
741st Tank Battalion, 15 June to 17 Aug. 44
759th Tank Battalion (Light), 18–28 June 44
HQ, 3d Armored Group, 17–29 July 44
744th Tank Battalion (Light), 18–29 July 44
759th Tank Battalion (Light), 27 July to 5 Aug. 44
Company D, 709th Tank Battalion, 22 Aug. to 21 Sept. 44
741st Tank Battalion, 8 Oct. 44 to 8 May 45

## 3D INFANTRY DIVISION

756th Tank Battalion, 13 July 44 to 1 July 45

## 4TH INFANTRY DIVISION

Task Force Barber (6th Armored Group), 9–12 June 44
70th Tank Battalion (–Company C), 9–13 June 44
70th Tank Battalion (–1 platoon), 13–16 June 44
70th Tank Battalion, 18 June to 16 July 44
70th Tank Battalion, 10 July 44 to 10 Mar. 45
759th Tank Battalion (Light), 11–21 Aug. 44
747th Tank Battalion, 28 Aug. to 15 Sept. 44
Task Force Rhino (incl. 70th Tank Battalion), 7–10 Mar. 45
70th Tank Battalion, 20–21 Mar. 45
70th Tank Battalion, 27 Mar. to 9 May 45
Company C, 772d Tank Battalion, 9–18 Apr. 45

## 5TH INFANTRY DIVISION

735th Tank Battalion, 13 July to 20 Oct. 44
735th Tank Battalion, 1 Nov. to 20 Dec. 44
737th Tank Battalion, 23 Dec. 44 to 11 June 45
748th Tank Battalion, 22–23 Mar. 45

## 8TH INFANTRY DIVISION

709th Tank Battalion, 13 July 44 to 26 Jan. 45
740th Tank Battalion, 6 Feb. to 13 Mar. 45
740th Tank Battalion, 6 Apr. to 12 May 45

## 9TH INFANTRY DIVISION

746th Tank Battalion (–Company A), 13–28 June 44
HQ, 6th Armored Group, 15–16 June 44
746th Tank Battalion, 28 June 44 to 10 July 45
Company C, 745th Tank Battalion, 17–18 Aug. 44

## 17TH AIRBORNE DIVISION

Company C, 707th Tank Battalion, 1–13 Jan. 45
761st Tank Battalion, 15–27 Jan. 45

771st Tank Battalion, 19 Mar. to Apr. 45
784th Tank Battalion (–), 10 Apr. 45


## 26TH INFANTRY DIVISION

761st Tank Battalion, 29 Oct. to 12 Dec. 44
735th Tank Battalion, 21 Dec. 44 to 25 Jan. 45
778th Tank Battalion, 29 Jan. to 16 Feb. 45
Company C, 778th Tank Battalion, 16 Feb. to 8 Mar. 45
Company B, 778th Tank Battalion, 11–18 Mar. 45
778th Tank Battalion, 19 Mar. to 20 July 45


## 28TH INFANTRY DIVISION

744th Tank Battalion (Light), 30 July to 27 Aug. 44
747th Tank Battalion, 15–26 Sept. 44
707th Tank Battalion, 6 Oct. 44 to 8 Jan. 45
2 platoons Company B, 709th Tank Battalion, 1–3 Feb. 45
777th Tank Battalion, 28 Feb. to 26 Mar. 45


## 29TH INFANTRY DIVISION

743d Tank Battalion, 17 May to 14 June 44
747th Tank Battalion, 17 May to 17 Aug. 44
Company A, 709th Tank Battalion, 23 Aug. to 21 Sept. 44
747th Tank Battalion, 28 Sept. 44 to 8 Mar. 45
744th Tank Battalion (Light) (–Company A), 30 Sept. to 3 Nov. 44
1 platoon, HQ, 739th MX Tank Battalion, 9–26 Feb. 45
747th Tank Battalion, 29 Mar. to 23 July 45


## 30TH INFANTRY DIVISION

743d Tank Battalion, 14–23 June 45
7th Armored Group, 20 Nov. to 17 Dec. 44
740th Tank Battalion, 19–28 Dec. 44
744th Tank Battalion (Light), 7–28 Feb. 45
744th Tank Battalion (Light), 9–30 Mar. 45
Company C, 736th Tank Battalion, 11–27 Mar. 45

## 35TH INFANTRY DIVISION

737th Tank Battalion, 9 July to 28 Aug. 44
737th Tank Battalion, 11 Sept. to 22 Nov. 44
737th Tank Battalion, 27 Nov. to 22 Dec. 44
Company C, 735th Tank Battalion, 3–12 Jan. 45
784th Tank Battalion, 3–28 Feb. 45
784th Tank Battalion (–Company A), 10 Mar. to 10 Apr. 45
Company A, 784th Tank Battalion, 25–26 Mar. 45
Companies B and C, 784th Tank Battalion, 12 Apr. to 9 May 45

## 36TH INFANTRY DIVISION

191st Tank Battalion, 26–31 Aug. 44
753d Tank Battalion, 15 Aug. to 26 Dec. 44
753d Tank Battalion, 4–29 Mar. 45
753d Tank Battalion, 29 Apr. to 13 June 45

## 42D INFANTRY DIVISION

191st Tank Battalion, 17 Feb. to 4 Mar. 45
749th Tank Battalion, 26–28 Mar. 45

## 44TH INFANTRY DIVISION

749th Tank Battalion, 23 Oct. 44 to 15 Feb. 45
772d Tank Battalion, 26 Mar. to 9 May 45

## 45TH INFANTRY DIVISION

191st Tank Battalion, 15 Aug. to 28 Nov. 44
191st Tank Battalion (–Company A and 3d Platoon, Company D), 29 Nov.
    to 21 Dec. 44
191st Tank Battalion, 22–27 Dec. 44
191st Tank Battalion (–Company B), 28–31 Dec. 44
191st Tank Battalion, 1 Jan. to 16 Feb. 45
191st Tank Battalion, 4 Mar. to 9 May 45

## 63D INFANTRY DIVISION

Company A, 749th Tank Battalion, 2–4 Mar. 45
70th Tank Battalion, 12–18 Mar. 45
740th Tank Battalion, 17–28 Mar. 45
753d Tank Battalion, 31 Mar. to 28 May 45

## 65TH INFANTRY DIVISION

Company C, 778th Tank Battalion, 7–11 Mar. 45
Company C, 748th Tank Battalion, 13–21 Mar. 45
749th Tank Battalion, 29 Mar. to 6 Apr. 45
707th Tank Battalion, 6 Apr. 45
748th Tank Battalion, 7 Apr. to 9 May 45

## 69TH INFANTRY DIVISION

Company A, 777th Tank Battalion, 6–8 Mar. 45
777th Tank Battalion, 29 Mar. to 15 June 45

## 70TH INFANTRY DIVISION

Company C, 753d Tank Battalion, 28 Dec. 44 to 2 Jan. 45
Company B, 191st Tank Battalion, 29 Dec. 44 to 1 Jan. 45
Company A, 753d Tank Battalion, 29 Dec. 44 to 2 Jan. 45
781st Tank Battalion (-companies A and D), 3–16 Jan. 45
749th Tank Battalion (-Company A), 16 Feb. to 15 Mar. 45
740th Tank Battalion, 15–16 Mar. 45
772d Tank Battalion, 22–24 Mar. 45

## 71ST INFANTRY DIVISION

749th Tank Battalion, 15–23 Mar. 45
761st Tank Battalion, 28 Mar. to 10 May 45

## 75TH INFANTRY DIVISION

750th Tank Battalion, 22 Dec. 44 to 26 Jan. 45
709th Tank Battalion, 31 Jan. to 11 Feb. 45

701st Tank Battalion, 18 Mar. to 2 Apr. 45
744th Tank Battalion (Light), 30 Mar. to 17 Apr. 45
Company B, 747th Tank Battalion, 3–7 Apr. 45
717th Tank Battalion, 17–18 Apr. 45
744th Tank Battalion (Light), 18 Apr. to 4 June 45

## 76TH INFANTRY DIVISION

3 tanks, Company C, 737th Tank Battalion, 11–13 Feb. 45
702d Tank Battalion (–Company C), 26 Feb. to 11 Mar. 45
17th Armored Group, 3–9 Mar. 45
Company C, 735th Tank Battalion, 28 Mar. to 2 Apr. 45
707th Tank Battalion, 2–4 Apr. 45
749th Tank Battalion, 4–9 Apr. 45

## 78TH INFANTRY DIVISION

709th Tank Battalion (–), 10 Dec. 44 to 25 Jan. 45
Mortar Platoon, HQ Company, 736th Tank Battalion, 11–21 Jan. 45
Assault Gun Platoon, HQ Company, 736th Tank Battalion, 11–21 Jan. 45
736th Tank Battalion (–), 25 Jan. to 1 Feb. 45
Mortar Platoon, HQ Company, 736th Tank Battalion, 25 Jan. to 3 Feb. 45
Company D, 736th Tank Battalion, 25 Jan. to 3 Feb. 45
Company A, 739th MX Tank Battalion, 27 Jan. to 6 Feb. 45
Company B, 774th Tank Battalion, 3–8 Feb. 45
774th Tank Battalion (–Company B), 3–24 Feb. 45
1 platoon, Company A, 738th MX Tank Battalion, 6–28 Feb. 45
Company B, 774th Tank Battalion, 13 Feb. to 24 Apr. 45

## 79TH INFANTRY DIVISION

749th Tank Battalion, 1–24 July 44
Company B, 749th Tank Battalion, 31 July to 1 Aug. 44
191st Tank Battalion, 1–22 Dec. 44
781st Tank Battalion, 22 Dec. 44 to 3 Jan. 45
761st Tank Battalion, 20 Feb. to 1 Mar. 45
717th Tank Battalion, 8 Mar. to 17 Apr. 45
744th Tank Battalion (Light), 17–18 Apr. 45
717th Tank Battalion, 18 Apr. to 20 May 45

## 80TH INFANTRY DIVISION

702d Tank Battalion (–Company D), 8 Aug. 44 to 27 Feb. 45
Company D, 702d Tank Battalion, 8 Aug. 44 to 1 Mar. 45
702d Tank Battalion, 11 Mar. to 7 July 45

## 82D AIRBORNE DIVISION

Company C, 746th Tank Battalion, 4–10 June 44
Company A, 746th Tank Battalion, 13–16 June 44
740th Tank Battalion, 30 Dec. 44 to 11 Jan. 45
740th Tank Battalion, 27 Jan. to 7 Feb. 45
Company B, 774th Tank Battalion, 9–19 Feb. 45
Company A, 740th Tank Battalion, 30 Apr. to 1 May 45
Company C, 740th Tank Battalion, 30 Apr. to 1 May 45

## 83D INFANTRY DIVISION

746th Tank Battalion, 5–16 July 44
70th Tank Battalion, 17–18 July 44
Company C, 749th Tank Battalion, 20–29 July 44
Company A, 709th Tank Battalion, 1–16 Aug. 44
Company C, 709th Tank Battalion, 12–16 Aug. 44
Assault Gun Platoon, 709th Tank Battalion, 13–16 Aug. 44
774th Tank Battalion, 28 Aug. 44 to 3 Feb. 45
736th Tank Battalion, 6 Feb. to 29 July 45

## 84TH INFANTRY DIVISION

Company A, 771st Tank Battalion, 19 Nov. to 20 Dec. 44
701st Tank Battalion, 10–20 Dec. 44
771st Tank Battalion, 20 Dec. 44 to 22 Mar. 45
771st Tank Battalion, 2 Apr. to 30 June 45

## 86TH INFANTRY DIVISION

Companies A and B, 740th Tank Battalion, 8–18 Apr. 45
787th Tank Battalion, 2–10 May 45

## 87TH INFANTRY DIVISION

761st Tank Battalion, 20–23 Dec. 44
761st Tank Battalion, 1–15 Jan. 45
761st Tank Battalion, 26 Jan. to 1 Feb. 45
735th Tank Battalion, 1 Feb. to 9 Mar. 45
Assault Gun Platoon, HQ Company, 735th Tank Battalion, 13 Mar. to
   9 May 45
735th Tank Battalion, 15 Mar. to 9 May 45

## 89TH INFANTRY DIVISION

748th Tank Battalion, 25 Mar. to 6 Apr. 45
707th Tank Battalion, 6–31 Apr. 45

## 90TH INFANTRY DIVISION

746th Tank Battalion, 11–12 June 44
712th Tank Battalion, 28 June 44 to 9 May 45?

## 94TH INFANTRY DIVISION

Company A, 748th Tank Battalion, 16–25 Jan. 45
Companies C and D, 748th Tank Battalion, 25–29 Jan. 45
Company B, 748th Tank Battalion, 29 Jan. to 21 Feb. 45
778th Tank Battalion (–Company C), 16 Feb. to 19 Mar. 45
778th Tank Battalion (–Company C), 23–24 Mar. 45

## 95TH INFANTRY DIVISION

735th Tank Battalion, 20 Oct. to 29 Nov. 44
778th Tank Battalion, 11 Nov. 44 to 28 Jan. 45
761st Tank Battalion, 2–13 Feb. 45
709th Tank Battalion, 16 Feb. to 21 Apr. 45
10th Armored Group, 7–13 Apr. 45

## 97TH INFANTRY DIVISION

782d Tank Battalion, 20 Apr. to 9 May 45

## 99TH INFANTRY DIVISION

2d Platoon, Company C, 741st Tank Battalion, 15–16 Dec. 44
Companies C and D, 741st Tank Battalion, 16–18 Dec. 44
Company A, 741st Tank Battalion, 10–28 Jan. 45
750th Tank Battalion, 28 Jan. to 5 Feb. 45
786th Tank Battalion, 23 Feb. to 9 May 45

## 100TH INFANTRY DIVISION

Company A and 1 platoon Company D, 753d Tank Battalion, 7–26
    Nov. 44
781st Tank Battalion, 7–21 Dec. 44
Company B, 749th Tank Battalion, 8–18 Jan. 45
781st Tank Battalion, 23 Feb. to 23 Apr. 45

## 101ST AIRBORNE DIVISION

Company D, 70th Tank Battalion, 6–16 June 44
759th Tank Battalion (Light), 28 June 44 to 8 July 44
Company A and 1st Platoon, Company D, 781st Tank Battalion, 26–28
    Jan. 45
Company A and 3d Platoon, Company D, 781st Tank Battalion, 6–7
    Feb. 45
774th Tank Battalion, 5–9 May 45

## 102D INFANTRY DIVISION

771st Tank Battalion, 4 Nov. to 20 Dec. 44
744th Tank Battalion (Light), 20–? Dec. 44
701st Tank Battalion, 19 Dec. 44 to 17 Mar. 45
Company C, 739th MX Tank Battalion, 20–27 Jan. 45
Company A, 739th MX Tank Battalion, 21–27 Jan. 45
701st Tank Battalion (–Company D), 4 Apr. to 2 July 45

## 103D INFANTRY DIVISION

Company B, 756th Tank Battalion, 15 Nov. 44 to 3 Feb. 45
781st Tank Battalion (–Company A and 2d Platoon, Company D), 17 Jan.
   to 5 Feb. 45
Company A, 191st Tank Battalion, 25 Jan. to 5 Feb. 45
Company C, 781st Tank Battalion, 7–22 Feb. 45
Assault Gun Platoon, HQ Company, 781st Tank Battalion, 17–22 Feb. 45
756th Tank Battalion, 22 Feb. to 31 Mar. 45
761st Tank Battalion, 10–28 Mar. 45
781st Tank Battalion, 23 Apr. to 5 May 45

## 104TH INFANTRY DIVISION

750th Tank Battalion, 16 Nov. to 23 Dec. 44
784th Tank Battalion, 31 Dec. 44 to 3 Feb. 45
750th Tank Battalion, 6 Feb. to 22 May 45

## 106TH INFANTRY DIVISION

Company C (–1 platoon), 740th Tank Battalion, 11–19 Jan. 45

**Note:** Armored attachments other than independent tank battalions are not listed here. American infantry and airborne divisions also received as attachments elements from American armored divisions and armored cavalry units, as well as the occasional British tank unit.

**Sources**
All except as noted below: Center of Military History Online, http://www.army.mil/cmh–pg/documents.

90th Infantry Division: 90th Infantry Division of the Texas Military Historical Society, http://www.cris.Companym/ ~Patriot2/90th/; History of the 712th Tank Battalion, 1 September 1944; AAR, 746th Tank Battalion; AAR, 6th Armored Group.

83d Infantry Division: Kevin Harris, *The Story of the 83d Division,* http://users.1st.net/bharris/83html/attached_and_supporting_units.htm.

Additions and corrections to entries for the 4th and 28th Infantry divisions are based on the AARs of the 747th Tank Battalion.

Additions and corrections to entries for the 102d Infantry Division are based on the AARs of the 701st Tank Battalion.

Addition to the 17th Airborne Division based on the records of the 707th, 771st, and 784th Tank Battalion.

## Appendix C

# INDEPENDENT TANK BATTALIONS BY CAMPAIGN

### NORMANDY (6 JUNE TO 24 JULY 1944)

70th, 709th, 712th, 735th, 736th, 737th, 741st, 743d, 744th (Light), 745th, 746th, 747th, 749th, 759th (Light), 774th

### NORTHERN FRANCE (25 JULY TO 14 SEPTEMBER 1944)

70th, 701st, 702d, 707th, 709th, 712th, 735th, 736th, 737th, 741st, 743d, 744th (Light), 745th, 746th, 747th, 748th, 749th, 759th (Light), 761st, 774th, 778th

### SOUTHERN FRANCE (15 AUGUST TO 14 SEPTEMBER 1944)

191st, 753d, 756th (Light)

### RHINELAND (15 SEPTEMBER 1944 TO 21 MARCH 1945)

70th, 191st, 701st, 702d, 707th, 709th, 712th, 717th, 735th, 736th, 737th, 738th, 739th, 740th, 741st, 743d, 744th (Light), 745th, 746th, 747th, 748th, 749th, 750th, 753d, 756th (Light), 759th (Light), 761st, 771st, 772d, 774th, 777th, 778th, 781st, 784th, 786th

### ARDENNES-ALSACE (16 DECEMBER 1944 TO 25 JANUARY 1945)

70th, 191st, 702d, 707th, 709th, 712th, 735th, 736th, 737th, 738th, 739th, 740th, 741st, 743d, 744th (Light), 745th, 746th, 748th, 749th, 750th, 753d, 756th (Light), 759th (Light), 761st, 771st, 774th, 778th, 781st

## CENTRAL EUROPE (22 MARCH TO 11 MAY 1945)

70th, 191st, 701st, 702d, 707th, 709th, 712th, 717th, 735th, 736th, 737th, 738th, 739th, 740th, 741st, 743d, 744th (Light), 745th, 746th, 747th, 748th, 749th, 750th, 753d, 756th (Light), 759th (Light), 761st, 771st, 772d, 774th, 777th, 778th, 781st, 782d, 784th, 786th, 787th

Source: Sawicki.

# GLOSSARY

| | |
|---|---|
| AAR | After-action report |
| AP | Armor-piercing |
| AWOL | Absent without leave |
| CDL | Canal Defense Light, code for spotlight tanks |
| CG | Commanding General |
| CO | Commanding officer |
| DD | Duplex Drive amphibious Sherman tank |
| HE | High-explosive |
| HEAT | High-explosive antitank |
| HVAP | High-velocity armor-piercing |
| ICT | Infantry (regimental) Combat Team |
| KIA | Killed in action |
| KO | Knock out, destroy |
| LCT | Landing craft, tank |
| LD | Line of departure |
| LVT | Landing vehicle, tracked (or "Water Buffalo") |
| MG | Machine gun |
| MIA | Missing in action |
| MLR | Main line of resistance |
| MX | Mine Exploder |
| NBC | Non-battle casualty |
| NCO | Noncommissioned officer |
| OP | Observation post |
| Peep | Jeep, ¼-ton truck |
| PW or POW | Prisoner of war |
| S-2 | Intelligence staff |
| S-3 | Operations staff |
| SHAEF | Supreme Headquarters Allied Expeditionary Force |
| SNAFU | Situation normal, all fucked up |
| SP | Self-propelled |
| SWA | Seriously wounded in action |

| | |
|---|---|
| RCT | Regimental Combat Team |
| TAC | Tactical air command |
| TD | Tank destroyer |
| TF | Task Force |
| WIA | Wounded in action |

# BIBLIOGRAPHY

Allen, Col. Robert S. *Patton's Third Army: Lucky Forward.* New York: Manor Books Inc., 1965.

Ambrose, Stephen E. *Citizen Soldiers.* New York: Touchstone, 1997.

Anders, Dr. Steven E. "POL on the Red Ball Express." Quartermaster Professional Bulletin, Spring 1989. Quartermaster Museum online, http://www.qmfound.com/pol_on_the_red_ball_express.htm.

Anderson, Christopher J. *Hell on Wheels: The Men of the U.S. Armored Forces, 1918 to the Present.* London: Greenhill Books, 1999.

Anderson, Rich. "The United States Army in World War II." Military History online, http://www.militaryhistoryonline.com/wwii/usarmy, 2000.

Anderson, Trezzvant W. *Come Out Fighting: The Epic Tale of the 761st Tank Battalion, 1942–1945.* Salzburg, Austria: Salzburger Druckerei und Verlag, 1945.

*Armored Group, The.* The General Board, United States Forces, European Theater, 14 May 1946.

*Armored Special Equipment.* The General Board, United States Forces, European Theater, 14 May 1945.

Astor, Gerald. *A Blood-Dimmed Tide: The Battle of the Bulge by the Men Who Fought It.* New York: Dell, 1992.

Blanchard, W. J. Jr. "Home page of the 746th Tank Battalion." Battalion History, http://home.hiwaay.net/~blan/.

Blumenson, Martin. *United States Army in World War II, The European Theater of Operations: Breakout and Pursuit.* Washington, D.C.: Office of the Chief of Military History, Department of the Army, 1961.

Bradley, Omar N., and Clay Blair. *A General's Life.* New York: Simon & Schuster, 1983.

Chamberlain, Peter, and Chris Ellis. *Churchill and Sherman Specials.* Windsor, England: Profile Publications Ltd., n.d.

———. *Pictorial History of Tanks of the World 1915–45.* Harrisburg, Pa.: Stackpole Books, 1972.

Cole, Hugh M. *United States Army in World War II, The European Theater of Operations: The Lorraine Campaign.* Washington, D.C.: Historical Division, Department of the Army, 1950.

Cooper, Belton Y. *Death Traps: The Survival of an American Armored Division in World War II.* Novato, Ca: Presidio Press, Inc., 2000.

Elson, Aaron C. *Tanks for the Memories: An Oral History of the 712th Tank Battalion from World War II.* Hackensack, N.J.: Chi Chi Press, 1994.

Folkestad, William. *The View from the Turret.* Shippensburg, PA: Burd Street Press, 2000.

Green, Michael. *M4 Sherman: Combat and Development History of the Sherman Tank and All Sherman Variants.* Osceola, Wis.: Motorbooks International Publishers and Wholesalers, 1993.

Greenfield, Kent Roberts; Robert R. Palmer; and Bell I. Wiley. *United States Army in World War II, The Army Ground Forces: The Organization of Ground Combat Troops.* Washington, D.C.: Historical Division, Department of the Army, 1947.

Griess, Thomas E., ed. *The Second World War: Europe and the Mediterranean.* West Point Military History Series. Wayne, N.J.: Avery Publishing Group, Inc., 1984.

Hassett, Edward C., ed. *701st Tank Battalion.* Nürnberg: Sebaldus-Verlag, 1945.

Heintzleman, Al. *We'll Never Go Over-Seas.* 1982. Self-published.

Hughes, Dale Adams. *331 Days: The Story of the Men of the 709th Tank Battalion.* Tucson: Self-published, 1980.

Jensen, Marvin. *Strike Swiftly: The 70th Tank Battalion from North Africa to Normandy to Germany.* Novato, Ca.: Presidio Press, 1997.

Johnson, David E. *Fast Tanks and Heavy Bombers: Innovation in the U.S. Army 1917–1945.* Ithaca, N.Y.: Cornell University Press, 1998.

Liddell Hart, Sir B. H. *History of the Second World War.* New York: G. P. Putnam's Sons, 1970.

Linderman, Gerald F. *The World Within War.* Cambridge, Mass.: Harvard University Press, 1997.

MacDonald, Charles B. *United States Army in World War II, The European Theater of Operations: The Siegfried Line Campaign.* Washington, D.C.: Office of the Chief of Military History, Department of the Army, 1963.

———. *United States Army In World War II, The European Theater of Operations: The Last Offensive.* Washington, D.C.: Office of the Chief of Military History, United States Army, 1973.

Moore, Col. Roy Jr. *Chariots of Iron: The 735th Tank Battalion (M),*

*World War II, Europe.* Lopez Island, Wash.: Island Graphics and Advertising, 1991.

*Omaha Beachhead (6 June–13 June 1944).* American Forces in Action Series. Washington, D.C.: Center of Military History, 1984. (Online reprint of CMH Pub 100-1, http://www.army.mil/cmh-pg/books/wwii/100-11/100-11.htm.)

*Organization, Equipment, and Tactical Employment of Separate Tank Battalions.* The General Board, United States Forces, European Theater, 14 May 1946.

Reardon, Mark. *Victory at Mortain: Defeating Hitler's Panzer Counteroffensive.* Lawrence, Kans.: University Press, 2002.

Reynolds, Michael. *Steel Inferno: 1st SS Panzer Corps in Normandy.* New York: Dell, 1997.

*Rhineland.* The U.S. Army Campaigns of World War II Series. Washington, D.C.: Center of Military History, n.d. (Online reprint of CMH Pub 72-25, http://www.army.mil/cmh-pg/brochures/rhineland/rhineland.htm.)

Robinson, Wayne. *Move Out, Verify: The Combat Story of the 743d Tank Battalion.* Frankfurt am Main, 1945.

Rubel, Lt. Col. George. *Daredevil Tankers: The Story of the 740th Tank Battalion, United States Army.* Göttingen, Germany, 1945.

Ryan, Cornelius. *The Last Battle.* New York: Simon & Schuster, 1966.

Sawicki, James A. *Tank Battalions of the U.S. Army.* Dumfries, Va.: Wyvern Publications, 1983.

*Southern France.* The U.S. Army Campaigns of World War II Series. Washington, D.C.: Center of Military History, n.d. (Online reprint of CMH Pub 72-31, http://www.army.mil/cmh-pg/brochures/sfrance/sfrance.htm.)

Stanton, Shelby. *World War II Order of Battle.* New York: Galahad Books, 1991.

*Tank Gunnery.* The General Board, United States Forces, European Theater, 14 May 1945.

*Up From Marseille: 781st Tank Battalion.* Camp Cambell, Ky.: The Battalion, 1945.

*Utah Beach to Cherbourg (6 June–27 June 1944).* American Forces in Action Series. Washington, D.C.: Center of Military History, n.d. (Online reprint of CMH Pub 100-12, http://www.army.mil/cmh-pg/BOOKS/WWII/utah/utah.htm.)

Walker, John. "Homepage of the 750th Tank Battalion." (http://members.aol.com/InfDiv104/750Tank.htm.)

Whiting, Charles. *America's Forgotten Army: The True Story of the U.S. Seventh Army in WWII and an Unknown Battle that Changed History.* New York: St. Martin's Paperbacks, 1999.

Wilkes, Homer D. *747th Tank Battalion.* Scottsdale, Ariz.: Self-published, 1977.

————. *APO 230.* Scottsdale, Ariz.: Self-published, 1982.

Wilmot, Chester. *The Struggle for Europe.* Ware, England: Wordsworth Editions Limited, 1997.

Wilson, Joseph E. Jr. "Black Panthers Go to Combat in World War II." The History Net on About.com. (http://www.afroamhistory.about.com/library/prm/blblackpanthers1.htm.)

Wilson, Ulysses Lee. *U.S. Army In World War II: The Employment of Negro Troops.* Washington, D.C.: Office of the Chief of Military History, United States Army, 1966.

Wolfert, Ira. "Sure Surprised Hell Out of the Germans!" *Tulsa Tribune,* 24 July 1944.

Zaloga, Steven J. *The Sherman Tank in U.S. and Allied Service.* London: Osprey Publishing, Ltd., 1982.

# NOTES

## CHAPTER 1: GENERAL McNAIR'S CHILDREN

1 Robinson, 30–31.

2 *Organization, Equipment and Tactical Employment of Separate Tank Battalions,* Appendix 2.

3 Christopher J. Anderson, p.6.

4 Johnson, 141 ff.

5 Ibid., 145.

6 Greenfield, Palmer, and Bell, 56–61, 321–326.

7 Greenfield, Palmer, and Bell, 326–327; Sawicki, 16; *Organization, Equipment and Tactical Employment of Separate Tank Battalions,* 4.

8 *Armored Special Equipment,* 35–38.

9 Jensen, 4–5.

10 Rich Anderson.

11 Ibid.

12 Elson, 5.

13 Sawicki, 14.

14 Rich Anderson.

15 Greenfield, Palmer, and Bell, 328.

16 Stanton, 282.

17 History, 5th Armored Group.

18 *The Armored Group,* 3.

19 Headquarters Armored Force, AG 320.2/58, *Reorganization of GHQ Reserve Tank Battalions, and Enlisted Cadres for Newly Activated Battalions,* 16 March 1942.

20 Blanchard.

21 Robinson, 14.

22 Diary of the 747th Tank Battalion.

23 Wilkes, *747th Tank Battalion,* 6.

24 *Tank Gunnery,* 18.

25 Jensen, 56.

26 Zaloga, 24.

27 Johnson, 122.

28 Zaloga, 19, 26; 2d Armored Division report to General Eisenhower, March 1945.

29 Commander's Narrative, 191st Tank Battalion.

30 AAR, 743d Tank Battalion, May 1945.

31 Zaloga, 20.

32 Moore, 67–68.

33 Green, 35.

34 Cooper, viii.

35 Ambrose, 65.

36 Unit Journal and History, 737th Tank Battalion.

37 AARs, 750th Tank Battalion.

38 2d Armored Division report to General Eisenhower.

39 Folkestad, 33.

40 2d Armored Division report to General Eisenhower.

41 Cooper, 257.

42 AARs, 743d Tank Battalion.

43 Green, 40.

44 S–3 Journal, 3d Armored Group.

45 AAR, November 1944, 756th Tank Battalion.

46 Walker. Unit history, 750th Tank Battalion.

47 AAR, 709th Tank Battalion, Annex 3.

48 AAR, March 1945, Company C, 753d Tank Battalion.

49 Green, 29.

50 Chamberlain and Ellis, *Pictorial History of Tanks of the World 1915–45*, 182.

51 Zaloga, 21.

52 Green, 101.

53 2d Armored Division report to General Eisenhower.

54 2d Armored Division report to General Eisenhower.

55 Rubel, 157.

56 AAR, 741st Tank Battalion.

57 Rubel, 157; AAR, October 1944, 702d Tank Battalion.

58 Green, 93–94, 101.

59 S–3 Journal, 3d Armored Group; S–3 Journal, 70th Tank Battalion; S-4 Reports, 774th Tank Battalion.

60 S–3 Journal, 737th Tank Battalion.

61 S–3 Journal, 741st Tank Battalion.

62 AAR, 743d Tank Battalion.

63 AAR, 3d Armored Group.

64 S-3 Journal, 3d Armored Group.

65 Green, 102.

66 S-3 Journal, 6th Armored Group.

67 S-3 Journal, 3d Armored Group.

68 Johnson, 192–193.

69 AAR, 709th Tank Battalion, Annex 3.

70 *Tank Gunnery,* 25–26.

71 *Tank Gunnery,* 15.

72 *Tank Gunnery,* 26.

73 Rubel, 158.

74 *Tank Gunnery,* 27; *Organization, Equipment, and Tactical Employment of Separate Tank Battalions,* Appendix 3.

75 S-3 Journal, 3d Armored Group.

76 AAR, 10 January 1945, 736th Tank Battalion; AAR, March 1945, 753d Tank Battalion.

77 AAR, 741st Tank Battalion; Moore, 59.

78 AAR, 746th Tank Battalion.

79 *Organization, Equipment, and Tactical Employment of Separate Tank Battalions,* Appendices 2 and 3.

80 Ibid., 4.

81 Chamberlain and Ellis, *Churchill and Sherman Specials;* Memo by Major William Duncan, 743d Tank Battalion: "Results of Training, Tests, and Tactical Operations of DD Tanks at Slapton Sands, Devon, England, During Period 15 March - 30 April 1944," dated 30 April 1944 and contained in the records of the 753d Tank Battalion.

82 Jensen, 125.

83 Wilkes, *747th Tank Battalion,* p. 6 and supplement; Conversation with Mrs. Wilkes, 10 November 2001.

84 Unit History for March 1944, 746th Tank Battalion.

85 Robinson, 16.

86 S-3 Journal, 745th Tank Battalion.

87 AAR, May 1945, 753d Tank Battalion.

88 *Organization, Equipment, and Tactical Employment of Separate Tank Battalions,* 4.

89 Diary of the 747th Tank Battalion.

90 Wilkes, *747th Tank Battalion,* 6.

## CHAPTER 2: DDs AT D DAY

1 S-3 Journal, 743d Tank Battalion.
2 Heintzleman, 26.
3 Jensen, 134.
4 Griess, 295.
5 Ibid.
6 Griess, 296.
7 Ibid.
8 History of the 6th Armored Group; AAR, 70th Tank Battalion.
9 Jensen, 135–140.
10 Ibid., 144.
11 History of the 6th Armored Group; Jensen, 147.
12 AAR, 746th Tank Battalion.
13 Griess, 297.
14 *Omaha Beachhead*, 38.
15 AAR, 3d Armored Group.
16 Interview with Sgt. Maj. Paul Ragan (ret.), 22 December 2001.
17 AAR, 741st Tank Battalion; Heintzleman, A14.
18 Heintzleman, 28.
19 Interview with Paul Ragan.
20 Interview with Paul Ragan; Unit Journal, 741st Tank Battalion.
21 *Omaha Beachhead*, 39.
22 Griess, 297.
23 Robinson, 22.
24 Personal reports, records of the 741st Tank Battalion.
25 Ibid.
26 Ibid.
27 AAR, 741st Tank Battalion.
28 S-3 Journal, 743d Tank Battalion.
29 Robinson, 26–27.
30 *Omaha Beachhead*, 81.
31 Unit Journal, 741st Tank Battalion.
32 S-3 Journal, 743d Tank Battalion.
33 *Omaha Beachhead*, 107–108.
34 AAR, 3d Armored Group.
35 AAR, 745th Tank Battalion.
36 AAR, 747th Tank Battalion.
37 Sawicki, 22.
38 *Omaha Beachhead*, 107–108. *Utah Beach to Cherbourg*, 53 ff.

## CHAPTER 3: THE BOCAGE: A SCHOOL OF VERY HARD KNOCKS

1 Robinson, 52–53.
2 Blumenson, 177.
3 Griess, 307–308.
4 AAR, 746th Tank Battalion; History of the 6th Armored Group.
5 Utah Beach to Cherbourg, 63.
6 S-3 Journal, 743d Tank Battalion.
7 S-3 Journal, 745th Tank Battalion.
8 *Omaha Beachhead*, 93; Robinson, 36–37.
9 Wilkes, *747th Tank Battalion*, 11 ff, supplement.
10 Wilkes, *747th Tank Battalion*, supplement; Wilkes, *APO 230*, 62–63.
11 S-3 Journal, 747th Tank Battalion.
12 AAR, 3d Armored Group.
13 Robinson, 48.
14 AAR, 6th Armored Group.
15 746th Tank Battalion Report, 10 July, 83d Div. G-2, G-3 Journal File, cited by Blumenson, 132.
16 *Tank Gunnery*, 11.
17 Blumenson, 36–39, 178.
18 Blumenson, 175.
19 Unit Journal, 737th Tank Battalion.
20 AAR, 746th Tank Battalion; History of the 6th Armored Group.
21 737th Battalion History, 3–4.
22 Blumenson, 43.
23 S-3 Journal, November 1944, 774th Tank Battalion.
24 Robinson, 40.
25 AAR, 741st Tank Battalion.
26 S-3 Journal, 743d Tank Battalion.
27 Robinson, 56.
28 AAR, August 1944, 741st Tank Battalion.
29 AAR, July 1944, 6th Armored Group.
30 AAR, 6th Armored Group.
31 Linderman, 32–33.
32 Robinson, 34–35, 38.
33 AAR, July 1944, 746th Tank Battalion.
34 Robinson, 34–35, 38.
35 AARs, 741st and 749th Tank battalions.
36 Heintzleman, 39.
37 AAR, January 1945, 736th Tank Battalion.

38 *Organization, Equipment, and Tactical Employment of Separate Tank Battalions,* 6.

39 AAR, 6th Armored Group.

40 Battle Report, 747th Tank Battalion.

41 AAR, 749th Tank Battalion.

42 Wilkes, *747th Tank Battalion,* 27.

43 S-3 Journal, 3d Armored Group.

44 S-3 Journal, 745th Tank Battalion; Blumenson, 43.

45 S-3 Journal, 6th Armored Group.

46 Wilkes, *747th Tank Battalion,* 24–25.

47 Wilkes, *747th Tank Battalion,* 25.

48 Blumenson, 85.

49 Jensen, 156.

50 Wilkes, *747th Tank Battalion,* 32.

51 Undated memorandum, "Method of Operation, 737th Tank Battalion."

52 *Organization, Equipment, and Tactical Employment of Separate Tank Battalions,* 4.

53 1st Division assault maps.

54 Jensen, 144.

55 Ambrose, 34.

56 Wolfert.

57 Blumenson, 205; AAR, 749th Tank Battalion.

58 Wolfert.

59 Jensen, 144.

60 Blumenson, 96.

61 S-3 Journal, 12 July 1944, 741st Tank Battalion.

62 Wilkes, *APO 230,* 75–76.

63 AAR, 749th Tank Battalion.

64 AAR, 741st Tank Battalion.

65 AAR, 743d Tank Battalion.

66 Wolfert.

67 AAR, 3d Armored Group.

68 AAR and S-3 Journal, 747th Tank Battalion.

69 Wilkes, *747th Tank Battalion,* 18.

70 S-3 Journal, 747th Tank Battalion.

71 AAR, 741st Tank Battalion.

72 AAR, 3d Armored Group.

73 Christopher Anderson, 29.

74 Griess, 317.
75 S-3 Journal, 745th Tank Battalion.
76 S-3 Journal, 747th Tank Battalion.
77 AARs, 6th Armored Group and 749th Tank Battalion.

**CHAPTER 4: OPEN-FIELD RUNNING**
1 Blumenson, 181.
2 The following description of Cobra relies heavily on Blumenson, 218–240.
3 Robinson, 64.
4 Blumenson, 240; Griess, 331.
5 Blumenson, 243.
6 Ibid.
7 Jensen, 190–191; AAR, 70th Tank Battalion.
8 Blumenson, 308.
9 Robinson, 66.
10 Blumenson, 244.
11 Ibid., 297–298.
12 Robinson, 70–71.
13 Blumenson, 268.
14 AAR, 741st Tank Battalion.
15 AAR, 749th Tank Battalion.
16 AAR, 6th Armored Group.
17 AAR, S-3 Journal, 741st Tank Battalion.
18 Blumenson, 251–252.
19 AAR, 745th Tank Battalion.
20 Allen, 71–74.
21 AAR, 749th Tank Battalion.
22 Moore, 70.
23 Moore, 72–73.
24 AAR, 747th Tank Battalion.
25 Blumenson, 208.
26 *Organization, Equipment, and Tactical Employment of Separate Tank Battalions*, 8.
27 Both quotes from S-3 Journal, 747th Tank Battalion.
28 S-3 Journal, 746th Tank Battalion.
29 Wilmot, 400.
30 Liddell Hart, 557.
31 Blumenson, 402–409; Hughes, B-2.

32 AAR, 709th Tank Battalion.

33 Griess, 334–335.

34 Reardon.

35 Wilmot, 401; Griess, 335.

36 Reynolds, 260.

37 Wilmot, 401–402.

38 Wilmot, 401–402; Griess, 335.

39 Blumenson, 466.

40 Blumenson, 469, 472.

41 Reardon, *Victory at Mortain,* 112–114.

42 S-3 Journal, 743d Tank Battalion; Folkestad, 58.

43 AAR, 737th Tank Battalion.

44 Reardon, note to the author, 14 June 2001.

45 Reardon, 188.

46 Jensen, 193–195; AAR, 70th Tank Battalion.

47 Allen, 83.

48 Allen, 87.

49 Wilmot, 424.

50 Elson, 66–68.

51 Griess, 338–340.

52 Blumenson, 689.

53 AAR, August 1944, 746th Tank Battalion.

54 AAR, 743d Tank Battalion.

55 AAR, August and September 1944, 743d Tank Battalion.

56 AAR, September 1944, 747th Tank Battalion; Wilkes, 747th Tank Battalion, 33–34.

57 Wilkes, *APO 230,* 115.

58 Griess, 342.

59 Jensen, 205 ff.

60 Heintzleman, 49.

61 S-3 Journal, 741st Tank Battalion.

62 AAR, 70th Tank Battalion; Jensen, 216.

63 Elson, 74–81; AAR, September 1944, 712th Tank Battalion.

64 AAR, 749th Tank Battalion.

65 MacDonald, 386.

66 S-3 Journal, AARs, 743rd Tank Battalion.

67 Allen, 107.

68 AAR, 743d Tank Battalion; Robinson, 86, 89.

69 S-4 Report, 702d Tank Battalion.

70 Anders.
71 AARs, 743d, 745th, and other tank battalions.
72 AARs, 191st and 753d Tank battalions.
73 AARs, 191st, 753d, and 756th Tank battalions.
74 AAR, 753d Tank Battalion.
75 AAR, Company C, 753d Tank Battalion.
76 *Southern France*, 13 ff; Whiting, 49 ff.
77 AAR, 756th Tank Battalion.
78 AAR, 191st Tank Battalion.
79 AAR, 191st Tank Battalion.
80 AAR, 191st Tank Battalion.
81 AAR, 753d Tank Battalion.
82 AAR, 191st Tank Battalion.
83 *Southern France*, 28.
84 AARs and S-3 Journal, 753d Tank Battalion.
85 AAR, 753d Tank Battalion.

## CHAPTER 5: HITTING THE WEST WALL

1 Allen, 115–120.
2 MacDonald, *The Siegfried Line Campaign*, 35.
3 AAR, October 1944, 737th Tank Battalion.
4 MacDonald, *The Siegfried Line Campaign*, 106.
5 Whiting, 100.
6 Wilkes, *747th Tank Battalion*, 35–36.
7 S-3 Journal, 746th Tank Battalion.
8 AAR, 747th Tank Battalion.
9 Wilkes, *747th Tank Battalion*, 44.
10 AAR, 747th Tank Battalion.
11 Wilmot, 478–479. MacDonald, *The Siegfried Line Campaign*, 31 ff.
12 MacDonald, *The Siegfried Line Campaign*, 34–35.
13 Robinson, 97–98.
14 MacDonald, *The Siegfried Line Campaign*, 37 ff.
15 AAR, 746th Tank Battalion.
16 MacDonald, *The Siegfried Line Campaign*, 48.
17 AAR, 747th Tank Battalion.
18 Interview with Al Heintzleman, 8 December 2001; Letter from Thornton's nephew, Mr. Paul McDaniel, 6 June 2001; Interview with Paul McDaniel, 22 December 2001.

19 Wilkes, *747th Tank Battalion*, 37–38.

20 MacDonald, *The Siegfried Line Campaign*, 55 ff.

21 *Armored Special Equipment*, 26–27.

22 Chamberlain and Ellis, *Churchill and Sherman Specials*.

23 Jensen, 225.

24 S-3 Journal, 3d Armored Group.

25 S-3 Journal, 3d Armored Group.

26 AAR, 70th Tank Battalion.

27 S-3 Journal and AAR, 741st Tank Battalion; AAR, 70th Tank Battalion.

28 Jensen, 226.

29 Wilkes, *747th Tank Battalion*, 44, 58.

30 *Armored Special Equipment*, 28.

## CHAPTER SIX: TWO GRIM MONTHS

1 *Rhineland*, 13.

2 AAR, 745th Tank Battalion.

3 MacDonald, *The Siegfried Line Campaign*, 310.

4 Ambrose, 149–151.

5 MacDonald, *The Siegfried Line Campaign*, 231 ff.

6 Ibid., 260 ff; AAR, 743d Tank Battalion.

7 MacDonald, *The Siegfried Line Campaign*, 306.

8 AAR, 743d Tank Battalion.

9 MacDonald, *The Siegfried Line Campaign*, 312 ff.

10 *Rhineland*, 15.

11 Ambrose, 153.

12 *Rhineland*, 17.

13 AAR, 746th Tank Battalion.

14 *Soixante-Dix: A History of the 70th Tank Battalion*, 11. *Soixante-Dix* is an informal battalion history contained in the 70th's official records.

15 Bradley and Blair, 343.

16 AAR, 746th Tank Battalion.

17 AARs or S-3 Journals of units cited and of 3d Armored Group.

18 AARs and S-3 Journal, 3d Armored Group.

19 *Organization, Equipment, and Tactical Employment of Separate Tank Battalions*, 6.

20 Unit History, December 1944, 781st Tank Battalion.

21 Wilkes, *747th Tank Battalion*, 44; Undated memorandum, "Method of Operation: 737th Tank Battalion," 5.

22 Drawn heavily from MacDonald, 341 ff.

23 AAR, 707th Tank Battalion; S-3 Journal, 3d Armored Group.

24 MacDonald, *The Siegfried Line Campaign,* 395; Wilmot, 566–568.

25 General History, 70th Tank Battalion.

26 Wilmot, 568; MacDonald, *The Siegfried Line Campaign,* 412 ff.

27 MacDonald, *The Siegfried Line Campaign,* 470–471.

28 Jensen, 252.

29 Jensen, 252–255; AAR, November 1944, 709th Tank Battalion.

30 MacDonald, *The Siegfried Line Campaign,* 415 ff.

31 Ibid., 476 ff.

32 Ibid., 424 ff.

33 AAR, 750th Tank Battalion.

34 MacDonald, *The Siegfried Line Campaign,* 440 ff.

35 AAR, 747th Tank Battalion; MacDonald, *The Siegfried Line Campaign,* 497 ff.

36 Recommendations for Tank Operations Based on Battle Experience, 747th Tank Battalion, 4 December 1944.

37 Battle Lessons, 747th Tank Battalion, 1 January 1945.

38 MacDonald, *The Siegfried Line Campaign,* 527 ff.

39 AAR, 747th Tank Battalion.

40 AAR, 743d Tank Battalion; Robinson, 111 ff; MacDonald, *The Siegfried Line Campaign,* 501 ff.

41 Macdonald, *The Siegfried Line Campaign,* 530–532.

42 *Armored Special Equipment,* 5–8.

43 MacDonald, *The Siegfried Line Campaign,* 581 ff.

44 Ibid., 596 ff; Company AARs, 709th Tank Battalion.

45 AAR, 712th Tank Battalion.

46 Cole, 264–265.

47 Ibid., 266.

48 *Armored Special Equipment,* 10.

49 Cole, 275.

50 Battalion History, 737th Tank Battalion; Allen, 122.

51 Cole, 278; Elson, 82 ff.

52 Battalion History, 737th Tank Battalion; Allen, 122.

53 Allen, 125.

54 Ibid., 128 ff; Wilmot, 565–566.

55 AAR, 737th Tank Battalion.

56 S-3 Journal, 11 November 1944, 737th Tank Battalion.

57 Battalion History, 737th Tank Battalion.

58 Wilson.

59 Cole, 421.

60 Ibid., 380 ff.

61 Ibid.

62 Ibid.

63 Ibid., 447–448.

64 AAR, 735th Tank Battalion.

65 AARs, 702d and 743d Tank battalions; *Armored Special Equipment*, 41.

66 Zaloga, 17.

67 AAR, February 1945, 737th Tank Battalion; AAR, January 1945, 702d Tank Battalion.

68 AAR, February 1945, and S-3 Journal, March 1945, 737th Tank Battalion.

69 Allen, 142–143.

70 Ibid.

71 *Rhineland.*

72 Wilmot, 569; Griess, 230.

## CHAPTER 7: HITLER'S LAST GAMBLE

1 Wilmot, 577.

2 Ibid., 576.

3 Astor, v.

4 AAR, S-3 Journal, 741st Tank Battalion, unless otherwise noted.

5 Heintzleman, 61–63.

6 AAR, 741st Tank Battalion; Heintzleman, 67–68.

7 Heintzleman, 64.

8 Ibid., 64–65.

9 Battle casualty reports, 741st Tank Battalion.

10 AAR, 707th Tank Battalion.

11 Griess, 379.

12 Griess, 379.

13 *Soixante-Dix;* AAR, 70th Tank Battalion.

14 The following account is taken from the AAR, 743d Tank Battalion, unless otherwise noted.

15 Robinson, 126.

16 Robinson, 127.

17 AAR, 743d Tank Battalion.

18 The following account is taken from Rubel. His book is essentially

a compilation of the battalion's AARs, augmented by his personal anecdotes as battalion commander.

19 Interview with Harold Bradley, 29 December 2001.
20 Ibid.
21 Ibid.
22 Reardon, note to author.
23 Rubel, 67.
24 AAR, 745th Tank Battalion; Wilmot, 594.
25 AAR, 750th Tank Battalion.
26 Interview with Harold Bradley.
27 Rubel, 72–73
28 Allen, 174–179.
29 Wilmot, 599.
30 The following account is drawn from the AAR of the 735th Tank Battalion.
31 AAR, 735th Tank Battalion.
32 The following account is drawn from the battalion history, 737th Tank Battalion.
33 Griess, 384.
34 AAR, 743d Tank Battalion.
35 Whiting, 107 ff; Griess, 387.
36 Whiting, 116 ff; *Up From Marseilles,* 12.
37 AAR, 753d Tank Battalion.
38 *Up From Marseilles.*
39 Whiting, 116 ff; Griess, 388; AAR, 709th Tank Battalion.
40 AAR, 756th Tank Battalion.
41 Griess, 388.
42 MacDonald, *The Last Offensive,* 1; Griess, 385.
43 MacDonald, *The Last Offensive,* 27.
44 AAR, 712th Tank Battalion.
45 MacDonald, *The Last Offensive,* 35.
46 AAR, January 1945, 750th Tank Battalion.
47 Rubel, 92, 98–99.
48 AAR, January 1945, 750th Tank Battalion.
49 Rubel, 72.
50 Robinson, 133.
51 Rubel, 92–93.
52 AARs, 741st Tank Battalion.

53 AARs, 743d Tank Battalion.
54 AARs, 749th Tank Battalion.
55 AAR, Company A, 753d Tank Battalion.
56 AAR, 743d Tank Battalion.
57 AAR, 750th Tank Battalion.
58 AAR, 741st Tank Battalion.
59 Rubel, 101.
60 Rubel, 93; AAR, 740th Tank Battalion.
61 Rubel, 101.
62 MacDonald, *The Last Offensive*, 43.
63 AAR, January 1945, 70th Tank Battalion.
64 MacDonald, *The Last Offensive*, 46; AAR, 743d Tank Battalion.
65 MacDonald, *The Last Offensive*, 42 ff.

## CHAPTER 8: THE REICH OVERRUN

1 Rubel, 105.
2 Ibid., 108–109.
3 MacDonald, *The Last Offensive*, 58 ff; Battalion history and S-3 Journal, 774th Tank Battalion.
4 Robinson, 144.
5 This and the following account drawn from the AAR, 743d Tank Battalion.
6 AARs, 743d, 737th, and 701st Tank battalions.
7 AAR, 743d Tank Battalion.
8 MacDonald, *The Last Offensive*, 136–137.
9 Griess, 397.
10 MacDonald, *The Last Offensive*, 156–157.
11 Rubel, 126.
12 Ibid., 130–131.
13 Ibid., 143.
14 Ibid., 144.
15 Ibid., 53–154.
16 AAR, 750th Tank Battalion.
17 Battalion history, 774th Tank Battalion.
18 AAR, 741st Tank Battalion.
19 Battle casualty report, 741st Tank Battalion; AAR, 743d Tank Battalion.
20 MacDonald, *The Last Offensive*, 99 ff; Battalion history, 737th Tank Battalion.

21 MacDonald, *The Last Offensive*, 116 ff.

22 Battalion history, 737th Tank Battalion.

23 Battalion history, 737th Tank Battalion.

24 Griess, 399.

25 Allen, 244.

26 Battalion history, 774th Tank Battalion.

27 Operational Notes Number 8, 21 March 1945, 746th Tank Battalion.

28 Allen, 263; Battalion history, 737th Tank Battalion.

29 Liddell Hart, 678.

30 Liddell Hart, 678–679.

31 Robinson, 156–157.

32 Whiting, 181 ff; AAR, 756th Tank Battalion.

33 AAR, 756th Tank Battalion; *Armored Special Equipment*, 19–20.

34 AAR, 748th Tank Battalion.

35 Armored Special Equipment, 23.

36 Ibid., 38.

37 Wilmot, 684; Cooper, 247 ff.

38 MacDonald, *The Last Offensive*, 364.

39 Rubel, 177.

40 Ibid., 180–181.

41 Ibid., 183.

42 Ibid., 172 ff; Griess, 407.

43 Rubel, 203.

44 Ryan, 280.

45 AAR, 737th Tank Battalion.

46 Griess, 406–407

47 Ryan, 285 ff; MacDonald, *The Last Offensive*, 387; AAR, 736th Tank Battalion; AAR, 709th Tank Battalion.

48 AAR, April 1945, 702d Tank Battalion.

49 *Soixante-Dix*.

50 Battalion history, 781st Tank Battalion; *Up From Marseille*, 22; Whiting, 193 ff.

51 AAR, 756th Tank Battalion; Whiting, 197 ff.

52 AARs, 735th and 746th Tank battalions.

53 Griess, 406–407

54 Griess, 408.

55 *Up From Marseille*, 25.

## APPENDIX A: BATTALION PROFILES

1 *Soixante-Dix,* official history of the 70th Tank Battalion.

2 *191 Tank Bn.,* contained in the battalion's official records.

3 Hassett; AARs, 701st Tank Battalion; *Armored Special Equipment.*

4 Battalion records, 702d Tank Battalion.

5 Official History, S-3 Journal, and AARs, 707th Tank Battalion.

6 Official History, S-3 Journal, and AARs, 709th Tank Battalion.

7 Official History, S-3 Journal, and AARs, 712th Tank Battalion.

8 *717th Tank Battalion Record.*

9 General Orders and AARs, 735th Tank Battalion.

10 History, AARs, and S-3 Journal, 736th Tank Battalion; *Armored Special Equipment.*

11 History, AARs, and S-3 Journal, 737th Tank Battalion.

12 Unit Journal, History, and AARs, 738th Tank Battalion; *Armored Special Equipment.*

13 Unit Journal, History, and AARs, 739th Tank Battalion; *Armored Special Equipment.*

14 Unit History and AARs, 740th Tank Battalion; Rubel; *Armored Special Equipment.*

15 Unit History and AARs, 741st Tank Battalion.

16 Unit History and AARs, 743d Tank Battalion.

17 *The 744th Light Tank Battalion's VE Day Reminiscence,* 744th Tank Battalion.

18 Unit History and AARs, 745th Tank Battalion.

19 Unit History and AARs, 746th Tank Battalion.

20 Unit History and AARs, 747th Tank Battalion.

21 Unit History and AARs, 748th Tank Battalion; *Armored Special Equipment.*

22 Unit History and AARs, 749th Tank Battalion.

23 Unit History and AARs, 750th Tank Battalion.

24 Unit History and AARs, 753d Tank Battalion.

25 Unit History and AARs, 756d Tank Battalion.

26 Unit History and AARs, 759th Tank Battalion.

27 Trezzvant W. Anderson; Ulysses Lee Wilson, 661 ff.

28 General Orders and AARs, 771st Tank Battalion.

29 Unit History and AARs, 772d Tank Battalion.

30 Unit History and AARs, 774th Tank Battalion.

31 Unit History and AARs, 777th Tank Battalion.

32 Unit History, AARs, and S-3 Journal, 778th Tank Battalion.

33 *Up From Marseille.*
34 Battalion history and AAR, 782d Tank Battalion.
35 AARs, 784th Tank Battalion.
36 Battalion history and AARs, 786th Tank Battalion.
37 Battalion history and AARs, 787th Tank Battalion.

# INDEX

FNU = First name unknown

Aas, (FNU), Lt.: 72.
Air support, tactical: 40, 60–61, 65, 94–95, 102–103, 107, 122–123, 128–129, 252–253.
Airborne divisions, American 17th: 221; 82d: 42–43, 59, 211–212, 220, 225–226, 229–230; 101st: 41–42, 212.
Airplanes, spotter: 122, 128, 232.
Alexander, (FNU), Pvt.: 69.
Ambleve River: 209.
Angelletti, (FNU), Sgt.: 196.
Armored divisions, American 2d: 5–6, 22, 93, 100, 146, 166, 215, 245, 249; 3d: 5, 17, 19, 93, 100, 105, 107, 132, 145, 215, 235, 245; 4th: 16, 100, 104, 212, 215–216, 237, 239, 242; 5th: 8, 28, 101, 109, 132, 139, 160, 167, 230; 6th: 100, 221; 9th: 193, 203, 239–240; 10th: 7, 184, 203, 238; 11th: 221.
Armored Force: 4, 6.
Armored group: 7–8.
Artillery
    Cooperation with: 10, 64, 122, 128–129, 136, 178, 232;
    Tanks firing as: 3, 10, 26, 66–67, 99, 185.
Austria
    Salzburg: 227.

Barcelona, (FNU), Lt.: 49.
Barton, Raymond, Maj. Gen.: 96.

Bauer, (FNU), Lt.: 180.
Bayerlein, Fritz, Gen.: 95.
Bazooka
    American: 183, 195;
    German: 17, 19–21, 47, 58, 69, 86, 99, 102, 112, 137–138, 140, 149, 175, 179–180, 203, 221, 246–247, 251.
Belgium
    Arlon: 213; Bastogne: 16, 189, 200–201, 212, 215; Brussels: 102, 192; Bullingen: 195–196; Bütgenbach: 211; Celles: 215; Charleroi: 127; Charleyville: 127; Dellev: 213; Dickweiler: 202; Dinant: 192; Goronne: 220; Heeresbach: 225; Houffalize: 219, 222; Krinkelt: 195, 198; La Gleize: 205, 210–211; Lierneux: 211; Malmedy: 204, 211; Masta: 204–205; Mons: 127; Namur: 192, 215; Neufchateau: 201; Osweiler: 202; Rocherath: 194–199; Sprimont: 208; St. Vith: 189, 222; Stavelot: 204–206; Stoumont: 205–207; Wirtzfeld: 195, 198.
Benson, (FNU), Sgt.: 68.
Berry, (FNU), Capt.: 209.
Blanford, William O., Lt. Col.: 162.
Boardman, Jack, Cpl.: 77–78.

Bocage (see hedgerows)
Bock, Abe, Lt. Col.: 213.
Bolt, Gerald, Sgt.: 52.
Bradley, Omar N., Lt. Gen.: 35, 59,
 67, 93, 100, 106, 145, 150,
 182, 222, 226, 229–230, 245.
Bruck, John, Lt.: 75.
Bulkan, (FNU), Capt.: 72.
Bulvin, (FNU), Capt.: 163.
Bussel, George: 114.
Buza, (FNU), Sgt.: 44.

Call, (FNU), Sgt.: 50.
Camp Polk, Louisiana: 9.
Camp Shanks, New York: 29.
Camouflage: 89, 221, 224.
Canal Defense Lights (CDLs): 5–6,
 207, 245.
Case, (FNU), Sgt.: 197.
Castignoli, (FNU), Sgt.: 84.
Casualties: 16–18, 52, 67, 101, 116,
 120, 138–139, 147, 157–158,
 162, 216, 224, 236, 247.
Chaffee, Adna: 3.
Chance, R. H., Col.: 203.
Chestnut, (FNU), PFC: 69.
Cobra, Operation: 89, 91, 93–101.
Collins, J. Lawton, Maj. Gen.: 100,
 140, 219.
Colmar Pocket: 187, 216, 218–219.
Cota, Norman, Maj. Gen.: 61–62,
 156.
Covington, (FNU), Lt.: 135.
Coy, (FNU), T/5: 242.
Culin hedgerow device: 88–89,
 97–98, 104.
Czechoslovakia: 248, 253.

De Gaulle, Charles, Gen.: 113, 216.
Deaver, Herman, Sgt.: 85, 163–164.
Desert Training Center: 9.
Dew, Joseph H., Lt.: 134–135,
 195–198, 236, 251.
Dickson, (FNU), Sgt.: 195.
Dixon, Forrest: 115.

Doctrine, armored: 4, 13.
Dragoon, Operation: 117.
Duckbills (see grousers)
Duncan, William, Lt. Col.: 99,
 204–205.

Eisenhower, Dwight D., Gen.: 35,
 59, 91, 111, 113, 116, 125,
 204, 216, 218, 227, 230, 239,
 249, 254.
Elbe River: 227, 248–249.
Elder, (FNU), Capt.: 70.
Elsenborn Ridge: 189, 194, 224.
Engineers: 41, 54, 85–88, 135–137,
 147, 198, 231–232, 234,
 240.
England
 Fairford: 29.

Fair, (FNU), Sgt.: 48–50.
Fasoli, Nello J., Sgt.: 220–221.
Ferish, (FNU), Cpl.: 69.
Field telephone, tank-mounted:
 77–78.
Fitzgibons, (FNU), Lt.: 70.
Flamethrowers: 139–141.
Fleig, Raymond, Lt.: 154–156.
Fleming, (FNU), Sgt.: 247.
Fort Dix, New Jersey: 29.
Fort Driant, France, siege of:
 178–181, 185.
Fort Knox, Kentucky: 6, 9.
France
 Alencon: 109; Allencourt:
 119; Angers: 101; Argentan:
 105, 108–109, 111; Avranche:
 100, 103–104, 109; Belfort
 Gap: 121, 187; Besançon: 91;
 Bitche: 187; Bois L'Eveque:
 113; Bouzanville: 213; Brest:
 103–104; Brittany: 100–101,
 103–104; Caen: 55, 108;
 Cambernon: 100; Carentan
 plain: 67; Caumont: 73–74;
 Cherbourg: 35, 55, 65–67,

115; Colmar: 187, 216, 218–219; Cotentin Peninsula: 16, 100; Cour de Precuire: 102; Coutances: 100; Dijon: 119; Falaise: 91, 104–105, 108–111; Fonteny: 183; Formigny: 59; Frescaty: 184; Gaborg: 33; Hautes Vents: 71; Isigny: 1, 63; La Desert: 68; La Fied: 121; La Parque: 65; La Viqosrie: 72; Landrecies: 112; Landres: 114; Laneuville: 183; Le Mans: 108; Les Bessardierre: 102; Les Moulins: 53; Lorient: 103–104; Lovdier: 102; Lyon: 91, 118, 120; Mackwiller: 224; Mairy: 114; Marigny: 95; Marseilles: 117; Maizières les Metz: 182; Metz: 104, 116, 128, 143, 145, 178, 183–184; Montelimar: 118; Mortain: 104–108, 111; Noroy le Bourg: 119; Osmanville: 60, 63; Paris: 35, 91, 101, 109, 111, 113–114; Pas de Calais: 35; Pommereuil: 113; Sarreguemines: 16, 183, 215; Sessenheim: 217; St. Amand: 102; St. Gilles: 96; St. Jean de Daye: 58, 69, 72; St. Laurent-sur-Mer: 53; St. Lô: 55, 75, 84, 91, 93–94, 96, 98; St. Malo: 103–104; St. Marie du Mont: 43; St. Mere Eglise: 43, 59; St. Nazaire: 103–104; St. Pois: 95; St. Sauver: 119; St. Tropez: 117; Strasbourg: 143, 187, 216; Tessy-sur-Vire: 96; Toulon: 117; Tournai: 127; Vierville (-sur-Mer): 33, 54, 60; Villedieu: 96; Vire: 105–106; Wissembourg: 187.

French divisions
  1st Armored Division: 118;
  2d Armored Division: 109, 113, 187.
Fries, Stuart G., Lt. Col.: 24, 31–32, 61, 63, 81.

Galbreath, (FNU), Lt.: 179.
Gale, George P., Lt.: 62.
Gen. Headquarters (GHQ): 4–5.
German divisions
  1st SS Panzer: 105; 2d SS Panzer: 105–106, 205–206, 215; 2d Panzer: 97, 105, 215, 220; 11th Panzer: 118, 238; 12th SS Panzer: 194; 17th SS Panzergrenadier: 27, 216; 21st Panzer: 216; 89th Infantry: 154; 116th Panzer: 105, 154, 243; 212th Volksgrenadier: 202; 352d Infantry: 47; Panzer Lehr: 95.
Germany
  Aachen: 18, 130, 132, 143, 145–148, 156, 231–232; Aldenhoven: 165; Altdorf: 164; Bad Salsig: 245; Berlin: 248–249, 253; Bettendorf: 163; Bitburg: 237–238; Bremen: 227; Cologne: 145, 227, 235–236; Dillingen: 186; Distroff: 184; Dorstewitz: 251; Düren: 166, 234; Düsseldorf: 234, 247; Echternach: 192, 202; Eisenach: 227; Eschdorf: 214; Erfurt: 227, 250; Frankfurt: 227, 242; Geilenkirchen: 156; Germeter: 151–152; Gibelsrath: 234; Groskampenberg: 134, 136; Hamburg: 227; Hamich: 159; Harsfelt: 133; Heckhuscheid:

Germany *(cont'd)*
136; Heilbronn: 251–252;
Hombert: 247; Hongen: 163,
204; Honnef: 240; Hürtgen:
160; Jülich: 161; Kalenborn:
240–241; Kassel: 227, 250;
Kesternich: 167; Kleine
Lengdon: 251; Kleinhau:
160; Knapsack: 235;
Koblenz: 182;
Kommerscheidt: 153–155;
Leipzig: 227; Lippstadt: 245;
Lucherberg: 159; Luebeck:
227; Magdeburg: 227, 253;
Mainz: 245; Manderscheid:
238–239; Mariadorf: 164;
Mechernich: 236;
Monschau: 189, 192, 211,
230; Muenster: 227; Munich:
227; Neuhof: 229;
Niederpallen: 214;
Nürnberg: 252; Oberbrugge:
247; Olpe: 245–246;
Oppenheim: 242; Pattern:
165; Puffendorf: 166;
Rahrbach: 246; Remagen:
227, 240, 245; Rohe: 232;
Saarlautern: 186–187, 212;
Schevenhutte: 150;
Schleiden: 162–164;
Schmidt: 153–155; Siegen:
245; St. Goar: 245;
Steinstrasse: 232; Stolberg:
156–157, 159; Strass: 166;
Stuckange: 212; Torgau: 253;
Trier: 177, 182, 238;
Udenbreth: 229; Vicht: 150;
Volkenrath: 159; Vossenock:
150–153; Welschen Ennestt:
246; Wetter: 247;
Windhagen: 241–242;
Worms: 227, 242–243;
Wulfen: 253; Wuppertal: 246;
Wurselen: 164; Zweifall: 150.
Gerow, Leonard, Maj. Gen.: 54.

Gifford, Jim: 109–111.
Gillem, Alvan C., Maj. Gen.: 24.
Goodwood, Operation: 95.
Graves, Arthur, Cpl.: 52.
Grenade, Operation: 233.
Grousers: 21, 218, 223.

Hamilton, James, Jr., Lt. Col.: 84.
Hansen, Jean, Lt.: 70, 205–206.
Harris, (FNU) "Cowboy", Lt.: 214.
Harz Mountains: 28, 253.
Hedgerows: 30, 41–42, 55–89.
Hembre, (FNU), T/5: 71.
Hendrix, (FNU), Sgt.: 220–221.
Hobbs, Leland, Maj. Gen.: 209.
Hodges, Courtney, Lt. Gen.: 153.
Hoffer, Steve, Cpl.: 50–51.
Holcombe, (FNU), Sgt.: 46, 51.
Homme, (FNU), T/4: 69.
Howard, (FNU), Lt.: 254.
Hunter, (FNU), Lt.: 70.
Hürtgen Forest: 129, 143, 148–153,
157–160, 166.
Huya, (FNU), T/5: 217.

Infantry (see tank-infantry
cooperation)
Infantry divisions, American
1st: 10, 47, 64, 73, 82, 93–94,
100, 132, 145, 147, 159, 204,
211; 2d: 64, 75, 97, 99, 102,
167, 193–194, 211, 251; 3d:
117, 252; 4th: 30, 42, 54, 66,
81–82, 93, 96, 102, 108, 114,
129, 139, 157–158, 160, 193,
202–203, 226, 243; 5th: 14,
101, 177–178, 184, 212, 215,
226, 237, 239, 242; 8th: 97,
100, 115, 160, 230, 234–235,
245, 247; 9th: 43, 66, 93,
95–96, 132, 145, 148,
150–153, 159, 204; 26th: 183,
212–213, 221; 28th: 114, 132,
135, 139, 153–156, 160, 193,
199–201; 29th: 31–32, 40, 61,

64, 130, 160, 166; 30th: 64, 93–94, 96, 105–108, 146–147, 160, 164, 204–205, 209, 211, 222, 231–233, 243–244; 35th: 18, 68, 107, 215, 233; 36th: 117, 122–123, 217, 221; 44th: 217; 45th: 117–118, 217, 252; 65th: 244; 70th: 217, 243; 75th: 211, 218–219; 76th: 238; 78th: 167, 230, 236, 240; 79th: 100, 109, 217, 244, 247; 80th: 111, 212, 226, 237, 249; 83d: 81, 101, 104, 158, 166, 177, 219, 249; 84th: 219; 87th: 221; 89th: 244; 90th: 43, 82, 101, 109, 114, 177, 182, 184, 186, 221, 237; 94th: 238; 95th: 184, 186; 99th: 167, 193–194, 208, 211; 100th: 217, 251; 103d: 217, 253; 104th: 7, 18, 159–160, 211, 234–235; 106th: 189, 193.

Infantry regiments, American 2d: 212; 7th: 244; 8th: 54; 9th: 65; 10th: 14; 11th: 178, 184; 12th: 108, 202–203; 22d: 42, 102; 23d: 98, 102, 194; 26th: 74; 30th: 244; 38th: 75, 98, 194; 39th: 150–152; 47th: 95; 60th: 130, 150–151; 104th: 213; 109th: 199, 201; 110th: 137, 199–200; 112th: 153–154, 199; 116th: 46, 60; 117th: 204; 119th: 99, 206, 209; 121st: 246; 122d: 106; 175th: 61, 162–163; 309th: 231; 310th: 231; 320th: 107–108; 395th: 194; 504th Parachute: 225.

Johnson, (FNU), Sgt.: 218.
Jones, (FNU), Lt.: 69, 179.

Kall River: 154, 156.
Kegut, (FNU), Lt.: 67.

Kieltyka, Al: 158.
King, (FNU), Capt.: 51.
Kirk, (FNU), Pvt.: 69.
Kolf, (FNU), T/4: 72.
Korrison, David, Lt./Capt.: 72, 165.
Kroeger, (FNU), Cpl.: 197.
Kyll River: 237–238.

Landing Vehicle, Tracked (LVT): 233, 244.
Larsen, (FNU), Sgt.: 49–50, 70.
Larson, (FNU), PFC: 70.
Leclerc, Jacque, Maj. Gen.: 113.
Leet, (FNU), Sgt.: 214.
Loopey, Charlie W., Sgt./Lt.: 208–210, 225, 230, 235, 246–247.
Luxembourg
    Bergdorf: 202; Berle: 221; Boulaide: 201; Buchholz: 200; Clerf: 200; Consdorf: 202–203; Detrange: 215; Diekirch: 201; Drauffel: 200; Ettelbruck: 201; Hoscheid: 200; Hosingen: 200; Marnach: 200; Osweiler: 202–203; Rippweiler: 221; Urspelt: 200; Vichten: 201; Wiltz: 200–201; Wilwerwiltz: 200.

M3 Grant medium tank: 5, 12.
M4 Sherman medium tank
    Armament: 13–14, 22–26; Armor protection: 18–21; Assault gun, 105mm: 26; Duplex Drive (DD): 30, 41–47; Jumbo: 20–21; Maneuverability: 21–22; Mine-clearing: 6, 166.
M5 light tank: 26–27.
M24 Chaffee light tank: 27–28.
M26 Pershing heavy tank: 25–26.
M32 tank recovery vehicle: 28.

Macht, (FNU), Lt.: 70.
Main River: 242.
Maintenance of tanks: 65–66, 76,
    115, 121–123, 202–203,
    214–215, 252.
Maloney, (FNU), Sgt.: 214.
Marshall, George C., Gen.: xix.
Mazzio, (FNU), Sgt.: 198.
McDonough, (FNU), Lt.: 49.
McMichael, (FNU), T/5: 70.
McNair, Lesley J., Lt. Gen.: xix,
    4–7, 13, 94–95.
Mechanized Division, 7th,
    American: 10.
Mercer, (FNU), Lt.: 43.
Merk, Bill, Sgt.: 114.
Meuse (Maas) River: 127, 189, 192,
    215.
Miller, (FNU), Capt.: 70, 72, 99,
    147.
Miller, Victor, Lt.: 195.
Mittendorf, (FNU), Lt.: 70.
Model, Walter, Feldmarschall: 226,
    245.
Moder River: 218.
Montgomery, Sir Bernard Law,
    General/Field Marshall
    (Monty): 35, 59, 95, 105, 109,
    111, 116, 219, 227, 230, 232,
    234, 239, 242–245.
Mortar platoon: 28.
Moselle River: 120, 127, 130, 182,
    184, 238–239.
Mosey, (FNU), Sgt.: 69.
Mulde River: 227, 248.

Nash, Cecil: 158.
Neckar River: 251.
Netherlands
    Antwerp: 143, 189, 192;
    Arnhem: 92; Maastricht: 127;
    Nijmegan: 234, Venlo: 234.
Nichols, Wallace J., Lt. Col.: 82,
    146.
Night attacks: 164.

Nordwind, Operation:
    189–191,216–218.
Norris, (FNU), Lt. Col.: 75.

Ocasio, (FNU), Cpl.: 241–242.
O'Davaney, Clint, Sgt.: 215.
Oliver, (FNU), Lt.: 69.
Olson, (FNU), Sgt.: 181.
O'Neil, (FNU), Pvt.: 72.
Orner, Al: 158.
Ourthe River: 219.
Overlord, Operation
    General: 35–36, 40, 47–54;
    Omaha Beach: 33, 37–40,
    44–47; Utah Beach: 33,
    40–44.

Padgett, (FNU), Sgt.: 196.
Panzerfaust (see bazooka)
Patch, Alexander, Lt. Gen.: 187.
Patton, George S., Lt. Gen.: 3, 16,
    100, 103–106, 108, 113,
    116–117, 119, 127–128, 130,
    143, 177, 182–183, 186, 189,
    203–204, 212, 216, 221, 226,
    230, 237–238, 242, 244, 248.
Peel Marshes: 146.
Phillips, (FNU), Maj.: 99.
Planck, Ralph: 158.
Pierce, (FNU), Pvt.: 68.
Plagge, (FNU), Lt.: 43.
Powers, Charles B., Lt.: 209–210,
    225–226, 229–230, 234–235.

Quesada, Elwood, Maj. Gen.: 103.

Radio, link to infantry: 31, 78–79,
    117–118, 152–153.
Ragan, Paul, Sgt.: 46.
Randolph, George B., Lt. Col.: 225.
Red Ball Express: 116.
Reddish, Irvin, Pvt.: 52.
Reserve group (see armored
    group)
Reynolds, (FNU), Cpl.: 71.

Rhine River
  Crossing of: 239–245;
  Drive to Reach: 187,
  231–236, 239.
Rhone River: 118.
Riffle, (FNU), Cpl.: 68.
Robinson, (FNU), PFC: 50.
Rocket launchers: 185–186.
Roer River
  Crossing of: 231–234;
  Dams: 167, 227, 230–232;
  Drive to reach: 143, 156–167.
Rogers, (FNU), T/4: 50.
Roosevelt, Franklin D.: xix.
Rötgen Forest: 130.
Rubel, George K., Lt. Col.: 25,
  207–212, 220, 223, 234–235,
  247.
Ruhr basin: 227, 245–247.
Rusech, (FNU), Cpl.: 71.

Saar River: 130, 143, 182, 185–186,
  212, 216, 221, 238.
Sauer River: 189, 226, 237.
Service company: 28.
Sexton, (FNU), Sgt.: 217.
Shields, (FNU), Lt.: 43.
Siegfried Line: 116, 127–139,
  145–146, 148, 156, 237–238.
Simons, Donald S., Sgt.: 239.
Simpson, William, Lt. Gen.: 127.
Skaggs, Vernon D., Sgt.: 77.
Skaggs, Robert N., Lt. Col.: 198.
Skiba, (FNU), Sgt.: 50–51.
Skorzeny, Otto, SS
  Hauptsturmführer: 192.
Slapton Sands, exercises at:
  30–31.
Smith, (FNU), Sgt.: 43.
Snike, (FNU), Cpl.: 198.
Stewart, (FNU), Capt.: 62, 129.
Stimson, Henry L.: xix.
Streeter, H. S., Lt. Col.: 201.
Sutherland, Edwin M., Col.: 99,
  210.

T2, tank recovery vehicle: 28.
Tank battalions, American
  70th: 6–7, 9–11, 27, 29–30,
  40–42, 60, 66, 68, 81–82, 93,
  96, 108, 114, 140, 149, 152,
  157–158, 193, 201–204, 226,
  244, 250–251; 191st: 6–7,
  117, 121–123, 217; 701st:
  5–7, 26; 702d: 6–7, 111, 116,
  185, 226, 237, 249–250;
  707th: 7, 140, 153–156, 193,
  199–201; 709th: 7, 20, 24, 97,
  104, 140, 157, 160, 167, 218;
  712th: 7, 68, 82, 109–111,
  114–115, 177, 182, 184–185,
  221, 225, 237–239; 717th:
  254; 735th: 6–7, 101, 152,
  177–181, 184–187, 212–215,
  221, 252–253; 736th: 5–7, 26,
  28, 244, 249; 737th: 7, 14, 18,
  23, 68, 82–84, 87, 107–108,
  152, 182–183, 215, 223–226,
  237–239, 242, 248; 738th:
  5–7, 166; 739th: 5–7, 139,
  166, 233, 245; 740th: 5–7, 22,
  25, 28, 83, 204, 207–212,
  220–224, 229–230, 234–235,
  245–247; 741st: 7, 9–10,
  22–23, 30, 37–40, 44–46,
  47–54, 63–66, 75, 77–78,
  85–88, 97–102, 114, 116,
  133–137, 139–140, 167,
  193–199, 224, 236, 244, 251;
  743d: 7, 9–11, 14, 17–20, 23,
  29–30, 32, 40, 44, 46–47,
  52–54, 59–60, 63–66, 68–75,
  77, 87, 94, 96–97, 99, 101,
  106–107, 112, 116, 140,
  146–148, 152–153, 160,
  164–166, 167–177, 185,
  204–207, 209, 216, 222,
  224–226, 231–233, 236,
  243–244, 253; 744th (Light):
  7, 166; 745th: 7, 28–29, 32,
  54, 59, 79–80, 82, 100,

Tank battalions, American *(cont'd)*
145–146, 159, 204, 208, 211,
253; 746th: 7–9, 27, 29–31,
33, 42–44, 59, 65–68, 73, 76,
81, 93–96, 103, 130, 145,
148–152, 204, 240–242, 252;
747th: 7, 10, 24, 29–32, 54,
60–66, 78–81, 84–85, 87–88,
101–103, 112–113, 129–130,
135–138, 140, 160–164, 166,
244, 253; 748th: 5–7,
244–245; 749th: 7, 68, 77–79,
84–85, 99–100, 115, 217, 224;
750th: 7, 18, 20, 140, 159,
211, 219, 222, 224, 230,
234–236; 753d: 7, 20, 32,
117–119, 122–123, 185, 217,
224; 756th: 7, 20, 117–121,
219, 243, 252; 758th (Light):
8; 759th (Light): 7; 760th: 9;
761st: 7–8, 82, 183, 221;
771st: 7, 219; 772d: 253;
774th: 7, 23, 140, 152, 177,
219, 230–231, 236, 240–241,
253–254; 777th: 7; 778th: 7,
184, 186, 238; 781st: 6–7,
153, 185, 217–218, 229,
251–252, 253; 784th: 7–8,
234; 786th: 7; Establishment
of: 3, 6–7; Organization of: 1,
5–6.
Tank crew, organization of: 12.
Tank group (see armored group)
Tank destroyers, role of: 13, 128.
Tank-infantry cooperation
Effective: 1–3, 96, 128–129,
215; Problems with: 30–32,
60, 68, 99, 129, 213, 235;
Steps to improve: 130,
210–212.
Thornton, James G. Jr., Capt.:
45–46, 64–65, 75, 99–100,
114, 133–134.

Tichnor, (FNU), Lt.: 72.
Town, (FNU), Lt.: 179–181.
Training
Amphibious: 10; Standard:
9–10; Gaps in: 10–11, 31.
Tribby, (FNU), Lt.: 220–221.
Tunisia
Pichon: 11.

Upham, John, Lt. Col.

Van Loon, William H., Lt.: 239.
Van Voorhis, Daniel: 3.
Von Kluge, Günther,
Feldmarschall: 95, 97,
105.
Von Rundstedt, Gerd,
Feldmarschall: 95, 192,
226.
Vosges Mountains: 121, 128, 143,
187, 216–217.

Wacht am Rhein, Operation:
191–192.
Walker, Walton, Maj. Gen.: 184.
Wandzala, (FNU), Pvt.: 72.
Wilkes, Homer, Lt.: 10, 31–33,
60–64, 80–81, 84–85,
112–113, 129, 138, 163–164,
244.
Williams, (FNU), Lt.: 69–70.
Wilson, (FNU), Lt.: 65, 99.
Wilson, Ray, Sgt.: 195.
Winoski, Harvey E., Lt.: 239.
Woljlechowski, (FNU), Sgt.:
138.
Würm River: 147.

Young, Charles, Capt.: 45, 135.

Zurman, (FNU), Capt.: 238.
Zussman, Raymond, Lt.:
119–120.